A HISTORY OF THE

OGADEN (WESTERN SOMALI) STRUGGLE FOR SELF-DETERMINATION

PART II (2007–2021)

Mohamed Mohamud Abdi

CLEAR PRESS

Birmingham – UK

Published by Clear Press, an imprint of Safis Publishing Limited, Birmingham, UK.
www.clear-press.net

ISBN   978-1-906342-37-1 (paperback)
          978-1-906342-38-8 (ebook)

First Edition

Version Identifier: 21060701

Contents

Introduction

This is the second part of the historical work titled "A History of the Ogaden (Western Somali) Struggle for Self-Determination)". It is a continuation of part I, which started the history from the 14ᵗʰ century and ended it at the time of its publication, in 2007. As this is a continuation of the first part and not a new topic, it is necessary to read that first part before starting this one. The events of this history have been related and written in chronological order; therefore, understanding it requires the events to be read in the sequence in which they happened.

As mentioned in the main introduction of the work in part I, this history concerns the Ogaden/western Somali region and the inhabitants' resistance to the Ethiopian rule there. The region, which today is officially called the Somali state by Ethiopia, is also known by other names. These names include the Ogaden and Western Somali; however, the inhabitants have not yet voted for a name of their own choosing for their land. The liberation movements call the region both the Ogaden and Western Somali. In the first part, we used the two names that the liberation movements used interchangeably, and in this section, we have added the Somali state since that official name is gaining ground.

Whatever one calls it, that piece of territory, which is inhabited by the Somalis, is geographically situated in the Horn of Africa. It shares borders with Djibouti, Somalia, Kenya, and the country that rules it, namely, Ethiopia. Due to the lack of a reliable census, the population was estimated, in 2007 (at the time of the publication of the first part), at about 4–5 million. No censuses have been taken since then, but the official estimation of the population today is about 8 million.

Historically, the region was part of the Greater Somali Nation before the scramble for Africa, and the people lived there largely free, except for some attacks from the Christian Kingdom of Abyssinia on the western part between the 14ᵗʰ and 16ᵗʰ centuries. The Islamic Sultanate of Adal defended the region from those aggressions and eventually defeated Abyssinia by the middle of the 16ᵗʰ century. After the defeat, the Abyssinian aggression ceased and did not return until the 19ᵗʰ century when Menelik II took control of the Abyssinian Kingdom.

Abyssinia's aggression resumed during the last two decades of the 19ᵗʰ century. The Christian Kingdom frequently attacked and terrorised the Somali region and, with the help of the main European powers (namely, France, Britain, Italy and Russia), conquered most of it by the end of that century and completed its occupation in 1927. After that annexation, the region changed hands several times. It was under Italian occupation between 1935 and 1941, and Britain took over the Somali state in 1941 but handed over most of the region to Ethiopia in 1948. The last part (the Haud and Reserve Area) was ceded to Ethiopia in a treaty signed between Ethiopia and Britain in 1954, and the takeover was completed in 1955. Ethiopia has ruled the region since then, except for a short period during the 1977–78 Ogaden War in which Somalia controlled most of it.

The struggle for the liberation of the Ogaden began during the 14th century as a resistance to the expansionist campaigns of the Christian Kingdom of Abyssinia, which intensified after Ethiopia completed her occupation of the region and continues to this day. Ethiopia took over the region without the consent of its inhabitants in a harsh and violent manner, and she introduced repressive policies from day one of her occupation. The people of the region rejected both the occupation and the ensuing repression, reacting with protests and armed resistance. As detailed in part I, the pan-Somali Dervish resistance, led by Sayyid Mohamed Abdille Hassan, replaced Adal in the defence of the Somali territories, and it began its first operation in the Ogaden. Another pan-Somali resistance movement, namely, the SYL, followed in the footsteps of the Dervishes. The resistance movements of Nasrullah/the Ogaden Liberation Front (OLF), the Western Somali Liberation Front (WSLF) and the Ogaden National Liberation Front (ONLF) have all replaced one another in the Ogaden region since the 1950s. Somalia and Ethiopia have also fought twice (in 1964 and between 1977 and 1978) over the Ogaden issue. Over the centuries, the struggle has taken various forms and survived different generations, with many ups and downs, but it has not yet achieved its goal of liberation.

The main reasons for the lack of success of the struggle were, as detailed in part I, a misconception about this just cause, the world powers' backing of Ethiopia and the inhabitants' inability to end the occupation militarily or reach out to the wider world and gain the support of the international community. Ethiopia presented the Ogaden conflict as a border dispute between Ethiopia and Somalia in which the latter was the aggressor and branded the liberation movements as terrorists or agents of the aggressor. Ethiopia was extraordinarily successful in this misrepresentation: she got the backing of her position on the conflict from the African Union, the superpowers and nearly all of the world powers, and this broad support enabled her to also cover up her human rights violations in the region.

The Somali people in the Ogaden, however, never gave up hope and remained defiant—despite the odds against them. They refused the subjugation and resisted the occupation via all possible means. The struggle for freedom and human dignity began as a reaction to the occupation and the subsequent humiliations and gross violations of human rights. The struggle for the liberation of the region was mainly driven by two forces: the society's dream to regain its independence and the often harsh realities on the ground. Both forces affected the struggle directly and indirectly by interacting with one another and, in turn, influencing the struggle. The dream for self-determination has, itself, been guided mainly by nationalism, religion and—most important of all—the need to safeguard human rights. These pillars of the dream have been the main fuel for the struggle machine; that is, they have provided the rationale for the liberation struggle. Although the dream was stronger during some periods than others, it never died because of the violations of human rights.

In the first part, we investigated the historical development of the society's struggle to regain its independence. The core of our investigation was how the dream of freedom lived through different generations of the society in the region during the occupation period, what prompted the formation of freedom fighters, both armed and unarmed, and how they performed. Taking armed conflicts and political, social and human rights activism as indicators of the level of the struggle—as well as the strength of the dream to live in freedom— the achievements and challenges of the struggle for self-determination were examined using observations, eyewitness accounts, and historical data. Based on the findings, it ended with a prediction about the future of the struggle.

In this part, we will continue our investigation; we will examine how the lives of those in the society have changed since then and the evolution of the struggle for freedom, which was meant to help them. Just as we did in the first part, we will conclude with a prediction about the future of the struggle and the status of the Somali state.

1

The Obole Battle

On 24 April 2007, a commando unit of the ONLF stormed an oil exploration site in Obole, near Dagahbur. In a press release on 25 April 2007, the ONLF claimed to have killed nearly 200 Ethiopian soldiers in that operation and to have removed 7 Chinese workers from the place to ensure their safe return. The 7 Chinese were handed over to the International Committee of the Red Cross (ICRC) afterwards. For its part, the Ethiopian government admitted to the operation but reported the killing of 74 workers, including 9 Chinese workers.

Whatever the claim or counter claim, this battle, which was the last incident reported in part I of this historical work, was not noticeably big in operational terms; however, it was a turning point in the conflict, and its impact on the region was immense. The battle and the ensuing publicisation of its aftermath were not only a big embarrassment for the Ethiopian government in its relationship with China, but because of the operation, the regime was also forced to change its war strategies. The battle also opened a new front in the struggle for self-determination, and the consequences of the struggle and the lives of the Somali people in the region have been very grave.

As mentioned in the preceding part, neither the exploration of natural resources nor the involvement of foreign companies was new. In fact, the Ethiopian Emperor, Haile Selassie, used the Ogaden's natural resources as a bargaining chip in his efforts to reoccupy it. He did so by promising exploration concessions to American companies on the condition that the US government back his claim to the region. In a meeting in Cairo in 1945 between the American President and the Ethiopian Emperor, Haile Selassie told President Franklin D. Roosevelt that he would give US companies exploration rights in the Ogaden, that is, if the US could help him in the reoccupation of that region, and he fulfilled that promise a few years later after he secured America's backing.

Since the 1950s, foreign companies from both the west and the east have been exploring the resources of the region; however, the scale and intensity of the exploration reached unprecedented levels during the Ethiopian People's Revolutionary Democratic Front (EPRDF)-led regime. In the past, the presence of liberation movements and their warnings to foreign companies discouraged those companies from undertaking large exploration activities or starting an extraction; however, because of the competition amongst themselves after the Asian companies joined the scramble, and due to misinformation from the Ethiopian government about the situation on the ground, some companies dared to take the risk.

The freedom fighters saw the danger of foreign companies looting their resources before them, and so, they had to react to that threat. According to the ONLF, these foreign companies and the Ethiopian government ignored their repeated warnings and continued their illegal operations there, and thus the military operation was unavoidable since it was the only warning that they would understand. The battle was the first of its kind, launched for the defence of the natural resources of the region, and as a result, it became the symbol of that new front.

After this battle, most of the companies halted or cancelled their exploration activities in the Ogaden region and many of them annulled their contracts with the Ethiopian government. This was a heavy blow to the Ethiopian government and its projects there, and hence a reaction was inevitable. But the question was in what way would it respond? Would it be sensible enough to admit its mistakes and correct them by taking a peaceful approach and engaging in dialogue with the people of the region? Or, would it continue its suppression and aim for a military resolution? It chose the latter and vowed to wipe out the resistance movements once and for all, and in so doing, introduced new methods of warfare and policy strategies, which we will detail in the next chapter.

2

The Aftermath of the Obole Battle

In the wake of the Obole battle, the Ethiopian government decided to eradicate the rebels. To achieve that goal, it did two things: it waged war against the whole population and established a paramilitary militia, which was exclusively recruited from the inhabitants of the region. The aim of this collective punishment was to ensure the total surrender of the inhabitants and, at the same time, deny the rebels a hiding place and cut their supply lines. The creation of the militia was intended to destroy the unity of the Somali society by creating internal conflicts and to get a fighting force on her behalf, too. In the following sections, we will examine both the successes and the failures of those policies.

2.1 The All-Out War against the Civilian Population

The war against the defenceless civilian population consisted of terror, trade blockades and the disruption of livelihoods. Oppression and state terror were not new to the region as, since the start of the Ethiopian occupation, human rights violations persisted. However, the severity and magnitude of these violations increased dramatically with the new crackdown. The government saw the whole population of the region as backers of the rebel movement, which it was determined to wipe off the face of the earth. By carrying out a crackdown on the whole society and destroying its fundamental livelihood, the government believed that it could achieve victory over these resistance movements.

Since nearly everyone was declared a suspect, particularly in the zones where the resistance movements operated (such as Dolo, Jarar, Nogob, Qorahay, Faafan, Afdheer and Shabele), each army centre began to attack and round up the people nearest to them. The captives were then given unimaginably harsh treatment, both collectively and individually. The punitive measures that were enforced included public execution, detention, torture and body dismemberment. The army would kill some of them on the spot, while others were taken to detention centres and tortured before eventually being killed there or being taken to other prisons. The terror campaign spared no one: the elderly, the sick, women and children were amongst the victims.

The inhabitants of the region have often been displaced internally within the region or externally by fleeing to other countries. In the past, they used to flee to neighbouring countries to escape conflict and repression, but for the survivors of this war, there was nowhere to go—this was because of the blockade Ethiopia imposed on the region and because of Ethiopia's dominance of the Horn. The Ethiopian government closed the borders, and in addition to this, demanded from the various regional administrations in Somalia—which it effectively controlled—to return the people fleeing from persecution in the Ogaden region. The Ethiopian agents also operated in the whole region of the Horn of Africa and hunted dissidents everywhere in that part of the African continent.

Not only were the movements of the people restricted, but the essential goods that the inhabitants depended on, which used to come mainly from Somalia, were barred. All goods and items entering the region without the approval of the army were confiscated, as reported by the Human Rights Watch (HRW):

> The trade embargo was rigorously enforced through the confiscation of trucks and supplies that violated the embargo, as well as occasional killings of livestock and people who sought to evade it. The army patrols the main roads in the area and has set up checkpoints at entry points into towns to prevent embargo violations.
>
> Within weeks of the April 2007 Obole attack, the armed forces began confiscating commercial vehicles that moved goods into conflict-affected zones of Somali Region. In May 2007, the last major trade convoy left Hargeisa in Somaliland, consisting of 18 trucks stocked with food items and clothing. All 18 trucks were stopped and confiscated by the army near Dhagahbur, and were taken to the military base in Dhagahbur. At the end of September 2007, four months afterwards, all 18 trucks remained confiscated at the military base, according to their owners.[1]

As a result of the blockade, essential food items, clothes and many other consumer goods disappeared from the markets in the region. Consequently, the prices of the few goods that were smuggled rose sharply. As shown by the estimation of an interagency United Nations humanitarian assessment mission to the Somali region, conducted in late August and early September 2007, the trade embargo reduced the flow of commercial goods from 80 to 90 per cent and led to a rise in food prices of about 95 per cent. According to the same assessment, between

---

[1] Human Rights Watch, Collective Punishment: War Crimes and Crimes against Humanity in the Ogaden area of Ethiopia's Somali Region (New York: Human Rights Watch, 2008), 83.

60 and 80 per cent of the region's population depended on the sale of livestock for their income, and that trade was also severely affected by the embargo.

In addition to this, the government harassed and killed herders of livestock and farmers for allegedly supporting the resistance, and it frequently confiscated livestock and harvested crops. Farming, livestock and trade, which are the main livelihoods of the people there, were severely affected by this war. All three sectors were disrupted by these punitive measures, and as a result, the already weak subsistence economy dwindled further.

The collective punishment was also institutionalised by the regional parliament when it passed two laws in 2007. One of the two laws made the family and clan of a rebel movement member liable for the damage of his/her actions, by forcing them to compensate for the loss of lives or property. The other law required the suspension of budgetary subsidiaries to the districts where the insurgents were operating.

As part of the campaign to starve the people and hide the war crimes it was carrying out on the ground, the Ethiopian regime expelled, in mid-2007, the ICRC from the region. It accused the organisation of collaborating with the ONLF and spreading baseless accusations against the Ethiopian government. The ICRC was the only international organisation working throughout the region at the time. In addition to monitoring the conditions of the prisoners, its assistance activities there included sanitation projects and the construction of boreholes and wells. The Ethiopian regime also severely restricted the operations of the few remaining NGOs in the region, which included Médecins Sans Frontières (MSF) and Save the Children, and afterwards, also expelled the MSF.

Despite the Ethiopian government's attempts to hide the abuse it had been carrying out, the crackdown and the subsequent human rights violations drew the attention of international rights campaigners, international organisations and world media to the region. The Obole battle—in which 9 Chinese workers were killed—opened a new front over the natural resources of the region and triggered the new world's attention. The large diaspora community from the region, in the west, also made huge efforts to highlight the plight of their people. As a result of the unprecedented world attention, human rights organisations, international humanitarian organisations and international media all began to report on the human rights violations in the Somali region. In fact, the US House Foreign Affairs Subcommittee on Africa, Global Health, and Global Human Rights held a hearing about the human rights abuses within the region.

During the crackdown, several human rights campaigners reported severe human rights abuses by the Ethiopian army in the Ogaden, including gang rape, extrajudicial killing, body dismemberment, village burning, forced displacement and carpet bombardment. According to the rights groups, the terror campaign was a deliberate effort to mete out collective punishment against a civilian population suspected of sympathising with the resistance.

In mid-2007, both the HRW and the Ogaden Human Rights Committee (OHRC) published lengthy reports regarding the human rights situation in the region. They documented, amongst other things, the effects of the collective punishment measures, such as embargoes, forced displacement, the burning of villages and the confiscation and destruction of properties. The reports also gave detailed accounts of the scope and methods of human rights abuses perpetrated against the people as individuals and groups, and in particular, they highlighted the systematic abuses of extrajudicial killing, arbitrary detention, illegal imprisonment and sexual abuse.

The British newspaper The Independent likened the situation in the Ogaden to that of the Darfur region because of the similarity of the human rights violations (for instance, village burning, gang rape, extrajudicial killing and more). It warned of a looming catastrophe within the Somali region of a magnitude that was similar to the Darfur crises. Other international media outlets that reported on the issue included Reuters, The Guardian and Al Jazeera, and they published similar reports about the human rights situation in the region.

Many international media outlets reported on the conflict following the Obole attack. However, the contribution of The New York Times was the most significant, as it publicised both the cause and the brutality of the regime. With the help of the ONLF, The New York Times secretly visited the Somali region in May 2007, with the aim of finding out the truth about the situation within the region. An ONLF team, consisting of two underground units based in Addis Ababa and Jigjiga, and coordinated by Bashir Farah, secretly escorted The New York Times' journalists.

ONLF underground units smuggled The New York Times team, which consisted of Jeffrey Gettleman, the chief correspondent in the Horn, and two other journalists, to the base of the ONLF army in the region. The team stayed with the ONLF for about 9 days, making documentaries about the rebels, their cause and the lives of the population. They interviewed the villagers, the rebels and the people they met in the cities.

Unfortunately, the team was detained in Dagahbur upon their return from the rebels' camp, and their equipment—including most of their recordings—was confiscated by the Ethiopian authorities. However, the team managed to send some of the materials to New York before their arrest, and using those materials, the newspaper was able to produce written and visual documentaries about the brutality of the Ethiopian forces, the crackdown on the civilian population and the root causes of the conflict.

In June 2007, the newspaper published an article with the headline "Fear and Crises of Army Brutality" and released a video, titled "Rebels with a Cause". In the article and video, the newspaper reported on the human rights abuses that the atrocious Ethiopian regime was committing in the region, which included indiscriminate killings, village burnings, mass arrests and imprisonments with no judicial processes. The New York Times' reporters had interviewed villagers and ONLF militants. The latter told the newspaper that the organisation had been formed to resist the oppression and that they took arms to defend their people from the tyrannical regime.

The newspaper not only shed light on the human rights abuses that were going on in the region, but it also pointed out the indirect involvement of the US government in these human rights violations, resulting from its support of the regime in Addis Ababa on the pretext of the so-called war on terror campaign, of which the two governments cooperated. The report was part of the information used by a congressional subcommittee hearing on the matter, which was held in that same year.

In September 2007, a United Nations fact-finding mission stated that the situation in the Ogaden had deteriorated rapidly and called for an independent investigation into the allegations of human rights abuses by Ethiopian forces in the Somali state. John Holmes, the UN's Under-Secretary-General for Humanitarian Affairs visited the Somali region on 27 November 2007, and he described the situation of the Somali state as 'potentially serious'. In the same month, the UN's Office for the Coordination of Humanitarian Affairs (OCHA) announced they were opening aid facilities in the region.

On 10 July 2007, the US House Foreign Affairs Subcommittee on Africa, Global Health, and Global Human Rights and other international organisations held a hearing about the violations of human rights in Ethiopia, in which the Ogaden crisis was at the top of the list. Fawsia Abdulkadir, from the OHRC, was one of the people who testified in that hearing. Abdulkadir presented a broad picture of the human rights situation in Ethiopia and detailed the gross human rights violations that were taking place in the Somali region. Drawing a parallel between the Ogaden crisis and the situation in Darfur, she argued that the violations in the Ogaden region amounted to genocide and elaborated, in detail, the basis for that view. In her concluding remarks, she urged the committee to act upon their findings and intervene on behalf of the victims.

Despite this unprecedented world attention, history repeated itself. Just as it was used to misrepresent the cause of justice of the Somali people under Ethiopian rule in international arenas, the Ethiopian government again succeeded in misleading the world—by covering up its abuses and persuading the West to finance the campaign on terror. The big powers of the West were in alliance with Ethiopia on the so-called war on terror, and for Ethiopia, the crackdown was part of that war. The Western countries ignored the call for an international independent investigation because they did not desire a confrontation with Ethiopia for two reasons. Firstly, Ethiopia had already expelled the ICRC and the MSF, and they argued that a confrontation with the regime would trigger a further expulsion of desperately needed aid agencies, and secondly, they saw Ethiopia as an important ally in the anti-terror campaign. Thus, instead of condemning them, they helped the regime get away with its violations, and rather than imposing sanctions on them, they ended up funding the terror campaign against civilians.

The tragedy was aggravated by the West's indirect support of Ethiopia's human rights abuses. The Western governments not only tolerated the crackdown, but they also rejected the subsequent human rights abuses committed by the Ethiopian regime and described the violations as unsubstantiated. Additionally, they indirectly supported the crackdown by covering up the massacres of defenceless civilians and the destruction of their livelihoods by framing the terror campaign as a development and peace-building programme and funding it.

As was its aim, the war against the civilian population destroyed the economy of the region by disrupting their livelihoods. The collapse of the economy and the lack of available alternative resources led to persistent hunger and periodical famine. The war on terror also affected the people mentally by traumatising them. The multiple cruel punishments inflicted on them, combined with the abduction, torture and killing of loved ones in front of them, immensely affected their mental health. Eventually, the devastating war and consequent hunger enabled the regime to weaken the resistance and force the population to physically submit to its authority.

The crackdown devastated the economy and destroyed many lives. However, it did not kill the spirit of the people, and despite the severity of the punishments, they never gave up hope. Unlike the body, the human mind cannot be enslaved by force, and as a result, the people did not give up their dream of self-determination. Oppression is the main seed of anger, and repression fuels grief, which, in turn, increases the determination to resist. As a result, the violence and crackdowns that successive Ethiopian regimes always resorted to when dealing with the conflict did not work.

The resistance started as a reaction to the inhumane treatment of the inhabitants, and military force and human rights violations led to further resistance. Thus, despite the increase in human suffering, the long-term effect of the crackdown on the civilian population was as expected: an increased determination to get rid of the oppressor. In other words, it only made the resistance more determined to fight. Ethiopia has not taken any lessons from the history of this conflict, and the overall result of this vicious circle of state oppression and violence, triggering armed resistance and more repression in return, has been further bloodshed.

By forcing the inhabitants into physical submission to its authority, the terror campaign achieved much of its short-term objectives. However, it did not bring a resolution to the conflict. The key question of how to resolve the problem remained unanswered. A just solution to the problem was not the intention of the Ethiopian regime, and therefore, a negotiated settlement was out of the question for the regime. Instead of accepting reality and finding a solution, it went ahead with its old policies of imposing its will through military means and embarked upon new strategies to enforce them. Besides that, the scramble for the Ogaden's resources opened a new fight, which Ethiopia wanted to win quickly, to show her investors that she was in control of the situation. The new elements of the warfare strategy included the indigenisation of the conflict and the creation of a paramilitary militia. To add insult to injury, the regime in Addis Ababa contemplated the establishment of a local killing force at the peak of the crackdown, as detailed in the next section.

2.2 The Establishment of the Special Police Force (Lyu Police)

The paramilitary militia, known locally as the "Lyu Police", which means Special Police, was created in 2007. At the time, Ethiopia was fighting within Somalia following her invasion of the country in December 2006.

Ethiopia and her militia allies in Somalia were waging war on Al-Shabab and anyone opposed to her invasion. From there, the idea came to create a similar militia that would carry out the dirty jobs for her in the Ogaden.

The Ethiopian military had been fighting the ONLF army since 1994 but had still not defeated the rebels. Because of that failure, the regime in Addis Ababa changed its military tactics and, instead, put its weight behind the Special Police Force to make the new warfare strategy successful. Ethiopia wanted to show the governments and companies involved in the scramble for the Ogaden's natural resources rapid security improvements, and for that reason, she gave priority to the operations and funding of the new militia. In other words, the recruitment and funding of the Special Police Force were given the highest priority, and the methods of the recruitment process and the rules of engagement were made extraordinarily special.

2.2.1 Recruitment for the Special Police Force

Recruitment for the new force started with the enlisting of the destitute on the streets and prison inmates. Taking advantage of their vulnerability, the government recruited its first group from the destitute but did not get enough people. Thereafter, forced recruitment became the primary method of drafting recruits for the Special Police Force.

The Somali state has not seen real peace for more than a century, and because of that, it is one of the poorest regions in Ethiopia, despite the richness of its natural resources. The terror campaign and collective punishments led to more despair, hunger and famine—and more prison inmates. The consequent ever-increasing vulnerability of the inhabitants enabled the Ethiopian regime to exploit them and garner recruits for the paramilitary militia, which had been established to terrorise and kill them. Many youths joined the Special Police Force out of despair or for security reasons. Because of widespread unemployment and the conflict-ridden situation, most youths had no other option than to join either the resistance movements or the Special Police Force. In addition to this, any youth who was not a member of the Special Police Force automatically became a suspect and was seen by the security forces as a member of the resistance movement. For that reason, some joined the militia to escape the persecution of the regime's forces.

The army would round up people from the towns and villages and take them to training camps, and because of the threat of imprisonment or execution, they could not resist. Government employees were required to report for duty on short notice. As several international aid agencies reported in December 2007, the Ethiopian government was forcing local civilians, including health workers, to fight alongside the troops against the rebels. According to the same reports, soldiers barged into hospitals to draft recruits and threatened health workers with jail if they did not comply.

2.2.2 The Rules of Engagement for the Special Police Force

After a short period of training, they were sent to the streets to patrol and were given full powers to arrest, kill and imprison without charge. Besides that, they were given more powers than the military army to do similar jobs and were told that they would be rewarded according to the magnitude of the atrocities they committed: the higher the violations of human rights they perpetrated, the higher the rank they achieved. As expected, these criminals in uniform used their newly found powers to terrorise communities, rape women, confiscate property, detain and kill innocents, burn villages and carry out many more crimes.

In addition to this, the members of the force were required, by the authority, to prove the violations they had committed. To demonstrate the human rights violations they perpetrated, they were given orders to take pictures of the victims and send them to their commanders, who, in turn, were to report them to the regional president. The government ordered every one of them to commit abuses against the civilian population, and anyone who did not comply was punished. The aim behind this policy of forcing militia members to commit crimes was to make each one of them guilty and, consequently, an enemy of society. By doing so, the force became the only safe haven in which the soldier could stay. In a way, it was also another control mechanism that was used to make them insecure and irrational actors.

After the first phase, in which they exercised terror practises on their own community—a practice they excelled in—they were sent to the forests to fight the liberation fronts. At the time, the ONLF army was strong, and indeed, they were able to defeat the federal regular army. The morale of the regular army was incredibly low at the time because of the many years of fruitless war in a never-ending conflict. The army began to desert and some of its officers openly advised the government to find a political resolution to the problem. The Special Police Force was no match for the ONLF army, and as expected, it encountered defeat after defeat in the initial stages of the war with the rebel movement.

The special force and its patron turned their guns against the civilian population after their defeat by the rebels. They knew that the rebels lived on the support of the population, and killing the population was the means to cut that supply line. The regular army started the war against the defenceless civilians prior to the establishment of the Special Police Force; however, gradually, the new force took over that function. Because of their background and local knowledge, the paramilitary militia became more effective at punishing the population than the regular army.

Unlike the military confrontation between the army and the resistance movements, the collective punishment of the civilian population yielded early results for the perpetrators. Mistrust and division within the society came to the surface in a short period due to the atrocities committed by the Special Police Force. Before the creation of that army, the conflict had been between the Ethiopian government and the inhabitants of the region. However, the killing of the Special Police Force of its own people on behalf of the Ethiopian regime changed the picture of the conflict and made the war an internal one. To frame the war as an internal regional conflict, the Special Police Force was instructed to do the dirty work of human rights violations for the federal army, and the state's administration was given the political responsibility of those violations. The collective punishment carried out by the Special Police Force on the civilian population and the takeover of the leadership of the offensive against the resistance by the same force were the means to indigenise the conflict and achieve total victory over the inhabitants of the region.

As the junior partner of the regular army, the paramilitary militia, in the beginning, took a supportive role in security operations. However, as the new force grew, it gradually replaced the federal security forces in two main areas of engagement: the fight against the resistance movements and the collective punishment of the civilian population. The military waged parallel wars against the civilian population and the rebels, and it regarded the two offensives as complementary to one another, whereas the Special Police Force saw the collective punishment of the population as the primary instrument to quell the rebellion, as well as a means to suppress the voice of general discontent. As detailed in the following chapters, it became effective in both areas.

2.2.3 Funding Sources for the Special Police Force

Because of the totalitarian system of the government in Ethiopia and the lack of an independent audit, it is hard to get reliable data on defence spending or the source of income for military operations in Ethiopia. And it is nearly impossible to get a true picture of the funding for the Special Police Force because of the sensitivity and importance of the issue at stake. In addition to these reasons, war, corruption and the possible involvement of other governments and foreign companies complicate things even further.

However, we know that the scramble for natural resources was a decisive factor in establishing the Special Police Force, and it is highly likely that the scramble involved foreign parties (governments and companies) taking part in the funding and training of the Special Police Force. Independent sources have also revealed Western donor countries contributing to the force.

Whoever financed it, that is, all of the parties involved in the scramble for the Ogaden's natural resources counted on the success of the Special Police Force, and they were not outsiders wishing them victory but active participants of the war against the owners of those resources. Some of these involved parties such as the governments of China and Djibouti. Neither hid their intention on the matter nor their consequent actions on the ground. These two governments made arrangements with the regime in Addis Ababa on how to extract, transport, refine, export and share the revenue of the Ogaden's natural gas amongst themselves. They completely disregarded the people of the Somali state, viewing them as militarily insignificant, and were convinced they could get away with the robbery of the Ogaden's natural resources.

Ethiopia and the West were allies in the so-called war on terror, and Ethiopia took advantage of that alliance by making its massacre of the inhabitants of the Somali region a part of that war.

Even though the British government denied it, a leading British newspaper, namely, The Guardian, reported on 10 January 2013, that Britain had financed the Special Police Force. The report was based on internal government documents, seen by The Guardian, outlining a government tender to train security forces in the Somali region. The newspaper detailed the amount of the funding (between £13 million and £15 million), its intended beneficiary and the purpose of the donation:

> The Guardian has seen an internal Department for International Development document forming part of a tender to train security forces in the Somali region of Ogaden, which lies within Ethiopia, as part of a five-year £13m–15m "peace-building" programme.
>
> The document notes the "reputational risks of working alongside actors frequently cited in human rights violation allegations". DfID insists that the training will be managed by NGOs and private companies with the goal of improving security, professionalism and accountability of the force, but Human Rights Watch has documented countless allegations of human rights abuses.[2]

---

[2] Ben Quinn, 'UK tenders to train Ethiopian paramilitaries accused of abuses', *Guardian*, January 10, 2013, https://www.theguardian.com/world/2013/jan/10/ethiopia-forces-

From the report, Britain not only promised to contribute huge amounts of money, but it also misrepresented the reality of the situation by framing the terror campaign against the civilian population as a peace-building programme. Thus, financial contributions to the Special Police Force from the governments and companies that were directly involved in the scramble were highly likely.

Whatever the source of the funding, the Ethiopian government gave the responsibility of administering the budget of the Special Police Force to the regular army's headquarters in Harar. The army division head in Harar also oversaw the operations of the Special Police Force in collaboration with the head of the Somali Regional State. Despite the existence of a state assembly and a state administration, the head of the army division was the real ruler of the Somali state, even though he was not answerable to it politically.

---

human-rights-funding

3

The Escalation of the Crackdown

The war against defenceless people, which the federal army had started, escalated with the Special Police Force's takeover of most of the security operations within the region. The new militia army energised the security forces and widened the scope and intensity of the crackdown. Soon, the paramilitary militia had developed new punishment methods, such as the systematic use of rape, and strengthened the punitive measures that were already in use. As a result of the accelerated crackdown, existing prisons were enlarged and new ones were built to make room for the ever-increasing population of prison inmates. In addition to this, public places and private homes were used as prisons after ordinary (that is, regular) prisons became too overcrowded.

From their first encounter with the perpetrators to the end of their ordeal, victims underwent different types of abuse depending on the place or phase they were in. Whatever one might call these places where the abuse occurred (that is, a detention centre, a prison or a public or private place), the same criminals were in charge and gross human rights violations took place at all of them. In the following sections, we will highlight these places and some of the routine punishments that were carried out in each.

3.1 Open-Roof Prisons

Open-roof prisons were the starting point of human rights violations. Here, victims were apprehended, abused and kept until the next phase of their mistreatment. Very often, they would also return to these prisons after the end of their jail terms. These types of prisons were not specific buildings or locations but anywhere people lived their normal lives and carried out their daily routines, such as workplaces, mosques, markets or the local streets. In other words, a whole region could be an open-roof prison.

The victims could be a father in his home, a shopkeeper in his shop, someone walking down the street, a farmer working on his farm or a herder grazing his livestock on the land. Each one of these victims would encounter the most excruciating abuse on the spot, whether that was psychological, physical or economical.

For example, before arresting a father, the perpetrators would first rape his female family members in front of him and attack him as soon as he reacted, often killing him on the spot or torturing him and dragging him away. Some of the females, including the wife of the victim, could be taken as permanent wives. The goods of shopkeepers, the crops of farmers and the livestock of herders were often confiscated upon the owner's arrest. The victims could be handcuffed on the streets or killed on the spot.

Public execution in the towns was a frequent practice that was used by both the military and the Special Police Force. Prior to their murder, victims were paraded around the main parts of the town, and after the public execution, their bodies were displayed and left in the open for many days. This was to check for and hunt down anyone showing grief over the atrocity. In any case, no one would be able to help the victim, as any attempts to relieve or remove the body would have fatal consequences. The aim of this type of terror was to transform large towns into prisons so that no one would feel immune to the atrocities of the terrorists.

Although victims lived in open spaces, they were under constant watch and were unable to move freely. They were frequently abused both physically and verbally, and for that reason, we call these places open-roof prisons.

3.1.1 Stories from the Open-Roof Prisons

We will present in this section some real stories from open-roof prison victims and their families. The short narratives of these victims, and the related issue of property confiscation that follows, do not cover everything, but they provide a broader picture of the gravity of the abuses and shed some light on the precarious situation victims found themselves in.

3.1.1.1 The Magan Family Story

Magan was a farmer who used to live in a village called Dulcad. At the time, there was frequent fighting between the Ethiopian army and the resistance movements in the area. Because of the ongoing conflict, the resistance movements ordered people to evacuate the area and warned that anyone found there would be treated as an enemy collaborator. The inhabitants left the area promptly as they were told, taking some of their belongings with them. However, they left the newly harvested grain behind, which they depended on to survive.

The villagers dispatched a camel-led caravan consisting of four

24

women, two teenage girls and their transport camels to their village to collect some of the grain they had left behind. While loading the grain onto the backs of the camels, an armed group from the resistance came to the village. The group seized the women and accused them of being enemy collaborators. They killed the four women but spared the lives of the two girls because of their age.

One of the women and one of the girls were Magan's wife and daughter, respectively. After the death of his wife, Magan moved to another village that was 50 miles away from where he used to live. He started a new life by reorganising his livelihood and family life. He cultivated the local land to make a new farm and married again.

One day, his newly wedded wife went out to fetch water. On the way to the water well, she passed by an Ethiopian army makeshift camp and, after a while, saw an armed man approaching her. She ran away from him by circling and hiding around a thick tree. His aim was to first rape her and then kill her. As some villagers who watched the incident from a distance reported, he did the latter but failed to rape her. In his disappointment, he shot her in the head out of anger and she died instantly.

A few weeks later, the resistance movement ambushed the makeshift camp of the army near the village. The Ethiopian army accused Magan of helping the resistance in the attack. They severely tortured him and afterwards jailed him. They also burned his farm—the only livelihood he had.

He was sentenced to life imprisonment and spent many years in solitary confinement. However, because of ill health, he was eventually released. After his release, he had no normal life due to his poor health. He was frail and eventually died in the village from the injuries of the torture he had received. He left behind seven children who had nothing to inherit and who had lost both of their parents as well as their livelihoods.

Although Magan spent many years in a locked jail cell, it was within the open prisons where he experienced the most painful periods of his tragic life. It was there that he lost both his wives and his livelihood twice. His agony and suffering also ended there. He had not only been caught in the crossfire, but he was a victim of both the resistance and the government army and could not find anyone to turn to for aid. Similarly, nowhere was safe for him as both the Ethiopian army and the resistance movement had made him a target.

3.1.1.2 The Geedi Family Story

Geedi lives in a village called Carroguduud. One day, the Special Police Force stopped two teenage boys on the main street and killed them on the spot. The paramilitary militia later informed Geedi what they had done to the boys and where he could collect their bodies. One of the boys was his son and the other was his nephew.

A few days later, the Special Police Force came to the home of Geedi's eldest son who was married. They took him to an unknown destination. After many years of relentless searching, the family found him in the central prison of Jigjiga, which was known as Jail Ogaden. The young man was freed on general amnesty some years later, but he was re-arrested a few days after his release and again taken to an unknown destination. Two days later, the Special Police Force told Geedi where they had murdered him and dumped his body.

All three victims were murdered for allegedly supporting the ONLF. Geedi, who himself experienced detention and torture many times but survived, lives today with the killers of his sons in the same village. Most of these criminals have left the force, but some of them are still in uniform. None of these perpetrators has shown any remorse, and they all claim that they were simply following the orders of their commanders.

On the one hand, Carroguduud village is an open space with no walls surrounding it, and on the other hand, it was and continues to be an actual prison for the family both physically and mentally. The family was powerless when the perpetrators of human rights violations were abusing them. Now they are powerless as they are unable to bring justice to the murderers of their children or get any reparations for their suffering. They were unable to flee from the village at the time of the slaughter of their children because the paramilitary force made them captives. And it has also made them too weak to do anything about the injustice today.

3.1.1.3 The Asker Family Story

Asker was a nomad whose main livelihood was livestock, which included camels, goats and sheep. One day, the paramilitary force came to his home, attacked him and instantly began to torture him. While beating him, they kept asking him about the whereabouts of the rebels, and he told them that he had not seen them. They continued their torture until he became unconscious and afterwards took him to a detention centre.

He was accused of giving food and shelter to the resistance movement and was sent to the central jail, where he was sentenced to many years of imprisonment. After spending many years in jail, the political climate of

Ethiopia changed, and he gained his freedom as a result of the ensuing reform.

Asker wished to return home after the release, but he could not find anywhere to return to. Upon his release, he learnt that his wife and daughter had been taken as wives by the perpetrators, and both women were raising the children of the criminals who had raped them. He was also told that some of his sons had been killed by the same criminal gangs and that the rest of his family had fled the country. In addition to this, his livestock and belongings had been confiscated by the criminals in uniform.

The open-roof prison Asker returned to was, in many ways, worse than the ordinary one he had left. Even though he had experienced extremely harsh punishments there, he was unaware of what had happened to his family, which was the only hope he had been holding on to. He is physically and mentally frail and needs rehabilitation. His livelihood has gone, and the survivors of his family have either fled the country or have been captured by the very same criminals who ruined his life.

The worst thing about this type of prison is that he will spend the rest of his life there because of the new relationship he shares with the criminals. His wife and daughters are the mothers of the perpetrators' children. He is the stepfather and grandfather of those children, and they are a constant reminder of his ordeal.

In many ways, the situation of these women is a more challenging one than that of Asker's. Despite the stigma associated with illegitimate children, as mothers, they should love and raise their children like any other parent, and of course, the old Asker family should function like any other family. On the one hand, the women are committed to the original Asker family as mother, daughter and sister, and on the other hand, they are part of the families of the perpetrators who destroyed their real family. They have been torn apart physically and mentally by their conflicting commitments, which also serve as constant reminders of the unimaginable abuses they were subjected to.

3.1.1.4 The Galool Family Story

The Galool family used to live in a small village called Buuraley. Their main livelihood was livestock, which consisted of cattle and sheep, and they had a small farm in which they grew grain. The family consisted of a mother, a father and four sons. They had a happy life there until one of the sons joined the resistance movement. After he joined, everything suddenly changed, and the lives of the family were turned upside down.

One morning, the paramilitary militia—known as the Special Police Force—came to the village looking for Galool. As soon as they saw him, they apprehended him, beat him and demanded that he bring his son back from the resistance. The man told the militia that his son had made his own decision without consulting him, and for that reason, he could not bring him back. They began to torture him and told him that he would not live unless he accepted their demand. One of the sons who could not bear the pain of his father tried to defend him. They swiftly retaliated by shooting him dead. Subsequently, they left the father unconscious and took the other two sons with them.

A few days later, they came back to the village to again demand the return of Galool's son from the resistance. Just as they had done before, they tortured Galool—this time breaking his ribs and one of his arms. They also confiscated his livestock. The two sons they had previously taken with them were sent to jail within Jigjiga. On leaving, they told Galool that they would return again and again and continue punishing him until he brought his son back.

The son who had joined the resistance movement heard what had happened to his family, and although it made him sad, going back to the village was not an option for him. He knew that going back home would not make a difference to his family's situation and would only lead to the end of his life. He decided to carry on with his fight until he was victorious—a fight that ended his life before the defeat of his enemy.

The lives of Galool and his wife were devastated following the imprisonment of two of their sons, the death of the other two and the confiscation of what they owned. Their livestock was taken from them, their sons were gone and, because of the torture he had received, Galool became too weak to cultivate the land. As both their family and livelihood had been destroyed, their lives were ruined, and they became very fragile physically and psychologically.

Despite the difficult situation, Galool and his wife lived with a glimmer of hope of one day seeing their two sons who had been taken away from them, but that hope was soon dashed by the news that their sons were amongst many other inmates who had died in jail from starvation and torture. The couple could not cope with this unbearable tragedy, but help was also not available because the people they could turn to were experiencing similar tragedies.

Buuraley, the open-roof prison of the Galool family, was also home to many of their neighbours who were in similar situations. It was a typical village where similar tragedies occurred on daily basis, and because of the common gross violations of human rights that took place everywhere, there were no other places in the region to flee to or seek refuge. Therefore, the couple remained in the village. Everyone stayed in these open-roof prisons expecting a visit from the perpetrators at any moment and fearing that the worst would happen to them, that is, until the regime change.

3.1.1.5 The Biihi Family Story

Biihi joined the ONLF, and because of this, all the members of his extended family were arrested and detained. They were severely tortured in a detention centre, and during the interrogation, they were asked about the whereabouts of Biihi and the organisation he had joined. They demanded that the family bring Biihi back. His wife, who was pregnant at the time of her arrest, suffered a miscarriage before dying of a beating.

Biihi was eventually captured by the Special Police Force. They released the family after his capture but then rearrested them shortly afterwards. They also rounded up many of the inhabitants of the village. The authority demanded that the villagers buy a machine gun for the government, which they alleged had been taken by the ONLF rebel group. The villagers had to sell their livestock to procure the money for the gun they had been forced to buy.

They promised the authorities that they would purchase the gun as soon as they sold the livestock, but the government did not wait. They arrested all of them and confiscated their livestock. Thereafter, government soldiers killed all of the detainees. Biihi witnessed the scene of mass murder. One image from that horrible scene that has never left his mind was of twin babies lying on the body of their murdered mother seeking her help. The mass graves in which those victims were buried can be vividly seen from a distance.

3.1.2 The Property Confiscation Trap

All the successive regimes in Ethiopia used the confiscation and destruction of property as a collective punitive measure. However, during the nearly 30-year reign of the EPRDF, it was part of their daily routine. Resistance members, their families and suspected sympathisers of the resistance movement have been the main victims of property rights violations.

Property destruction took place in the form of burning farms and villages, the demolition of houses and the shooting or starvation of livestock. Harvested crops, livestock, houses, real estate, farms, vehicles and nearly everything owned by the people would be confiscated. Some of the confiscated properties were used by government agencies, such as the military and the Special Police Force, while others were sold to individuals often with regime connections. Victims of property rights violations often ended up in jail or fled the country, and many of them never returned. However, because of the frequency of these violations, victims could be found in every village and town in large numbers.

Violations of property rights are very widespread and most inhabitants of the Somali region have experienced this problem either directly themselves or indirectly through family members who have been victims. However, the conflicts related to confiscated property whose owners are still present and is being used by the perpetrators or by new buyers are amongst the most difficult and painful cases. The disputes that break out are often between an occupant of confiscated property—such as real estate, a farm or a house—who claims to have been given it by the government and the real owner of that property or between the new buyer of the confiscated property and the original owner. Since the conflicts are predominantly between the victims of human rights violations and the perpetrators of the abuses and their associates, the conflicting parties are not equal in terms of the power and resources they hold.

In many cases, the victims are just as powerless as they were when their property was first taken away from them. They see their desperately needed land, livestock or house in front of them, but they cannot exercise their property rights. And that powerlessness makes them prisoners even though they live in open spaces. They cannot forget the property they see before them, and they are unable to get it back legally or otherwise and, therefore, remain trapped by it. They feel imprisoned because of the deprivation of their property in the same way that a prisoner feels confined when he loses the freedom of movement. In both cases, the rights that have been taken away are what make them prisoners.

3.2 Ordinary Prisons: Jail Ogaden

Ordinary prisons are places of incarceration where the movement of an inmate is confined and restricted to a prison cell. Such jails existed at one point in every zone and town of the Somali region. The larger jails were in Jigjiga, Bayahow, Godey, Dagahbur, Qabridaharre, Wardheer, Dire Dawa and Fiiq. The recently closed Jigjiga Central Prison, also named Jail Ogaden, was the largest in the region.

It is not possible to cover everything that happened in these prisons in a single book; therefore, we will not be narrating stories from all the prisons listed here. Instead, we will take Jail Ogaden as an example since what happened at that jail is representative of what took place at other prisons in the region. Stories from that central jail should suffice.

The regional TV channel and other media outlets have made documentaries about this jail. They conducted interviews in which former inmates spoke about their experiences of that prison in detail. We will summarise some of those testimonies here.

The infamous central jail of Jigjiga, commonly known as Jail Ogaden, was a dreadful place. It was built in 1996 and closed for good in 2018. During this period, it was home to thousands of people, and because of the large number of people who were imprisoned there, nearly everyone in the region has either been imprisoned there themselves or knows someone who was imprisoned there. Victims were not imprisoned for any definable legal reason, and most inmates were never charged or convicted of any crime.

Far too many people have been imprisoned in Jail Ogaden for committing no crimes and have lived in unthinkable conditions. The inmates were abused physically, sexually and psychologically; they were subjected to unimaginable torture, including beatings, drownings and rape. They were starved, humiliated, had no access to medical care and were not allowed to contact their families. As a result of these inhumane treatments and punishments, many of them died and many others became disabled. Some of them also lost their reproductive organs because of the severe torture they were subjected to. They expected death to come to them at any moment, and some of them even wished death to come sooner rather than later because of their unbearable suffering.

As one inmate put it: 'Jail Ogaden was a place that nobody has ever seen or ever heard the like of before and no human being could ever even imagine'.

3.2.1 Testimonies
In this section, we will present twelve testimonies from prisoners to get firsthand accounts of the living conditions of the prison.

3.2.1.1 Halgan Hassan Ahmed
Halgan started his testimony by saying, 'I am very hesitant to talk about or share my experiences in that jail with someone else because it is so sad to be reminded of the horrors of that place. The people in charge of that horrible place were not aliens but our people: we knew each other, we worked together and we shared a common ethnicity, and that unpleasant reality also makes me reluctant to revisit that tragic place. But for the sake of creating a historical record, it is necessary to talk about it'.

He then continued his account by explaining how he was arrested. He recalled he received a phone call on 22 January 2015 from Mustafe Abdi, a member of the regional state cabinet whom he knew. After asking him about his whereabouts, the official told Halgan to stay where he was and wait for his arrival. That minister and Mukhtar Suubane, a high-ranking Special Police officer who accompanied him, told Halgan to bring his laptop and mobile phone with him. He and two other men, who had also been called to attend the meeting, were then taken to a house in Jigjiga, which was used as a transitional detention centre. As soon as they arrived at that house, they were interrogated by a team who had been waiting for them. They were accused of publishing a website called Fadumo Firimbi, which was critical of the Somali state president, a charge that the three men denied. The team searched their laptops and mobiles but could not find any evidence showing what they had been accused of.

The three men were then taken from the house by soldiers in vans to Jail Ogaden, where their clothes were stripped except for their underwear. The victims were then chained in the shape of a number eight: their legs and arms were tied together behind their backs and their chests were laid on the ground. They were left in that position for several hours until the chains began to cut into their skins. Bleeding and still in chains, the three men were then taken to a water reservoir where they were separated. Each man was taken by a team of 10 soldiers; the soldiers held them upside down and began to plunge the victims into the cold water. They forced them deep into the water ground until they were just about to drown before pulling them out again to check whether they would reveal any information. They repeated the process until Halgan fell unconscious.

The next day, he regained consciousness in a very cold cell. He did not know where he was until he saw some graffiti with the name of a friend of his on the door. That friend had told him about a punishment cell in Jail Ogaden in which he had once stayed, and when he saw the name, he understood where he was. For about 17 days, he stayed in that cell alone, naked and on a cold cement floor. He could not move because of the infected wounds that he had sustained from the incisions of the chains in both legs and arms. There was no toilet and he had to urinate and sleep in the same place.

Halgan was then moved from solitary confinement to another punishment cell along with six other inmates, where they stayed for nearly a month. The men were stripped of their clothes the day they were arrested, and they did not get them back; the cell was very cold during the night and extremely hot during the day. Beatings and many other types of torture were a daily routine. Often, they were tortured inside the prison, but sometimes punishments would take place outside such as at the water reservoir, as mentioned earlier.

One of the outdoor torture sites was a sewage dumping ground. One night, Halgan and his friends were taken from their prison cell to the sewage dump. When they arrived there, they were thrown into the sewage dump and interrogated by Shamahiye Sheikh Farah, who was the head of the central prison. Shamahiye Sheikh Farah was also in conversation with the regional president during the interrogation. Halgan heard the president asking whether they had revealed any information regarding the website. During the interrogation, two of the inmates sank into the sewage dump, but fortunately, they were rescued by some soldiers at the last minute, just as they were about to disappear into the sewage entirely.

For about seven months, Halgan and his friends were taken from one punishment cell to another: sometimes into solitary confinement but often together in an overcrowded cell. During the seven months, they did not take a bath, and in all of the cells they stayed in, there were no toilets and their food consisted of a loaf of bread and a handful of plain white rice. Constant beatings, starvation, sleep deprivation and drownings in water and sewage were amongst the daily punishments they received. Throughout that period, they did not even see the other inmates of the jail.

Afterwards, they joined the other inmates in the main halls. According to Halgan's estimation, the total number of inmates of Jail Ogaden at that time was about 5,000. Halgan's family were not aware of his whereabouts during the seven months, and they only learnt that he was alive when he made contact with the other prisoners of the jail. Aside from the occasional contact with his family, his situation did not change when he joined the other inmates in terms of punishments and general living conditions.

The torture inside and outside the jail continued after he was moved to the main halls. He faced some elements of the torture he was subjected to in the punishment cells, such as water torture, along with new torture methods, such as being forced to stand for several days. He added that the prison guards made torture their primary duty in the prison because they were obsessed with it, and there was not a single day without punishment. The various types of torture he experienced in the main jail are mentioned next.

On one rainy night, he was taken to a large water ground that was flooded with rainwater. He was taken there by several men in uniform who pushed him down into the water and held him there until he became unconscious. Part of his flesh remained on the ground when he was picked up the next day. On another occasion, Halgan and many others were forced to stand outside for five consecutive rainy days; each time one of them fell to the ground, the guards would beat him until he stood again. Another day, Halgan and friends of his were buried in wet sand. The sand that entered his body continued to come out of his ears for several months afterwards. He was also given a penalty of beatings and was confined to a toilet for four consecutive months for allegedly writing a book while in jail. He was thrown into a hole about eight metres deep and spent several days there.

The conditions of the rooms in the main halls were just as bad as the ones they had left and more overcrowded. First, Halgan was moved to the coldest cell in the whole jail along with the other inmates when they were transferred to the main jail. The room was in the middle of the building and never saw any sunshine. Later, he ended up in another cell marked for people who had been sentenced to death. Over 2,000 people—of whom over a dozen were insane—shared a death row cell of about 84 square metres.

While talking about some of the most horrifying scenes he had experienced in the jail, Halgan mentioned an incident that occurred in the toilet he was forced to stay in. The so-called toilets were not normal toilets but more like a dumping place for human waste, where human excrement lay everywhere. He was thrown into such a toilet after he had been savagely beaten. The place was not only full of excrement, but the one-square-metre toilet was also very narrow and too small for him. Because of the pain of the beating and the dirty narrow place he was confined to, he cried until he was joined by other prisoners in the same small toilet.

The prisoners who joined Halgan were two old sheikhs of whom the eldest was about 80 years old. Like Halgan, the two sheikhs had been tortured before they were thrown into the toilet. As soon as he saw the pain and suffering of those old men, he forgot his own pain and stood up to help the 80-year-old sheikh and tried, in vain, to find a place he could lay him down. The three men were on top of one another because of the narrowness of the place, and all three were in pain. Because of the high regard that the elderly and religious leaders have in society, Halgan instinctively tried to show the same respect and welcomed them in that terrible place. But he had nothing to offer them. Halgan said that the helplessness he felt and the suffering of that 80-year-old sheikh in that horrible place will never leave his mind.

Another scene that he will never forget was the torture of a friend who could not bear the punishments of prison and attempted suicide by cutting his throat. When they saw him cutting parts of his throat, the soldiers began to torture him instead of relieving him. He was bleeding because of the cut to his throat and the torture, and he was crying for help. But they did not allow anyone to talk to him, let alone help him. The bleeding body of that friend and the torture he was subjected to while in a coma, as well as his agony at that moment, are vividly fixed in his mind.

The rapid physical deterioration of the other inmates is another image that appears in his mind all the time. Because of starvation and continual torture, prisoners often physically changed in a short space of time. One after the other, they would lose the ability to stand or walk, and many of them become fully disabled for the rest of their lives. In addition to this, the reproductive organs of some of the prisoners were damaged by the torture, and as a result, they were no longer able to produce offspring.

Halgan was sentenced to seven years in prison, a sentence he believes was very lenient compared to the average sentences of other prisoners. After three and a half years, he came out of prison following the reform in Ethiopia and the regime change in the Somali state.

3.2.1.2 Siraje Adan Hassan

Siraje's account of jail starts with his arrest. Under the command of Colonel Mukhtar Mohamed Suubane, 20 soldiers broke into his house at around 2.00 am in a very violent manner. One of their vehicles hit the gate and they smashed the doors and windows with the bottom of their guns. He was in bed at the time with his wife and baby. They apprehended him violently and asked for his mobile and laptop. He handed over his mobile phone, but he did not have the latter.

One day after his arrest, they ejected his family from the house, which he owned, and turned it into a detention centre. According to the victim, the decision to kick the family out of their house and throw them onto the street was made by Mukhtar Mohamed Suubane and the Somali state president.

He was then taken to Jail Ogaden, which he called a concentration camp. He added that it was not a prison but a place to assemble people and then brutally kill them. Some of them were killed by drowning, some were starved to death and others died after being beaten. As soon as they reached the jail, the soldiers began to torture him. First, they tied his arms behind his back and then plunged him upside down into a barrel of water. Later, they covered his head with a plastic bag containing hot chilli pepper powder. He said there were some guards who never cut their nails and would use them as tools for torture. They used to scratch the body of the victims with their nails, and he was subjected to this as well.

The next routine punishment was water torture. Together with some of the other inmates, he was taken by the Special Police Force to a water reservoir where they were tortured and interrogated. Their heads were pushed deep into the cold water and then pulled out for a few minutes of questioning. The punishment continued for three consecutive days, repeating the same process of torture and interrogation.

He was accused of supporting a rebel group within the cabinet and for partaking in the publishing of a website, called Fadumo Firimbi. One day, he was visited in his cell by a woman and a man from the regional high court, who gave him a card and asked him to sign a piece of paper. When he asked what the paper and the card were for, they told him that he had been sentenced to 15 years imprisonment; the number on the card—5554—was his sentence number, and he was required to confirm that he had received his sentence card. Siraje asked them how he could be sentenced without attending court. Many prisoners who also received their sentences that day asked the same question without prior discussion. The prisoners all knew the justice system in the region, and while they were not expecting a normal court hearing or a just verdict, they thought they would at least be taken to court before being sentenced.

Afterwards, Shamahiye Sheikh Farah, the head of the prison, threatened and accused Siraje of spreading propaganda against the system and stirring up a rebellion inside the prison. The prison head also told Siraje point-blank that it would not make a difference whether he attended court or not as long as the sentence had been decided in advance. Siraje added that they knew General Abdirahman Labag'ole, the head of the Special Police Force, and Colonel Mukhtar Mohamed Suubane had the authority to sentence prisoners, and the courts would simply write what they dictated. In that sense, the head of the prison was right in saying that court attendance was not necessary.

Because of the question the prisoners posed, the authorities changed their minds, and in the evening of that day, the sentenced prisoners were taken to court. When they arrived, they were told that a total sentence of 230 years had been decided in advance and that they had been brought to the court merely to inform each person of his share of that total number. The judge added that they could divide the total number amongst themselves if they were not happy with the court's sentencing formula.

Siraje spent the first two months in the coldest room, which the prisoners had nicknamed the Titanic. It was in the centre of the jail and surrounded by other buildings; because of its location, it did not get sunlight. There were around 30 prisoners in that room. In the next cell, he stayed about a year. In both cells, there were no toilets, they had little to eat and were beaten daily; sometimes, they were tortured outside the prison.

The sewage dumping ground was one of the torture places outside the jail. One night, Siraje and his friends were taken there by a special force sent by the regional state president, who forced them to go into the dump. The victims were in chains and their arms were tied behind their backs. They were interrogated while inside the sewage and spent many hours there. Siraje was asked to reveal the website password for Fadumo Firimbi and his alleged connection with the cabinet group that opposed the president. Siraje was one of the victims whom Halgan said had to be rescued after sinking into the sewage dump.

Another form of punishment in the jail was enhanced interrogation in which the victim was examined under torture. When carrying out this type of punishment, all the inmates were assembled on one side to watch the torture and interrogation process. The victims were asked to admit to crimes they had not committed, and if they did not comply, they were beaten. Usually, this type of interrogation took the whole day or night, and no one was allowed to leave until the interrogation was over. This was a routine punishment for everybody.

On one occasion, a prisoner who was suspected of links with the rebel group ONLF admitted that he had buried weapons somewhere while undergoing enhanced interrogation. They took him to the site, but before they arrived, he told them that he had not buried anything and that he had only confessed to the crime because of the pain from the torture. After this incident, they introduced a new punishment regime for all alleged members of this rebel group. They brought in 300 new soldiers and began to torture the ONLF group. They brought all of the ONLF prisoners—over 1,000—into three rooms, which each had a normal capacity of 40 people. The punishment programme was to isolate them, starve them and torture them. In doing so, they were locked inside the three rooms without food and beaten daily. Because of the severity of the punishment, the inmates decided to block the doors to prevent the soldiers from entering the rooms and demanded to see the highest authority. Siraje later said that if the inmates knew the punishment programme had been prescribed by the highest authority, they would have not demanded to see them.

General Abdirahman Labago'le came to see them, and after meeting them, he decided to increase the punishments of the inmates: daily enhanced interrogations, constant beatings, different drowning methods and starvation. Siraje said one of the horrible memories of the torture of that group was the breaking of the prisoners' limbs. Two soldiers would sit on the legs of the victim and another soldier would hit one of the legs with heavy stones. They used to check the leg after they had hit it to make sure it was broken. He said that they knew the victims and would hear sounds of the bones breaking, but out of fear of punishment, they could not even show their grief. The victims could not express their feelings either, because they would break both legs if they cried.

A government employee group, of which Siraje was one, was accused of lecturing the ONLF group about their rights. Subsequently, the severe punishment that the ONLF group experienced was applied to the civil servant group, too.

People were dying in huge numbers in jail because of mass shootings and physical torture. However, starvation was the biggest killer. Siraje added that families had been bringing food for their loved ones in jail for about eight months, not knowing that it was being eaten by the prison guards while they were left to starve inside.

The most shocking scene that Siraje remembers is that of a young man who was beaten so hard that flesh from his buttocks and parts of his thighs fell from his body to the ground. He added that the young man is still alive and everybody can see the half-skeleton man.

Due to the regime change in the Somali region and the general reform in Ethiopia, Siraje was released from prison after three years and eight months.

3.2.1.3 Abdi-Hukun Ali Dubad

Abdi-Hukun Ali Dubad was arrested together with Halgan Hassan Ahmed and Khalil Haji Abdishukur. It was nighttime when they were arrested and brought to Jail Ogaden. As soon as they arrived, they were stripped of their clothes and tied into the shape of a number eight: their legs and arms were tied together behind their backs. It was a very cold night, and they had no clothes except for their underwear. Their punishment started with cold water torture; the soldiers first splashed cold water on the victims and afterwards took them to a water reservoir to torture them there. The prisoners were in chains and their limbs were tied together behind their backs when they were thrown into the cold water. They were kept submerged in the water to simulate drowning and remained in that position for some time. After being questioned for a few minutes, the torture was repeated, and the victims stayed in the water for several hours.

Abdi-Hukun, however, was lucky to escape most of the water

punishments that night because of a lung condition. A prisoner with a similar condition had died under such torture, and because of that incident, they took him from the water after he told them he had asthma. Despite the escape, Abdi-Hukun was not a happy man because of the torture of his friends: he grieved over their suffering. He was separated from his friends after the water reservoir visit and was taken to a solitary punishment cell.

The chains and consequent injuries inflicted on him during that first night in jail were very painful. His limbs had deep cuts from the tight chains, and the cold water increased the inflammation of the injury. Because of the wounds and ensuing infection, his fingers swelled, and the long-term consequences of the painful chains were very harmful. Many people lost their arms and legs because of the chains and became disabled.

After a week, he received a sentence of 13 years imprisonment. The decision was made without attending a court hearing, although he and his friends were later taken to court to formally hear the sentence they had received in advance. The judge was a local musician who was dressed as a judge but had no judicial education.

Abdi-Hukun was neither surprised by the way he was sentenced nor was he worried about it. The regime would frequently imprison people before they were charged, and very often, the crimes they were charged with were invented while they were in jail, which is what happened to him. Sentencing would also take place prior to court attendance. In short, he said that the message of the government to the public was 'not to cry over their torture, not to grieve over the murder of their family members and not pay attention to the abuses of the government'. He added that the people of the region had become 'laughing patients' as a result of that cruel message, that is, they pretended to be happy despite their immense suffering. He knew that such an oppressive regime would not last long, and for that reason, he was not worried about the lengthy sentence.

He spent several years in jail, and during that period, he experienced different types of torture: enhanced interrogation, beatings, starvation and near-drowning. Even though he was sentenced at the beginning of his imprisonment, the interrogation and torture continued until the day he was released.

Despite the punishments and harsh conditions, he believed his situation had been better than many of the other inmates. He described the situation of the women as unbearable. They were tortured like the other prisoners, and in addition to that, they were gang raped.

According to the victim, the place was not a jail, but an

experimentation centre, where all types of torture were practised. It was also a sealed place that was hidden from the rest of the world. Even the federal government, who initiated the abusive programme and on whose behalf all that brutality was carried out, was sometimes misled regarding the magnitude of the brutality. The Ethiopian Human Rights Commission (EHRC) used to visit the jail and stay for some days. Ahead of the EHRC and other dignitary visits, the jail was cleaned and painted, the inmates were given the freedom to go to the toilet and they were given clothes. However, they were warned of the consequences if they did not cooperate and talk positively about their personal treatment and the general condition of the jail.

Speaking on the bank of the sewage dumping ground where he had been tortured, Abdi-Hukun described in detail how that particular punishment happened. The bank of the sewage dump was very steep, and the victims were in chains. His biggest fear was falling from the steep hill on the sewage dump side and sinking into the sewage. After several hours of interrogation and near-drowning in the sewage, the inmates were laid down on the ground. The soldiers then walked on them while they lay there.

At the end of the torture, the team leader who was also the head of Jail Ogaden received a phone call from the president of the region. The team leader explained to the president the different punishments they had carried out in detail. He also told him that they did not manage to get any new information from them, despite the extreme torture.

The special presidential forces that picked them up from jail took them back and handed them over to the prison guards somewhere between the prison and the sewage dump. When they arrived at the jail, they were bleeding and unable to move because of the injuries from the handcuffs. The guards attempted to remove the handcuffs but could not find the keys. They waited in pain for several hours, but eventually, they managed to get rid of the chains.

As Abdi-Hukum predicted, the regime was ousted before the end of his sentence. After about three and a half years, he regained his freedom as a result of the regime change.

3.2.1.4 Mohamud Faysal Ahmed

Mohamud was in Jail Ogaden from 2011–2018. He told us that he could not reveal everything that he saw in jail but would mention some of the things that had happened to him and his inmate friends.

Starting with what happened to him, Mohamud said that of the many different tortures he experienced, the breaking of his leg was the most painful. Four men took part in that torture: some sat on him while the others performed the breaking action. They also refused to fix the broken bone at the right time. After nearly a month, they told him that he could repair his broken leg, but there were neither doctors to help him nor medical equipment that he could use. His inmate friends attempted to fix it using pieces of wood and their garments as a splint. Although it was not a proper fix, somehow it became walkable. One day, one of the officers called Nur Ilka'ase saw Mohamud walking and soon after ordered the guards to break his leg again. Because of the repeated bone fracture, his leg became deformed and unrepairable. The first incident took place at the beginning of his imprisonment and he was without a proper leg throughout his sentence.

The breaking of limbs was one of the routine punishments that took place. Guards would ask the victims to choose the leg or arm to be broken. But often, they would come back and break the other leg or arm, and he saw many people who had all of their limbs broken.

One of the most horrible crime scenes that he witnessed was that of a young man who was a Qur'an teacher. The man had been arrested in Jigjiga and was accused of affiliating with Al-Shabab. He watched the soldiers beat him to death. For six years, his family was not aware of his death.

He mentioned another incident in which a victim was beaten to death. The man was an ONLF suspect, and they killed him as they interrogated him. After the murder, they asked one another whether they had got the information they needed from him before his death. He added that the information was more important to them than his life.

Other shocking scenes he saw included a pregnant woman who lost her unborn child during a beating, without knowing when the baby came out of the womb. He also saw a man and his son-in-law stripped of their clothes and ordered to hold each other's genitals.

They used to assemble thousands of people for collective punishments, and by the end of the gathering, the majority of inmates could not walk and go back to their cells because of hunger. Dozens of inmates were dying every day—most of them because of the beatings they received and starvation.

Another strange punishment was not allowing people to talk. They were forced to pretend to be mute. If they were seen talking, they would be beaten. When this ban was lifted, victims unconsciously still used sign language for many months afterwards. Others were forced to make noises like animals.

Although the victims were suffering in jail, they were also hopeful.

They expected the struggle to succeed and for the situation to change for the better. However, despite the regime change, the return of the ONLF and the talk of the human rights violations that took place, they have not been given reparations and they have not seen any improvements to their lives. The criminals who made them suffer are free; they do not show any remorse and some of them even claim to be victims themselves. This harsh reality and faded hope make Mohamud sad today.

3.2.1.5 Muhumed Abdullahi Guuleed (Anni)

Muhumed was a well-known commander of the ONLF. He was arrested on 5 January 2014 near Gur'el, a village on the Somali side of the border between Ethiopia and Somalia. He was arrested by a Somali militia group who handed him over to the Special Police Force. The latter brought him to Jigjiga on 7 January 2014. He was interrogated on the first day by a team led by Abdirahman Labago'le. His imprisonment began the following day with severe torture.

The soldiers first tied his four limbs behind his back and covered his head. Then, he was taken to a place where he was given tools to dig his own grave while his face was still covered. They untied him so that he could dig, but they did not remove the cover from his face while he dug the grave. He repeatedly asked them to uncover his face so he could make a proper grave for himself, but they rejected that request. He dug for many hours, and he felt death getting closer the deeper the hole became. He knew of many people who had been buried in the graves they were forced to dig for themselves. When he completed the grave and thought his life was over, they lifted him from the hole and put him in a van. In addition to the emotional distress, he was tired, thirsty and hungry. But he was relieved that they had spared his life.

From there, they took him to the office of Abdullahi Yusuf Weerar, who was the then vice president and head of security. Abdullahi wanted to get information regarding the ONLF from the detainee and demanded him to cooperate and give the government details about the organisation and its operations. Muhumed refused to comply with that order.

The next destination was Jail Ogaden, where he spent the first six months in a solitary torture cell. Another inmate joined him in the cell and the two were there for another six months. He did not see light for the first 24 months of his 4-year imprisonment. During that period, he stayed in torture cells, including seven months of confinement in a toilet. He recalled that in both solitary confinement and the group cell, the punishments were too many to count and too painful to describe in detail. It is sufficient to mention the methods of the tortures they experienced in summary form.

They were forced to lay down in the sewage dumping grounds next to the jail and paint one another with human excrement. They were ordered to pretend to be mute and only use sign language for up to a year, or sometimes they were forced to pretend to be animals and make animal sounds instead of talking. For example, Muhumed was forced to be a sheep; every time they talked to him, he had to bleat instead of talking like a human being. Their limbs were broken. Both his arms were broken, and his right arm was broken three times, which practically made him disabled. Water torture was another form of routine punishment. Sometimes, the water torture was carried out inside the jail by plunging the victims into barrels full of water while they were being held upside down. The water torture also used to take place outside the prison at the water reservoir and sewage dumping ground. Using different tools, including sticks and water pipes, the prison guards used to beat the inmates, and sometimes they forced the prisoners to beat one another. For seven months, he was beaten three times a day. The heads of the victims were put inside plastic bags containing hot chilli pepper powder while their hands were tied or held by guards. Many victims died of suffocation from this type of torture. Some of the worst types of torture involved standing outside for many days or being confined to a room with narrow crooked walls where one could not stand properly, could not stretch out one's body and could not lie down.

People were dying every day because of the torture they received; however, beatings and starvation were the two most harmful punishments. They were not only the ones that caused the most deaths, but the deaths that were caused by these punishments were the most painful because of the long agony and suffering involved, which often meant that it would be weeks before the victims passed away. People were dying slowly from beatings and starvation, and their cries were getting lower and lower until their souls departed their bodies. And watching them die in that way was the most painful kind of death to witness.

Muhumed's imprisonment ended dramatically; in July 2018, weeks before the collapse of the Somali regional administration, Muhumed was forced to talk to the BBC Somali Service while in detention. During that month, the HRW published a damning report on the conditions of Jail Ogaden, and the authorities demanded him to refute the report and present a positive, albeit false, picture of the condition of the jail. In the interview, he said that he did not know anything about the conditions of the jail. The interviewer repeatedly asked him to give a description of life in the prison, but he declined to say anything.

His bravery surprised everybody and worried the audience of the radio programme, who knew what the reaction of the regime would be. However, they did not wait for the regime to react but took steps for immediate rescue. The interview took place outside the prison, and from there, they planned an escape route for him. They risked their own lives to save Muhumed's life. They cunningly lured the guards and managed to take him to a secret place in the city (Dagahbur) where he was interviewed. From that secret place, they planned the next steps, and in the end, they succeeded in bringing him to a hotel in Addis Ababa.

3.2.1.6 Abdifatah Matan Said

Abdifatah was arrested in 2015 in Addis Ababa where he was staying for security reasons. He had fled the Somali region to the capital, which he mistakenly thought would be a safe haven. With the help of the federal intelligence and Addis police, the Somali regional administration succeeded in arresting him in Addis Ababa. After two days of detention there, he was brought to Jigjiga, where he was first imprisoned in a local jail called Havana. In that prison, a police commissioner came and took him to Jail Ogaden.

As soon as he arrived, he was interrogated and asked to reveal the password of the website Fadumo Firimbi and the names of its publishers. After the interrogation, he was beaten and taken to a toilet where he stayed for 24 hours before being moved to solitary confinement in a cell. From there, he was then taken to a barrel full of water where his head was forced into the water and held until he nearly died. The punishment was repeated several times, and the victim was also interrogated while undergoing that torture. The questions he was asked included information about his family and other victims and their families.

Abdifatah was taken from solitary confinement to another punishment cell together with five other inmates. The room was about one square metre; it was very cold at night and extremely hot during the day. A woman from the court visited them in that cell to inform them of their jail sentences. When they asked how they could be sentenced before they had even attended court, she replied that they would be taken to the court shortly. On the evening of the same day, they attended court in which the main judge was a local musician called Abdul-Aziz. The judge formally read out the sentences that they had received in advance. Abdifatah was sentenced to 15 years imprisonment.

Of the many tortures he experienced in jail, one punishment that stands out was when he was thrown into a hole that was several metres deep. Using rope, the guards lowered him to the bottom of the hole, and once he had reached the bottom, they covered the hole. He was also given three months of beatings by an officer called Ilka-Case. Another officer, called Hassan, prescribed a special beating on the knees, and because of this beating, he could not walk normally. He was buried in wet sand and experienced water and sewage near-drowning several times. Their cell was a dumping ground for human excrement, and they were starved. He nearly died of suffocation inside a plastic bag containing chilli pepper powder. For nearly three years, he did not see his family. He could not perform his religious duties because he was either prevented from doing so or lacked the means.

The most shocking incident he remembered while in jail was the torture of a young woman. On a very cold night, the prison guards brought a woman to a nearby place where they stripped off her clothes and tied her limbs into the shape of a number eight: her hands and legs were tied behind her back and her chest was laid on the ground. As they started beating her, the young woman cried and begged them to lift her breasts off the ground. Calling them cousins, she further asked them whether they had mothers and sisters. The four officers—Nur Ilka-Case, Mukhtar, Shamahiye and Geel-Qaylo—who were carrying out the torture responded to her pleas by walking on her body.

3.2.1.7 Abdi Baaruud

When Abdi was arrested in Jigjiga, he was first taken to the provincial headquarters. His ordeal began with an interrogation in which he was asked about his role in an alleged conspiracy against the regional president. He denied any involvement in the alleged conspiracy. The officers told him that he was lying and began to threaten and punish him. They splashed hot tea on his face, stripped off his clothes and tied his legs and arms together before starting to beat him.

After the beating, they took him to a water reservoir. They repeatedly plunged the upper part of his body deep into the water ground while his four limbs were tied together behind his back. After several hours of such torture, they took him from the water reservoir bleeding and nearly unconscious.

After this ordeal, they took him to Jail Ogaden where he met the head of the prison. The head told him that he must either cooperate and admit to the charges against him or he would be forced to do so. Afterwards, they put him in a punishment cell in which some high-ranking officers visited him. The officers, Nur Ilka-Case and Yasin, told him to talk about the alleged coup d'état attempt against the regional president: the plan of operation and the intended weapons. In the same way as before, Abdi told them that he was not aware of any coup against the president, let alone having any part in it. He also told them that he had been severely tortured since his arrest for something that he did not know anything about. They laughed at him and told him that he had not yet been tortured.

Ilka-Case ordered the guards to torture the victim properly and bring him back afterwards. Eight men took Abdi to a torture cell and put a plastic bag with hot chilli pepper powder over his head. He inhaled the chilli pepper powder and lost a lot of oxygen. Because his arms and legs were tied, he could not remove the bag from his head. In his agony, he jumped and hit the ceiling with his head. At that point, the guards understood that he was about to die of suffocation and removed the bag from his head.

He was unconscious when they removed the bag, and as soon as he regained consciousness, they took him to a hole that was several metres deep. They lowered him using a rope, and when he reached the bottom of the hole they told him to unfasten himself. He told them that he would not do that since the rope was needed to lift him from the hole. They told him that he would never leave the hole and that he would die there. Because of the threat to kill him, he unfastened the rope. The hole was very dark; he heard noises inside, and it was very smelly. As they were covering the hole, one guard asked the other why they had put the victim in a hole full of snakes, and that made him very scared.

The guard wanted to scare the victim and force him to confess to crimes he had not committed; for that reason, he mentioned the snakes. Abdi, who was naturally very afraid of snakes, cried and told them that he would tell them anything they wanted. They lifted him for interrogation but he again failed to confess to the crimes they wanted. They returned him to the hole and he spent several days there. He found that he could not sleep because of its indescribably bad condition and was awake all of the time. He spent his time in the hole talking to himself constantly and asking contradictory questions, such as whether he had died and was in a grave and how he could hear noises and people talking if he was dead.

His next ordeal was in a punishment cell that was nicknamed the Titanic. There were about 30 inmates in the cell—all of them were well educated and most of them were civil servants. The cell was the coldest room in the jail; it was both a toilet and a place to stay. The victims were wearing only underwear. They had very little food to eat and beatings and other punishments were a daily routine. Security chief Abdirahman

Labago'le visited them in the cell while Abdi was there. He told the prison guards that the conditions of the inmates in the cell were not bad enough and ordered them to give the prisoners more punishments. Very often, other officers also used to recommend more punishments for the inmates whenever they saw them.

Because of the severe punishments that were imposed on them, some members of the ONLF group blocked the doors of their cells in protest and demanded to see the highest authority. Abdirahman Labago'le came to see them, and they demanded better living conditions. His response to their demand was to increase the number of punishments they received. He also extended these extra punishments to the civil service group, whom he accused of being behind the protest of the ONLF group. One of these extra punishments was to starve the inmates. They were not given food for several days and were told the only way they would get food was if they beat one another. They knew they would be punished if they did not do what they were ordered to and, thus, began to beat one another. The next punishment was sand torture. Abdi and his friends were buried in wet sand that covered every part of their body. They nearly died of suffocation inside the sand.

A new prison head called Hassan Ismail Ibrahim—known as Hassan Dheere—took over the administration of the jail and introduced extra routine punishments. These new torture methods included standing for several days and collective enhanced interrogations in which victims were interrogated one after another while being beaten at the same time. The standing for several days punishment was the worst type of torture Abdi experienced because of the long duration of the suffering. The physical and mental damage of this torture was great both in the short term and the long term. He then mentioned some of his fellow inmates who became mentally unfit after the standing punishment.

Another new torture device that Hassan Dheere introduced was forced dancing. He demanded the inmates—especially the civil servants—perform a dance for him every weekend. The officials would also watch this punishment as a form of entertainment. Additionally, putting the inmates in cages with hyenas and leopards was another torture device that the officers used as a means of entertainment.

Abdi said that the punishments they experienced in prison were too many to mention and are very painful to be reminded of. However, for the purpose of documenting this piece of history, it is important to talk about what they witnessed in jail as much as they can in order to educate future generations. While he does not remember everything, some of the terrifying punishments and events that do not leave his mind included bone-breaking, dragging, dehumanising acts, the hiding of one's illnesses, absurd charges, and the constant presence of death around him.

Abdi, whose own shoulder was broken during water torture, witnessed a coordinated campaign that involved breaking the limbs of the commanders of the ONLF group. He saw the breaking of the arms and legs of those inmates, and he remembered the guards asking the victims which leg or arm they preferred to be broken. He recalled instances of already broken limbs that were also broken again.

They would also drag people, which was one of the routine punishments the inmates encountered. However, the dragging of an elderly man called Abdulhakim Adhi-Didiye left a mark on Abdi. The gentleman was prescribed daily dragging as a special punishment. He said the contrast between his positive attitude and the torture he was experiencing was a very remarkable thing. Unlike many other inmates, he remained calm and pretended to be okay.

Very often, inmates were forced to eat human excrement, and the punishment for not complying with that order was to beat the victims on the mouth with sticks until all their teeth were broken. The inmates were also forced to pretend to be animals: they would sound and act like animals.

Abdi mentioned a good doctor called Hirsi who worked in the jail and who used to prescribe medicine for him and the other patients. Hassan Dheere heard about the prescriptions and one day came to the clinic asking which patients had gotten prescriptions. Because of the fear of being punished, the patients all denied that they were sick. He praised them for their denials and added that he could not tolerate sick people in his prison.

Most of the prisoners in the jail had not been charged, and if they were, they had not been given reasonable charges. The things they were accused of were absurd and baseless lies. Abdi described one of the absurd accusations for which a prisoner had been jailed; there was a teenage boy called Amin Yare who had been imprisoned because a friend of his had the flag of the ONLF as his WhatsApp profile.

Abdi's fellow inmates were dying in large numbers every day, and imminent death was something they all expected to happen to them all the time. However, a suicide attempt of a friend and the death of his wife became constant nightmares. Mohamed Abdullahi Amakag, who was in his cell group, tried to kill himself after both of his arms were broken. He recalls that he suddenly saw him covered in blood with even more blood gushing from his throat. Because of the severe punishments he was receiving, he had decided to end his life. When the guards arrived at the scene, they were told that Mohamed had tried to kill himself. They reacted to the suicide attempt by beating him instead of helping him. Additionally, Abdi's wife died while he was in prison; however, for several years, he was not aware of her death. His sister-in-law who was taking care of his children after the death of his wife also died before he was released.

He saw some of the perpetrators after his release, but they did not show any remorse. Yasin who used to punish him even denied that he worked in the jail. He concluded his testimony by saying that the perpetrators were ignorant idiots who knew the harm they had inflicted on others, and their refusal to repent was proof of their ignorance.

3.2.1.8 Ahmed Nuriye Yusuf

Ahmed was arrested on 10 September 2017 in Jigjiga and was first taken to a local jail called Havana. Although he came from the diaspora, he lived and worked for many years in the Somali region. He emphasised the importance of talking about the atrocities that happened in the region, both for historical record and for the sake of seeking reconciliation: 'The abuses that took place should be shown and made public, and the perpetrators must admit the violations they committed and show remorse before they are forgiven or punished for the crimes they committed'.

Ahmed was not told what he was accused of upon his arrest, and as he and many other victims testified, officers would frequently invent charges after the accused had already been imprisoned. The crimes they would be charged with were often deduced from the information they obtained through interrogation or that had been found on the private phones of the accused. Ahmed was first accused of anti-government propaganda. On his phone, they found an email that he had sent to his brother in the diaspora in which he mentioned the harassment and deportation of the Oromo people from the region. They used that email as evidence of alleged links with Jawar Mohamed, a well-known Oromo activist. They also accused him of distributing anti-government cartoons on social media. They planted some inflammatory material on his phone weeks after his arrest to build a case against him on the latter charge after they had failed to substantiate the alleged links with the activist.

Ahmed was transferred to Jail Ogaden, and following the transfer, they changed the charge against him from anti-government propaganda to tax evasion. They invented a new story in which they claimed the existence of an electronic store that supposedly belonged to Ahmed, which he had not paid any tax for several years. The victim did not have a store there; nevertheless, he was taken to court on a tax evasion charge. The tax revenue authority claimed that he had 6 million Ethiopian Birr of the alleged unpaid tax still due. The court case took eight months, and he was taken there two times a week. At the end of the trial, he was sentenced to five years imprisonment.

He saw many upsetting things while he was in jail. For instance, he noticed that one could not talk to or help a friend in need. The prison guards did not regard the inmates as human beings, but whenever they received visitors from the federal authorities or embassies, they pretended they were treating the inmates humanely. One example of this was during the visit of some dignitaries; they were allowed to go to the toilet when they wanted to and were given some clothes to wear.

Ahmed concluded his testimony by saying that 'the place was not a jail but a concentration camp'. All the torture methods used around the world, including those used in the concentration camps of Europe, were experimented with there, and he mentioned that some of these torture devices he had been subjected to personally. He had been beaten, had his head plunged into a water reservoir, thrown into a hole that was several metres deep and almost starved to death.

3.2.1.9 Mohamed Farah Hassan

Mohamed was arrested on 26 August 2006 while on a visit to the Somali region from the US, where he had lived since 1995. He was imprisoned in a local jail, known as Havana. After three months of imprisonment, the president of the Somali region visited him and told him that he had been arrested because of his prominent role in the ONLF rebel group. Although Mohamed sympathised with them, he was not a member of the ONLF.

The punishments he experienced in Jail Havana included beatings, having his clothes stripped and psychological abuse. He spent three years and nine months in that jail and was released after the US Embassy and a human rights group intervened. He was secretly rearrested in Addis Ababa two months after his release by the Somali regional authorities. They brought him to Jigjiga and imprisoned him in Jail Ogaden. After his second arrest, they did not allow him to have contact with anyone. The total length of his imprisonment in the two prisons was eight years.

Mohamed was tortured in both prisons, though the punishment in the latter was more severe than the former. He was beaten two times a week in Havana but this increased in Jail Ogaden. When he arrived at Jail Ogaden, they first put him in a hole for nine days. Afterwards, 13 other inmates joined him in the hole. They stayed there for six months, and the only food they received in the hole was dry bread and water. From there, they moved him to a punishment cell without windows where he was subjected to different types of torture, including having his head covered with a plastic bag containing chilli powder, being forced to stand for several days and starvation.

He also witnessed the humiliation and punishments of other prisoners. As part of their daily routine, the guards would gather people for what they called evaluation meetings, which were essentially enhanced interrogations. The victims to be examined were brought to the stage and the other inmates were called to watch the interrogation and torture of the victims. One night, they assembled 800 men in one place and stripped them of their clothes. They were then ordered to form a long line with each man holding the genitals of the man behind him. Women inmates suffered the most because, in addition to the usual torture, they were often gang raped.

While he was in jail, Mohamed was visited by either the regional president or members of his staff every week. The president told him that he would not leave the jail as long as he was in power because of his anti-government activities. The victim denied the charges against him and did not understand how he could harm the government since he was already in jail. Indeed, he even had his artificial leg taken from him; they took the prosthetic leg at the time of his arrest and had not returned it to him since.

When he came out of the jail, he found Jigjiga to be an open-roof prison. People could not talk to each other freely, and because of the widespread spy networks, they did not trust one another. People looked around before they talked and even within families discussions were extremely limited. They felt a constant fear because of the harassment, imprisonment and killing that took place there every day.

Another contributing factor to the imprisonment of the people in the city was the lack of a place to flee to. The historical safe havens for the Somali people fleeing Ethiopian persecution were the neighbouring Somali states. Djibouti and the regional administrations that were formed in Somalia after the collapse of the central government became agents for Ethiopia, blocking victims who had fled for their lives. They not only denied them the refuge they sought but also returned them to the place where they were persecuted.

3.2.1.10 Bishaaro Wa'di Shaqlane

Bishaaro was arrested and imprisoned several times. She was first arrested and jailed in a military camp in Qabridaharre in 2001. From there, she was taken to a jail in Jigjiga, called Asluubta, where she spent two years. In both places, she was savagely beaten and the total length of her imprisonment was nearly four years.

She was arrested again in 2006 by a force led by the then security chief Abdi Mohamed Omar. Officers Canjeex and Assad A. Cawar entered her home to apprehend her, while Abdi Mohamed Omar and a group of soldiers consisting of the federal army and local police waited outside. They took her and her sister to Havana, where she was brutally tortured. After the torture, they took her to a military camp in Jigjiga and dumped her there. The head of the camp asked about her and they told him that she had been dumped there by the regional administration. He was shocked by her condition and asked why they had dumped the victim after beating her so badly. She spent nine months in that military camp. Jail Ogaden was the next destination, and she was brought there by Abdirahman Labago'le who received the order to do so from Abdi Mohamed Omar. In that jail, she spent two years and experienced and witnessed unimaginable suffering. At that time, two brutal men called Abdi Bade and Aweys were the head and commissioner of the jail, respectively.

Bishaaro's last arrest took place inside Somalia. She was apprehended in Hargeisa in 2010 and was transferred to Jigjiga, the capital city of the Somali state, where she was imprisoned in Jail Ogaden. As mentioned in the previous testimonies, the various state administrations in Somalia used to round up the refugees who had fled Ethiopian persecution and hand them over to Ethiopian agents who were stationed in those states.

Bishaaro mentioned some of the countless punishments she was subjected to or witnessed while in captivity. While in Havana, Bishaaro was singled out one night for a beating that was supervised by the then security chief Abdi Mohamed Omar. It was carried out by men including Canjeex, Abdi Libah, Haadi and Mohamud. Her arm was broken in that beating. The fourth night after she had been dumped in the military camp in Jigjiga, she was taken by a group of federal policemen, who had been sent by the security chief, to a hole in Garabcase. They covered the hole after they put her inside and left her there the whole night. The next morning, they interrogated her and beat her until she became unconscious. On another day, the prison guards threw a bleeding woman whose skull had been cracked from a beating into the cell where Bishaaro and other female inmates were staying. The victim was called Nimco Badel. When they saw her, they were shocked and aggrieved at her suffering. They were not allowed to cry or sympathise with any of the victims, but somehow, they could not hide their sadness. Because of that uncontrollable feeling, they were beaten and Bishaaro had her hands and ankles cuffed. They then stripped off her clothes and dragged her to the jail sewage, where she was laid down, kicked and beaten. The tortures she experienced or witnessed were too many to count and too painful to describe in detail. However, she has managed to summarise the main punishments she faced while in jail.

Beatings were one of the main methods of torture that took place. She said all the inmates, male and female, were beaten every night. They used to start beating the men in the evening before moving on to the women later that night. The tools that they used for the beating included sticks and water pipes, and before they started the beating, they made the victims wet by splashing water on them. They also used pliers to squeeze the testicles of the men and the breasts of the women. Another painful and humiliating torture was tying the genitals of men together with a thin rope and forcing them to form a line while naked.

The women in the jail were of all ages—some of them were pregnant and some of them had children. There were several hundred children: some of them were born in the jail while others had been small babies when they arrived at the jail with their mothers. Before the beating of the women began, some were stripped of their clothes. During the beating, the children were left on their own. After the punishment, they used to take the young women to rape and impregnate them. Very often, the pregnant women would die during labour, and many of the newborn babies were taken to unknown destinations and most likely sold.

They used to throw people into a pool full of cold water, and most of the victims would die there. Because of starvation, disease and torture, the victims were so weak that they could not withstand the cold water.

Starvation was the biggest killer. The inmates were not given adequate food and their families were not allowed to bring them food either. The hunger led to the spread of many diseases, and the absence of medical care exacerbated the situation.

Large numbers of prisoners died due to starvation, labour complications, disease, beatings, drowning, dragging and other forms of torture. Just as their bodies were treated badly when they were alive, so too were they mistreated after death. The bodies of the people who passed away were not removed for several days. They used to assemble the bodies in one place and then put them into mass graves near the jail.

3.2.1.11 Amina Sh. Mohamed Ahmed
Amina was arrested and detained in Dagahbur but was imprisoned in Jigjiga, where she spent three and a half years in Jail Ogaden. Both her

detention and imprisonment started with water torture. She was taken to a water well on the outskirts of the city of Dagahbur. The soldiers lowered her into the well using a piece of rope that they tied around her shoulders until she reached the bottom of the well and was submerged in water. They left her in the well for a while and pulled her out when she was about to drown so that they could interrogate her. They repeated that process of torture and interrogation many times until she became unconscious.

When she regained consciousness, they interrogated her again, but she had nothing to reveal. Afterwards, they dug a hole and buried her there, covering her entire body except for a small part of her face. They then interrogated her in that situation, but the innocent woman would not accept being forced into a guilty admission.

After the torture, she was returned to the Rugta, which was the detention centre in Dagahbur where she was held. However, the torture continued, and they took her from the detention centre every night for that purpose. One night, while undergoing torture, Abdirahman Labago'le, the former Special Police Force commander, hit her on the head with a torch. The head injury caused by that hit left a mark on her head, and she still feels constant pain in her head because of it.

After nine days at the Rugta, she was taken to the provincial headquarters, where they assembled prisoners from different prisons and detention centres to take them to Jail Ogaden. Five days after their arrival at jail Ogaden, they were tortured. Amina and several other women had their limbs tied behind their backs and were then dragged into a sewage dump or on hot ash containing the smouldering remnants of firewood.

One of the women who was subjected to that type of torture was called Fardawsa and was carrying a small child. As a result of the torture, the child became sick and died shortly afterwards. The dead body was not removed from the cell, despite the request from the mother to bury her son. The women cried because of the refusal to bury the dead body, and when they heard the endless cries of the women, the guards took the body away. However, nobody knows whether they buried the body or threw it out to the hyenas and other predatory animals.

The punishments continued as part of the daily routine. One night, they assembled female inmates from the Jarar zone within one place and beat them extremely hard. Amina lost some of her teeth in that beating. The dragging on the sewage and hot ash was also part of the torture that night. A pregnant woman called Sureer-Quraysh Mohamed Haji was part of that women's group. As a result of torture, she died shortly after giving birth to twin boys who also died soon after they were born.

The abuses they experienced in that jail are too many to count. The guards and officers were not only killing and torturing the most beautiful and respectful women, but they were also abusing them sexually. As an example, Amina pointed to a young woman who sat beside her during the interview. She had been given to an army general as a gift; he abused her sexually on daily basis.

They were not only tortured physically but also mentally. For example, every time they were beaten or verbally abused, they had to applaud and show that they deserved the punishment to avoid further torture.

3.2.1.12 The Women's Group

The types of punishments presented above by those who gave the testimonies were common to both sexes. But in addition to that, women were subjected to other severe punishments, which included genital burning, rape, forced impregnation, health care deprivation during pregnancy and labour and abuse of their children.

Many women reported the burning of their private parts by guards in the detention centres and prisons throughout the region. The doctors who examined the victims also confirmed this tragic crime. The soldiers used to lower burning plastic bags onto the private parts of the women so that the burning drops penetrated their genitals. The burning not only led to the complete devastation of their reproductive organs but also caused many life-threatening health complications.

Rape was a routine form of torture carried out by the Special Police officers or overseeing authorities, and many of the victims were forcibly impregnated. After they became pregnant, they were not cared for or given access to medical help and were left on their own to give birth in the prison cells. Many of the women and the unborn children they were carrying would die during labour, and the children were neglected and often taken away from those who had managed to give birth.

Different women testified both in private and in public about the additional punishments they experienced. The regional TV station gathered a group of former women prisoners of Jail Ogaden and interviewed them. In that documentary interview, they not only revealed the womens' 'lion's share' of inhumane punishments, but they also showed how the punishments within the jail, which they described as a hell on earth, affected their bodies and altered their lives. As the result of the torture, all four women in that group (Maryama Ma'alin, Fadumo Hussain, Halimo Sheikh Ali and Roda Abdirahman) were fully or partly disabled. For example, one of the women could not stand as her legs had become lame from the torture, another woman could hardly move her nearly incapacitated upper half, a third woman has to wear adult nappies all the time because of the dysfunctionality of her bowels and the upper part of the breast of the fourth woman had been cut off by guards.

The main causes of disabilities were beating, burning, being forced to stand for many days and starvation. The prison guards used to beat every part of the victims' bodies, resulting in multi-body dysfunctionality. However, women topped the list of inmates whose internal organs had been damaged by torture. Because of the additional tortures such as gang rape and genital burning, many women lost their reproductive systems. Their kidneys, digestive systems, bowel tubes and other organs became dysfunctional, and they require constant medical care and support to stay alive.

3.3 The Massacres

Massacres are not a new phenomenon in the Somali region. The first Ethiopian occupation of the region at the end of the 19th century was preluded by raids and indiscriminate mass killings.

As documented in part I of this work, the Ethiopian army frequently raided many parts of the region. They inflicted horrible punishments on the inhabitants, including skin peeling. They also looted their properties and killed them in big numbers before they eventually occupied the territory.

The successive Ethiopian governments used violence and crackdowns as various means to maintain the occupation. Therefore, the killing of the people of the region never stopped since the first occupation attempt. However, during the TPLF reign, brutality and killing increased dramatically, and the regime also succeeded in recruiting a killing militia force known as the Special Police Force using the inhabitants of the region. Both the regular army and the Special Police Force carried out massacres frequently, and they were much larger than the ones perpetrated by the previous regimes.

The places where these mass killings took place include Galalshe, Gudhis, Ela-Obo, Dagahmadaw, Dagahbur, Qorile, Qabridahar, Baarta, Gunagado, Gurdumi, Wardheer, Shilabo, Jaama'-Dubad, Maracaato, Daratoole, Laasoole, Higlalay, Labiga, Bulaale, Dawa'aale, Dharkeenley, Ceelhaar, Qamuuda, Dalal, Wa'di, Jinoole, Aado, Balli-Garabey, Arraweelo, Hodayo, Lahelow, Warandhaab,Taaloole, Dundumo-Ad, Farmadow, Madah-Maroodi, Karin-Bil'ile, Shaygoosh, Dhanan, Qabribayah, Toon-Eeley, Laan-Jaleelo, Hero-Bikir, Garwaan, Lih-Irdood, Samo, Fooljeeh, Galadiid, Geerigo'an, Gabagabo, Dalaad, Jii'a.

Malqaqa, Godey, Xarshin, Mooyaha, Bula-Dari, Gaashaamo, Lababar, Alen, Quumada and Golhabreed.

The massacres that took place within the region during the EPRDF reign are too many to describe in detail here. Therefore, we will outline only some of them in this section. However, the following abridged massacre accounts that are presented here as examples can give you a broader picture of the mass killings perpetrated by that regime. The victims in some of the massacres have been identified, but it was not possible to get a full list of names of the victims for many incidents, including some of the places in which the biggest massacres occurred.

3.3.1 Wardheer

Many mass killings occurred in Wardheer and the areas around that district during the period of this book's focus. However, for the sake of brevity, only the largest one is mentioned here. The first big massacre perpetrated by the EPEDF regime in the Somali region took place in Wardheer on 22 February 1994. The army opened fire indiscriminately at a rally, where the leader of the ONLF, Sheikh Ibrahim Abdallah, was holding a speech. Their aim was to kill the leader as well as many of the supporters of the organisation as possible. They succeeded in killing many of his supporters but failed to kill him. He was defended by the supporters of the rebel movement who used themselves as human shields. A total of 81 people were killed in that massacre and several dozens were wounded. At the time of the massacre, the ONLF was not only a legal political organisation but the main ruling party of the Somali region.

3.3.2 Qabridahar

The Qabridahar massacre took place on 15 November 2005. Some inmates of the Birgaydhka barracks detention camp escaped and an army was sent in pursuit of the runaway prisoners. Within the operation area, the army came across a civilian population who were not involved in the jailbreak. The army opened fire indiscriminately on those civilians without warning and with no apparent reason. About 30 people were killed in that massacre and amongst the murdered people were volunteers who tried in vain to help the wounded victims. The dead bodies were denied a proper burial and were left in the open for several days, and the wounded were not allowed to be given medical help or any other relief.

The victims who died in the massacre include Abdullahi Ahmed Aqib, Abdullahi Gani Ali, Abdiaziz Muhumed, Abdullahi Ahmed Mohamed, Yusuf Mohamed Adan, Asad Mohamed Abdullahi, Bashi Mohamed

Hassan, Mohamed Mohumed, Abdirahman Hared Alaki, Geesh Olad, Anwar Sheikh, Arab Garwah, Amin Mohamed Abdullahi, Siyad Irgah, Bashi Hassan, Rage Moalim and Abdi Wali.

3.3.3 Farmadow

As reported by the OHRC, the Ethiopian armed forces carried out a cold-blooded massacre in Farmadow on 26 October 2005, killing 7 innocent civilians and wounding 15 others. The names of the dead were Abdi Aided Adair, Ahmed-Wail Mohamed Bedel, Abdi Haybe Ali, Wail Omar Gabled, Anise Abdi Sofe, Burale Abdi Rabb and Mohamed.

Although the authorities did not give any reason for the brutal murder of these innocent civilians, they always assumed the whole population of the region to be sympathetic or potential supporters of the resistance movements. Therefore, they used to carry out reprisal attacks on the civilian population whenever they were ambushed by rebels.

3.3.4 Shilabo

The OHRC reported the killing of six civilians and the wounding of many others in Shilabo by Ethiopian armed forces on 29 June 2005. According to the OHRC, the army opened fire on a group of civilians listening to the BBC Somali Service in a teashop for no apparent reason except that they were listening to an interview with an ONLF member. Five of those who were killed were Ali Adan Dhoorre, Hurre Ali Barre, Hassan Faqid Dhuhul and Sahardid Abdi Ali Horor. Ms Jamila Aden, the owner of the teashop, was seriously wounded.

3.3.5 Dagahbur

Between 19 and 21 June 2007, the Ethiopian armed forces carried out cold-blooded mass killings in Labiga and several other villages in the district of Dagahbur. They killed more than 30 civilians and wounded many more. Their villages were also burned and their livestock confiscated. The victims were all nomad pastoralists with no political affiliation, and they were not a threat to the regime. The authorities did not give any reason for the mass killings, but they always used to kill the people for allegedly sympathising or supporting the resistance movements, and there were rebel activities in the area at that time. The OHRC, which was monitoring the area at the time the mass killings occurred, managed to get the names of many victims in that mass slaughter.

The names of some of the murdered victims are Mrs Nimo Yassin, Ibrahim Ahmed, Mrs Fadumo Shire, Ahmed Abdi Hamud, Mohamed Abade. Ruqiya Adan, Abdi Ahmed, Mohamed Ahmed, Yusuf Ahmed

Khayr, Haji Ahmed Hussein, Muhyiddin Yusuf Omar, Mohamed Yusuf Omar, Muhiaddin's brother, Moallin Abdi Hashi, Mohamed Abdi Qarayare, Abdullahi Mohamed, Qorgab Ali Bashir, Miyir Yusuf Iley, Asad Yusuf Iley, Farhan Abdi Arab, Sharaf Moalin Abdi (his two young sons also died in the massacre), Abdullahi Muhumed Matan, Wayel Abdi Iman, Mohamed Abdi Hussien, Ahmed Abdullahi, Abdi Mohamed Hashi, Fathi Ali Shide, Mohamed Hassan Wahar, Abdullahi Ahmed Fure, Mohamed Mohamoud, Abdullahi Timojad and Abdullahi Muhumed Gahnug.

3.3.6 Qoriile

In July 2007, the Ethiopian army arrested dozens of people in Qoriile and its surrounding areas and detained them in their barracks. They were accused of being members or supports of the ONLF. The army severely tortured the detainees before killing most of them in the detention camps. The murdered victims were both hanged and shot, and the killings took place at different places within the Qoriile area over a period of one week.

The OHRC reported from the scene and compiled a list of the killed and missing people in that area. Their names of those who were murdered include Hanad Moallin Abdullahi, Fadumo Abdi, Hassan Abdi Abdullahi, Ilmoge Badal Abdi Abdullahi, Hassan Burale Ilmi-Yare, Ali Burale Ilmi-Yare, AhmedGani Guled Ali, Farah Hassan Halosi, Mrs Ayan Aw Ali God, Hussien Gahnug and Abdirashid Sheikh Mohamoud. Additionally, Qarjaf Haji Osman and Ina Arab Ismail were amongst those who were missing.

Another massacre took place in Qoriile in September 2012. Ethiopian armed forces arrested and detained over a dozen people in the military camps in Qoriile. They were severely tortured before they were massacred by the army.

The names of 12 of the murdered people are Faarah Yuusuf Khaliif, Faysal Irshaad Awlaad, Mawliid Hasan Abdi, Abdirahmaan Guleed Ali, Fadumo Guleed Ali, Saynab Abshir Aw Ali, Ugaaso Ma'allin Omar, Sureed Abdi Qaate, Iido Sheekh Abdi Cisman, Khadar Ahmed Guleed, Faarah Ali Goh and Ayaan Abdi Hiis.

3.3.7 Moyaha

The Ethiopian army carried out a wanton massacre in the village of Moyaha near the town of Ararso on 17 December 2008. The troops rounded up the villagers and opened fire on them indiscriminately. 48 civilians—mostly comprising children, women and the elderly—died on the spot and at least 50 people were wounded.

3.3.8 Gunagado

The massacre of Gunagado was not a one-day event, but a series of operations that took place over many weeks in different locations within the Gunagado district. It started with the killing of two elderly men who were beheaded in the town during the night at the beginning of February 2012. The two men were Abdiqadir Foollow, a clan chief, and Moalim Khadar the district commissioner. They were killed by the Special Police Force. However, the militia force blamed suspected members of the ONLF rebel group from the district for the killing of the two men to create conflicts amongst the people of the district. However, the internal fighting amongst the clans, which the authorities tried to instigate, did not materialise. Because of that failed plan, the authorities instructed the Special Police Force to carry out the mass killing it had initially intended to take place.

On 12 February 2012, the Special Police Force, under the command of Abdi Adan Waris, attacked the town, killing 14 people on the spot and injuring over 20 people. Some of those who were injured later died. The survivors fled from the town to other towns and districts after the massacre, and Gunagado became a ghost town that housed only dead bodies and predatory animals.

After the mass killing in Gunagado, the Special Police Force continued their operation in other parts of the district. They attacked the villages of Madheedh and Abshir. In Abshir, which lies 10 kilometres from Gunagado, they killed 10 people, and in the surrounding areas, they killed 2 more people. The total number of people killed in that operation of the Gunagado district was 49 people.

The names of the victims killed in the Gunagado district included Abdulqadir Guuleed Folow, Moalim Khadar, Abdi Arab, Abdi Ali Bade, Abdikafi Hassan Nur, Siyaad Abdi, Kafi Hassan, Abdihakim Mohamed Sh. Osman, Mukhtar Farah Ali, Bishar Mohamud Seed, Muhumed Hassan Nur, Ahmed Muhumed Mohamed, Maxamud Abdirashid, Miss Hamdi Abdideeq, the son of Wa'di Sirad, the son of Abdi Qodah and the son of Jama Gagaale.

3.3.9 Malqaqa

A series of massacres took place in the Gol-Jano district where Maqaqa is located, but the biggest one-day killings took place in the village of Malqaqa. The massacre of Malqaqa was triggered by an ONLF attack on a Special Police Force post in the area. The ONLF attack took place on

16 May 2010, and in that offensive, the rebel group claimed the killing of 200 Ethiopian soldiers. Whenever ambushed by a rebel group, Ethiopian forces would always react by carrying out revenge attacks on the civilian population. The Special Police Force accused the whole civilian population in the district of helping the ONLF in their attack. They claimed they had done so by failing to warn them of the rebel attack and by not providing information on the activities of the rebel group in the area.

On 17 May 2010, the Special Police Force carried out a killing campaign in the village of Malqaqa, in the Gol-Jano district, and its surrounding areas in response to the rebel attack. They fired indiscriminately on everyone they saw in the area and killed 83 civilians in a single day across three locations in Malqaqa. The killing of civilians continued in the following days and weeks, and in 11 other locations within the district of Gol-Jano, massacres were carried out by the Special Police Force. Altogether, 570 people were killed in the district in series of mass slaughters. The properties of the people were also destroyed. About 3,000 houses were burned and a large amount of livestock was killed.

A Swedish television channel, which reported on the massacre, interviewed an eyewitness who gave his account of what happened. Bashir Ali, who was fortunate enough to escape the bullets, witnessed the massacre. Describing the scene of the killing, Bashir said, 'They split up into smaller groups, advanced methodically and gunned down everybody in sight. I counted 73 dead'. Bashir added, 'They gathered several people in the monastery of Malqaqa and stoned them to death'.

The television channel also obtained video footage that had been smuggled out by Abdullahi Hussain, a defected Ethiopian civil servant who used to be the communication adviser to the former president of the Somali region, Abdi Mohamed Omar. The video footage showed a group of Special Police Force officers stomping on the head of a dead victim and poking his face with a stick. From the video, empty villages could also be seen where the inhabitants had either been killed by the Special Police Force or had fled in search of a safe haven. It also showed the president, accompanied by Abdullahi Hussein, visiting the area after the massacre.

During the visit, the president talked to the local people who, despite thanking him for the visit, could not hide their feelings regarding the massacre. As shown in the video, an elderly man grabbed the microphone and told the president that many people had been murdered in Galaalshe and Malqaqa since the Special Police Force had arrived in the area, and most villagers had fled from their homes out of fear. He also reminded the president of his responsibility to safeguard the lives of the people, their land and their religion and requested him to stop the killing of the inhabitants of the district.

According to Abdullahi Hussain, who was present at the meeting, the gentleman was arrested immediately after the cameras were turned off on the order of the president. But he did not know what happened to him after the arrest.

Malqaqa was again visited by a new regional president in 2019. The new president was enthusiastically welcomed by the crowds. The contrast between the two visits was noticeably big. In the first visit, they had received a murderer demanding them to be content with the massacre and applaud him for the killings that had been carried out. In the second visit, they welcomed a president whom they saw as one of their own and whom they could turn to for help, which they expressed both in words and their happy emotions when they met President Mustafe Muhumed Omar. However, the two visits were similar in one sense; both visits had been overshadowed by one event.

Despite the happy meeting with the new president, the atmosphere and emotions of both the visiting delegation and the local crowd were overshadowed by the reminder of the events that took place in 2010: the orphans that gathered in front of the delegation, the unavoidable talk that linked the present situation to the previous massacre and the facial and verbal expressions of the survivors all took the 2019 meeting back to the devastating events of 17 May 2010.

3.3.10 Jama'-Dubad

The background to this massacre was a dispute between the Federal Customs Agency and traders of chat (stimulant leaves used in east Africa and Yemen). The agency confiscated a van belonging to the traders, which the owners tried to retake by force. In the ensuing confrontation, fire was exchanged, but there were no casualties. The incident took place near Gaashamo, between the villages of Bode Dheere and Jama'-Dubad.

On the night of 5 June 2016, the Special Police Force attacked the village of Jama'-Dubad. After they parked their vehicles on the outskirts, they swept through the village on foot and opened fire before they had reached the inhabitants. They fired indiscriminately at the unarmed civilians, and in the ensuing bloodbath, they killed 21 people, amongst them women and children.

Some of the people ran to the mosque and others tried to hide in their homes, but there was no safe place in Jama'-Dubad that night. Only those who managed to run away from the village before the bullets hit them survived. The army shelled the mosque before entering it to forcibly remove the people. They gathered the victims in front of the mosque and then summarily executed them.

Nearly everybody who was found in the village was killed. 7 women and 14 men were killed on the spot that night. Amongst the women victims were a mother and her daughter. The daughter was shot in the head while carrying her toddler son in her arms, and she was murdered for weeping over her mother's murder. The toddler was wounded in the leg and chest. The victims were buried in two mass graves: one for each sex. Additionally, the people were told not to show any sadness or grief over the dead bodies.

The operation was requested by the Federal Customs Agency, apparently in response to the standoff with the traders, and was executed by the Special Police Force under the supervision of the federal army. Therefore, this was a well-coordinated Ethiopian government operation, involving both the federal and regional agencies. But the dispute could not justify the horrific attack on the civilian population that had nothing to do with the incident that took place outside the village.

However, the government was not apologetic about the mass slaughter. Instead of condoling with them, it blamed the local people for causing the incident that led to the tragedy, and instead of supporting the bereaved families, it demanded the locals to bring forward those it blamed to have triggered the massacre. The aim of the Ethiopian government behind the mass killings in the Somali region was to terrorise the communities, deter potential voices of dissent and force them to fight anyone who was opposed to the government.

3.3.11 Ela-Obo

In February 2007, government forces killed 19 people in Ela-Obo in three separate incidents that were all related to the forced relocation of villagers from Ela-Obo to Galalshe. In the first incident, six people were killed by forces after they objected to the forced displacement and requested to stay in their homes. The soldiers returned to Ela-Obo after learning that some villagers had remained in the area and killed everyone they found in the area in two different locations. The names of the people killed in Ela-Obo are as follows:

Deq Yusuf Lacag, Hassan Abdurrahman, Muhumed Omar, Haji Abdi Ibraahim, Khadar Keenadiid, Waajir Sheikh Osman, Ardo Muhumed Mohamoud, Hodan Muhumed Mohamoud, Abdullahi Hussein Abdi, Muhumed Hassan, Ahmed Nur Hussein Mataan, Abdi Aden Ahmed,

Nasir Osman Aden, Mohamed Abdi Saahid, Nur Ayaanle, Sheikh Mohamed Ali, Mohamed-gurey Ali Taraar, Mohamed Beddel Gaas, and two brothers from the Bashir Mukhtar family.

3.3.12 Other Mass Killings

Very often, the villages where the mass killings occurred were burned, and the livestock and the crops of the villagers were confiscated. Some of the slaughter places where village burning and/or the destruction and confiscation of property also took place, and where some of the victims were identified by the rights groups of OHRC and HRW, include the following:

- Aleen: Mrs Madina Dirshe Hirsi, aged 90; Ahmed Abdi, aged 72; and Abdullahi Moallin, aged 70, were all killed by the army in Aleen on 29 June 2007.
- Gumareey: Hassan Ahmed Jes, Taman Mohamoud and Omar Awil were murdered by Ethiopian forces in Gumareey on 23 June 2007.
- Daratoole: In Daratoole, the Ethiopian army killed Hudle Badal, Ali Jama, Abdullahi Yusuf, Fadumo Ali, Ali Mohamed and Qamar Omar on 2 June 2007.
- Qamuuda: On 25 July 2006, the army summarily executed Ruqiya Yusuf Ali, Madina Abdi Ali, Nasra Ali Farah, Hina Muhumed and Ardo Mohamed Rabi in Qamuuda. All the victims were women in that massacre.
- Madah-Maroodi: On 15 March 2005, Ethiopian government forces killed Mohamed Bedel Gani, Mohamed Dahir and Abdirashid in Madah-Maroodi.
- Karin Bil'illle: On 30 November 2004, in Karin-Bil'ille, Ethiopian armed forces killed Ahmed Nur, Ali Gurey, Mahad Ali Abshir and Wa'adi Guhad Adan.
- Golhabreed: On 7 April 2004, in Golhabreed of the Dhuhun district, Ethiopian government forces killed Mahamad Hussein Jama' and Fadumo Arab Shaafi, who was a pregnant mother. A baby boy, called Ahmed Mahamad Abdullahi, was also wounded.
- Labiga: On 5 March 2001, in the village of Labiga, armed forces of the government killed Ahmed Wariye, Abdi Madobe Ahmed, Yusuf Rabi, Farah Ali, Ali Ahmed, Mohamed Omar and Nur Ahmed Gaydh. They were all nomads.

- Obole: In March 2002, in Obole, Diirane and Ahmed Nur were arrested, had their property confiscated and were then shot dead.
- Garawo: On 27 April 2002, in Garawo, Mawlid Ahmed Ali, Abshir Ahmed Ali and Muhumed Adan were executed.
- Nusdariiqa: On 4 February 2003, in Nusdariiqa, Ethiopian armed forces killed Nur Abdi Osman, Abdihakim Sh. Mohamed, Rashid Ismail Mohamed, Mohamed Dahir Madobe and Abdi Ahmednur. They were all nomads who were accused of sympathising with the rebels.
- Dagahmadow Massacre: In a single day in 2009, 38 people were massacred and buried in a mass grave. Accused of supporting the ONLF, the victims were forced to dig their own graves before they were killed. In total, 116 people were slaughtered that week in the Dagahmadaw by the security forces.

4

The Decline of the Armed Struggle

The armed struggle led by Al-Itihad and the ONLF started as a reaction to the aggression of the EPRDF regime. Both organisations were state-recognised parties that were operating in the country legally and peacefully when the regime decided to eliminate them through military means. The latter was even part of the government and had the largest representation in the regional assembly when the EPRDF declared war on it.

The government first attacked the headquarters of Al-Itihad without provocation in August 1992. In the attack, 26 people were killed, including the organisation's chairman, Sheikh Abdullahi Bade, and vice-chairman, Sheikh Abdullahi Qasim. Following the attack, the organisation elected a new leadership, regrouped and began an armed struggle against the Ethiopian regime. The government, for its part, outlawed Al-Itihad and declared it a terrorist organisation.

Despite the unprovoked attack on Al-Itihad and the signs of insincerity from the regime in Addis Ababa regarding its democratic and self-rule pledges, the ONLF decided to take part in the December 1992 election and won over 80 per cent of the seats in the regional assembly. A regional administration headed by the ONLF, which consisted of several parties, was formed in January 1993. However, that administration only lasted seven months. Another coalition administration headed by the WSLF but dominated by the ONLF replaced that first administration. On 22 February 1994, government forces opened fire indiscriminately at a peaceful rally in Wardheer, killing 81 people. The ONLF leader Sheikh Ibrahim Abdalla, who was the main target, had been talking to the people there at the time of the attack. Thanks to his supporters who used themselves as human shields, he survived the attempt on his life. The ONLF was the main ruling party in the Somali region when the Wardheer massacre took place. However, after that incident, they were removed from the government and outlawed. That attack on the rally, the assassination attempts on the leader of the organisation and the removal of the organisation from regional leadership triggered the armed resistance, which the ONLF began in 1994.

The war was forced on both organisations by the EPRDF regime, and as detailed in part I, their armed struggles started in a humble manner. They were not ready for war militarily, economically or politically. But they had to defend themselves against the aggression imposed on them. The armed resistance started with low-intensity warfare, occasionally hitting the huge Ethiopian army with the classical guerrilla warfare of hit and run. However, the two organisations—in particular, the ONLF—gradually built military capabilities that paralysed the functioning of the state administration. The military engagement of Al-Itihad peaked in the middle of the 1990s but declined in the second half of that decade. The ONLF fought effectively between 1999 and 2007 and nearly defeated the federal army in the region. The Ethiopian regime did not think it would take a long time to defeat the two organisations when it was initiating the war, but it underestimated them.

Despite the frustration of the regime, caused by the failure of a swift victory over the rebels and the early successes of the armed resistance movements, the rebels eventually lost momentum on the battlefield. In this chapter, we will examine the disappearance of Al-Itihad from the resistance struggle and the downward spiral of the ONLF's military activities.

4.1 The Death of Al-Itihad

By the middle of the 1990s, the military campaign of Al-Itihad escalated and reached its highest level. However, soon after its peak, it decreased drastically, and by the end of the decade, its military activities had ceased. Gradually, the organisation lost its foothold in the Somali state and afterwards disappeared. The main reasons for the disappearance of the organisation were the lack of strong public support and the military defeat. The Ethiopian military, supported by the west, made relentless attacks on the organisation and eventually drove it from the region. The militants fled to Somalia and were not seen in the Ogaden region for several years. The US government added Al-Itihad to its list of terrorist organisations in 2001, and that move also dealt a further blow to the already defeated group.

In an attempt to make a comeback, the remnants of the organisation met in Somalia in 2005 and discussed a way forward. In their efforts to revitalise the organisation, the movement made some organisational changes at that meeting—the most important of which was the change of its name from the Ogaden Islamic Union (OIU/Al-Itihad) to the United Western Somali Liberation Front (UWSLF). The main reasons for the name change were to widen the support base of the organisation inside the Ogaden region, to maintain continued support from the wider Al-Itihad movement in the Horn of Africa and to get rid of the former terrorist-linked name.

The colonial name of 'Ogaden' is seen by some parts of the region as a divisive one because of its similarity with the clan's name of Ogaadeen. Neutralising that feeling of exclusivity, which some sections of society had about the name, was one of the main reasons the organisation changed it. They did this by dropping the word 'Ogaden' and using the word 'Somali' instead.

Another reason for the name change was a demand from the umbrella organisation to do so. Al-Itihad was a movement that operated in Somalia and the Ogaden. Although they had separate leaderships, the two groups of the Al-Itihad family were united by a religious view and were very much interlinked politically. The Al-Itihad of the Ogaden used to get support from their umbrella group in Somalia and used Somalia as both a retreat and safe haven. The Al-Itihad in Somalia, which always opposed the use of Ogaden as a name, increased the pressure on the sister organisation to change its name, and because of its weak position and dependency on the Somalia Al-Itihad, the former could not resist that demand any longer.

Following the 9/11 attacks, Al-Itihad was branded by the US department as a terror group. Because of the terrorism labelling, the organisation felt it would be unwise to continue carrying that brand name, and that was another factor that led to the change in the name of the organisation.

The organisation elected a new leader in 2006, and following that election, the organisation reappeared on the world's radar. The new leader Sheikh Ibrahim Mohamed Hussein, who had returned from exile in the US, appeared in the media following his return. Additionally, in 2007, the organisation reported military campaigns it claimed to have carried out inside the Somali region. By the middle of 2007, the organisation published targeted attacks it declared to have carried out on military camps and convoys in the Shabele and Nogob zones, killing hundreds of Ethiopian soldiers.

Despite the organisation's claim of successful military campaigns in the region after its return, the reality on the ground contradicted that assertion. Although it had made some organisational changes, and the organisation had reappeared in the media, the rebel movement was neither able to revitalise itself in time nor return to the battlefield effectively. The return of the UWSLF coincided with Ethiopia's scorched-earth operations in the region and the subsequent collective punishment of the population. The operations of the huge Ethiopian military, supported by the newly formed Special Police Force, pre-empted the organisation's efforts to get a foothold in the region. As a result of the new Ethiopian military campaigns, Al-Itihad neither regained the military capabilities it used to have in the 1990s nor could the organisation's estimated few hundred militants find a hiding ground to regroup.

Because of the crackdowns, the collective punishments and blockades in the region, the ensuing hunger and suffering—as detailed in chapter 2 and chapter 3—and the occupation of its retreat base (Somalia) by Ethiopia, the organisation realised that it could not continue the armed resistance. Although most of the leaders of the organisation were united in that realisation, they had differing views on how to end the insurgency. Some of them were of the view that Ethiopia could not be trusted and preferred to end the war by simply dispersing and disappearing to avoid humiliation and possible persecution. The chairman and his team believed that the EPRDF regime could be trusted and eventually decided to make peace with Ethiopia in 2010.

After talks in Djibouti, the government of Ethiopia and the UWSLF agreed to a ceasefire in March 2010, and the two parties signed a peace agreement in a hotel called Ghion in Addis Ababa on 29 July 2010. Sheikh Ibrahim Mohamed Hussein, the UWSLF chairman, signed the agreement on behalf of the organisation and Shiferaw Teklemariam, the minister of federal affairs, signed it on behalf of the government.

The main obligations of the UWSLF within the agreement were the termination of the state of insurgency, a peaceful approach to problem-solving and the acceptance of the Ethiopian constitution as the basis for exercising individual and national rights by the organisation. For its part, the government agreed in general to observe all the rights enshrined in the constitution, including the right to secession, as detailed in article 39 of the constitution. It also pledged to release all UWSLF prisoners and safeguard their right of return, which was also enshrined in the constitution, and to make appropriate arrangements for the reception and rehabilitation of the UWSLF members to ensure that they successfully integrated into society and participated in the development of the country.

The termination of the insurgency and the commitment to abide by the constitution meant the end of the resistance movement. From the articles of the agreement, it was clear that the UWSLF had to cease to exist as a movement, and the leader of the organisation indicated that reality in an interview with the BBC Somali Service following the signing of the agreement. In that interview, the chairman declared that from that day the members of his organisation would become part of the ordinary civilian population.

Following the peace agreement, Sheikh Ibrahim Mohamed Hussein and his team met Meles Zenawi, the then Ethiopian prime minister, on 12 August 2010. The UWSLF chairman was upbeat about the agreement and his subsequent meeting with the prime minister: he talked about the beginning of a new dawn and a brighter future for the Somali region. He claimed to have the backing of the population and the regional administration to make the peace deal, and he was confident that the Ethiopian regime was genuine about the agreement.

For its part, the Ethiopian regime called the peace agreement a step forward and welcomed the decision that the organisation had taken towards peace. On the other hand, it did not hide its negative view of the UWSLSF and the reasons it believed the organisation opted for peace. Meles Zenawi and other officials described the UWSLF as a defeated terrorist organisation that had been forced to lay down its arms by the Ethiopian army.

The contradictory remarks from the EPRDF regime regarding the agreement and the UWSLF were not surprising given its documented approach to peace and war. In public, it always presented itself as a promoter of peace, and the positive comments regarding the agreement and the demonising remarks about the UWSLF were meant to enhance that image. In other words, it wanted to tell the Ethiopian public and the world that it was prepared to reach out to even a militarily defeated terror organisation for the sake of peace.

The EPRDF regime attacked Al-Itihad, the OLF and the ONLF in the 1990s without provocation—even though they were legal parties and some of them were part of the government—while at the same time presenting itself as a peace-loving government. The regime's stated peace policies always contradicted its military practices, and its comments about peace with the UWSLF were in line with that well-known deceptive approach to peace.

The other message of propaganda that the government wanted to send out from the peace agreement was that peace had been achieved through the combination of credible military threats and peace talks. Additionally, it suggested that the other armed resistance movements should also opt for peace before they encountered unavoidable and ultimate defeat.

The UWSLF ceased to exist as an organisation and its members dispersed after they returned home. Some of the UWSLF militants joined the security services such as the Special Police Force or the intelligence, others became traders and business people and some returned to relief and religious education.

The government released some supporters of the UWSLF after the agreement, although the number of prisoners released is disputed. The government side claimed the release of over 600 prisoners, but independent sources put that number at less than 200.

Apart from the release of some prisoners, the agreement did not bring any positive change to the dire situation in the region. Despite the UWSLF leader's euphoric talk regarding the peace deal and Ethiopia's promises of improvements to life, the crackdowns and collective punishments continued and even increased after the signing of the peace agreement. The gross human rights violations (such as massacres, imprisonments, torture and more) that had persisted in the region continued unabated. Although the government would harm dissidents and their families inside Ethiopia, it was not able to reach them abroad prior to its invasion of Somalia at the end of 2006. However, it began to hunt for them in the neighbouring countries after that invasion, and during the big crackdown that started in 2007, the extended arm of the regime reached many places that used to be a safe haven for the dissidents.

Soon after the peace deal, the organisation ceased to exist, and its members melted into the regional system. As a result, the former UWSLF was not able to influence the system as a single entity. Some of the former leaders of the organisation, such as Sheikh Ibrahim and Ahmed Neshat, occasionally acted as advisors to the regional administration and had a good relationship with the president of the region.

However, the friendly relationship between the former UWSLF leaders and the regional administration did not last long. The former UWSLF leaders complained that the regional administration had failed to honour the terms of the peace accord and was still treating them like insurgents. They sent their complaint to the federal authority.

For their part, the regional administration officials accused the former UWSLF leaders of security breaches and meddling in the affairs of the state administration. The administration also accused Sheikh Ibrahim and his deputy Ahmed Neshat of taking part in a coup against the regional president in 2015. The former UWSLF leaders sought the help of the federal government in their dispute with the regional administration but failed in their attempt to get the federal government on their side.

As Sheikh Ibrahim later admitted in the interviews he gave, the so-called peace agreement did not work because of Ethiopia's refusal to implement it, and he was right in his evaluation of the deal. As it made clear on numerous occasions, the government of Ethiopia regarded the peace accord as a face-saving document for a surrendering organisation and never regarded the other party as a genuine peace partner. For that reason, it never tried to make it work.

In conclusion, the peace agreement failed to make any kind of impact on the two primary goals of the UWSLF when signing the agreement: the restoration of peace in the region and the peaceful propagation of Islam. The conflict and human rights violations increased after the signing of the agreement and the UWSLF's Salafi/Wahabi sheikhs were not given permission to preach Islamic teachings freely. To deny them a prominent position in the affairs of the religion, Abdi Mohamed Omar, the president of the region, promoted their opponents—the Sufis—and appointed them as leaders of the council of clerics.

4.2 The Military Defeat of the ONLF

The armed conflict between the EPRDF regime and the ONLF was triggered by the 1994 Wardheer massacre, as detailed above. In the massacre, the chairman of the organisation was the main target, and 81 people were slaughtered. What happened in Wardheer on 22 February 1994 was not a one-off assault but the beginning of an already planned war. Before the ONLF had the opportunity to respond to the Wardheer massacre, Ethiopian forces launched a large-scale military offensive on the organisation and detained many of its supporters in April 1994 across different locations. The ONLF embarked on a war that had been imposed on it since the day of the mass slaughter—a war the organisation was not ready to undertake for several reasons.

Firstly, the organisation was relatively new: it held its first general conference in 1992 and had no functioning leadership prior to this conference. At the time, the organisation was also mostly unarmed and lacked military capabilities. In short, the organisation did not have the means to fight the huge Ethiopian army.

Because of drought and the huge wave of returning refugees from Somalia following the civil war that began in 1991, the population needed relief and alleviation from their suffering but not war and displacement. In other words, the main preoccupation of the population was how to survive and cope despite their difficult circumstances. The ONLF knew that the people of the region could not bear the burden of another war, and for that reason too, they did not want an armed conflict with

Ethiopia.

The organisation preferred a peaceful resolution to the conflict and decided to abide by the constitution to achieve its goals. It took part in the 1992 election and was part of the government when the Wardheer massacre took place. Because of the organisation's commitment to a peaceful approach, war was not part of its plan. However, it had no choice but to try to defend itself against the aggression imposed on it.

Because of its lack of preparedness, the organisation's first defensive engagements with the enemy were not organised. The ONLF neither had a trained organised army nor did it have the weaponry to fight with. However, the necessity to defend against the ongoing aggression, made it possible to organise a fighting force in a short time. Even though they did not have proper military training, most of the male inhabitants of the region learnt the use of light weapons due to the persistent conflicts in the region, and that war experience proved to be the most useful resource the organisers of the new army could find.

The newly formed army of the ONLF was no match for the huge well-armed forces of Ethiopia. Given the political, diplomatic and economic support of the west to Ethiopia, the large well-equipped Ethiopian forces, the near-starved situation of the Somali region and the unequipped and untrained small force of the ONLF, the Ethiopian regime was not only convinced that it would eradicate the organisation, but it also expected an early ONLF surrender. In fact, in 1994, they even prematurely announced that they had destroyed the organisation.

Nevertheless, the small army of the ONLF resisted, and gradually the resistance movement increased its military capabilities. After two years, the liberation army was not only able to defend itself but launch targeted attacks on military positions in most parts of the region. In their attempt to eliminate the movement, Ethiopian forces conducted an intensive military campaign between 1994 and 1996 against the ONLF. However, the campaign failed to achieve its aim, and after that period, the engagement tactics of the conflicting parties in the region changed, with the ONLF taking the offensive position and the Ethiopian army taking the defensive position.

The ONLF militants became confident fighters, and the Ethiopian government realised that it had underestimated the military strength of the resistance movement. The two antagonist armies fought many battles during the last half of the 1990s, with heavy casualties on both sides, causing huge collateral damage to the lives and livelihoods of the inhabitants of the region. Despite its inferior position in terms of numbers, levels of training and weaponry, the ONLF succeeded in containing the movements of the Ethiopian forces outside the towns and operating in the rural areas almost freely. The second general conference of the organisation, which was held inside the region in 1998, was evidence of their victory on the battlefield.

On the diplomatic front, the ONLF developed relationships with several Ethiopian opposition organisations and the government of Eritrea. Their friendship with the latter was instrumental in upgrading the military capabilities of the organisation. Because of the similar colonial history of the Ogaden and Eritrea and their opposition to the regime in Addis Ababa, the two found common ground and their relationship was based on mutual interests. The two friends saw the defeat of the EPRDF regime as their common interest, and the realisation of that shared goal was the main factor that motivated the cooperation of the two parties. To defeat the common enemy, Eritrea opened its doors to the ONLF, supporting it with military training and some much-needed military hardware.

The increased military capabilities of the militant organisation were felt inside the Ogaden, as evidenced by the defeat of Ethiopian forces throughout the region and the abandonment of their positions in rural areas. Not only did ONLF militants contain the enemy forces inside the main urban centres, but their fighting morale deteriorated to the point that they avoided going to places where they suspected the presence of ONLF forces, and they began to defect to the ONLF in large numbers. The huge defeat of the Ethiopian forces by the ONLF's operation— codenamed Manded—in April 2005, which the international press reported, revealed the ONLF's new military power. According to Radio Horiyo, the Manded operation aimed to weaken enemy forces in the Qorahay and Dolo districts, and the fighting took place between ONLF units and the Ethiopian forces on 15 April 2005 at Alen and Garas Qalo. The ONLF claimed to have killed 60 Ethiopian soldiers and captured 2 Ural trucks.

The failures of Ethiopia's much-publicised operation in 2006, which involved several divisions of its best army was further proof of the resistance capabilities of the rebel movement. In May 2006, the Ethiopian government sent tens of thousands of its troops to the region in what it called a sweeping operation. The military offensive was partly prompted by the need to convince foreign oil companies, which it was trying to make deals with over the exploitation of the Ogaden's natural resources, that it was in control of the region, that it was safe to conduct explorations there and most importantly to weaken the ONLF. To the disappointment of the Ethiopian government, the ONLF forces got the upper hand, and the government forces were defeated everywhere in the region.

The new military power of the ONLF was felt in Addis Ababa, too, and was reflected on the political and diplomatic fronts. The ONLF become a major actor in the Horn of Africa, and that position was recognised by the EPRDF regime. The late Ethiopian leader showed his recognition in many speeches and press conferences he held, though he gave conflicting remarks on how to deal with the rebel movement. For example, in a press conference held on 17 July 2005, he stated his readiness to enter into negotiations with the ONLF. In another conference held on 4 August 2006, he vowed to wipe out the organisation. In his address before parliament in October 2006, Meles Zenawi listed the ONLF amongst what he called the destabilising forces in Ethiopia and, at the same time, declared his willingness to engage in peace negotiations with the resistance movement. This recognition of the ONLF in the Horn of Africa as a major player changed the image of the organisation and helped it to make a political impact in Ethiopia. Both the Ethiopian opposition and the regime in Addis Ababa recognised the ONLF as a contender and a possible future partner.

The Ethiopian regime continued to talk in contradictory terms regarding both making peace with the ONLF and fighting and eliminating the rebel movement until 2007 when it made its mind up to opt for the latter. The regime's propaganda regarding peacemaking with the rebels ceased after it decided to eradicate the resistance movement. The main reasons for their attempt to eradicate the rebel movement included the scramble for the natural resources of the region, Ethiopia's desire to deny the inhabitants of the region to have a say regarding their natural resources and the pressure on Ethiopia to show the governments and companies involved a safe environment to conduct explorations.

In winning the war it opted for, the regime contemplated new strategies. As explained in chapter 2, the new strategies included the indigenisation of the conflict and systematic collective punishments. To indigenise the war, the government decided to create a paramilitary militia recruited from the inhabitants of the region to fight the resistance movement. Collective punishment, which was meant to force the people into total surrender, was also to be carried out primarily by the new local militia.

The intertwined strategies of conflict indigenisation and collective punishment achieved some of their goals. The government succeeded in turning the war between the Ethiopian government and the resistance movement into a war between the local militia, known as the Special

Police Force, and the ONLF. By doing so, it made it an internal conflict between two indigenous forces.

In chapter 2 and chapter 3, we examined in detail how the twin strategies of the indigenisation of the conflict and the collective punishment, in general, undermined the unity of the people and destroyed the lives and livelihoods of society. In this section, we will look at their negative impacts on the struggle for freedom and especially on the military capabilities of the ONLF.

The killing and punishment of the society by a group of their own led to suspicion and mistrust amongst the people of the region. In the past, the inhabitants of the region saw themselves as local comrades and the Ethiopians as foreign invaders. However, that view was changed, or at least shaken, when some of the local comrades turned their guns against their own people and became enemies of their former comrades. The definition of 'enemy' also changed with the appearance of the local enemy, and the differentiation between the foreign enemy and the local enemy became extremely difficult. As former comrades became enemies of one another, it also became difficult to distinguish between an enemy and a friend.

The lost trust amongst locals undermined the struggle in several ways. It made information sharing, especially intelligence information about the enemy, difficult for the resistance, and it made it easier for the enemy to infiltrate local resistance movements and their supporters and monitor the communities and intimidate them. The mistrust amongst the locals and the ensuing government infiltration enabled the Ethiopian regime to penetrate the ONLF itself and acquire firsthand intelligence about the operational and organisational structure of the rebel movement. As a result of the information it gathered about the ONLF through infiltration, it carried out successful surprise attacks on ONLF targets and pre-empted many operations of the movement.

The ONLF lost some of its best army commanders and some of its most influential leaders due to surprise attacks carried out or guided by the new local enemy, namely, the Special Police Force. The many political leaders and army commanders martyred in raids by the Special Police Force and their associates include Mohamed Sirad Dolaal, Abdullahi Guud Adde, Mohamed Ahmed Basey, Mohamed Hirsi Olhaye, Ganey Ali Aar, Mohumed Abdi Aar, Dahir Iid, Mohamed Hussein Yusuf, Sheikh Abdi Izi, Ahmed Nuur Muuse and Sheikh Deeq Mohamed.

The bodies of Sheikh Deeq Mohamed and two of his companions who were killed with him in July 2016 were put on display in the region, and graphic footage of regional cabinet members stomping on the dead bodies was shown on regional media outlets. This inhumane act showed not only the brutality of the regime's dehumanisation campaign but also demonstrated the success of the conflict indigenisation strategy.

Mukhtar Mohamed Suubane's case is a clear example of the damage caused by the new local enemy to the struggle and the negative impacts of the infiltration on the resistance movement. He was a member of the ONLF army and was amongst the militants sent to Eritrea for training. His group returned home from Eritrea in 2010, and upon their arrival, the group encountered an attack from the Ethiopian army on the border between Somalia and Ethiopia. Apparently, Ethiopian intelligence had information about their return journey and was following their movements closely. The militants entered the Somali peninsula through the Red Sea and entered the Somali Ogaden region from the north. The two armies clashed at the border, and the casualties were heavy on both sides. Some of the ONLF army units managed to enter the region unharmed, but many of them were killed while others, including Suubane, were captured by Ethiopian forces.

The Ethiopian government was informed of the returning rebel army by the Somaliland administration, whose army fought alongside the Ethiopian forces against the ONLF militants. In addition to the information provided by the Somaliland authorities, reports from different sources indicated that some undercover agents within the organisation, including Suubane, had also helped the Ethiopian intelligence in that operation. Both the reports and what happened after his capture indicated that he had been an informer the entire time and was the one who revealed the primary intelligence regarding that operation. He not only switched sides immediately, but he took a leadership role in the war against the ONLF and the people of the region within days of his capture.

Suubane was released from jail a few days after his capture, and he was appointed as a security adviser and intelligence chief soon after he left prison. His prompt nomination to the top security job after his capture showed that he was an informer who had been planted in the resistance movement. As a security adviser to the president of the region, he became a prominent figure in the security sector within a short time, and he was assigned to lead the fight against the ONLF. The inside information regarding the ONLF, which he gained through his membership in the rebel army, was crucial both for his appointment to the new position and in carrying out that task.

He led operations against his former comrades and was successful in those operations. Most of the members of the unit he led were defectors from the ONLF, which he had mainly recruited from the prisons. Because of their background, they knew the hideouts of the rebels, their supply lines, their daily schedules, their supporters' networks and the local terrain—some knowledge they used effectively. They ambushed the rebels in their hideouts, cut possible escape routes and by collectively punishing the inhabitants and especially the supporters of the rebel movements, which they knew, denied the rebel movement from getting the support they used to get from the local people. In a short period, the team succeeded in isolating the rebel movement, both geographically and socially, and thereby contributed to the military defeat of the ONLF. Although the operations of the unit were not the only factor that caused the military defeat of the organisation, they were decisive in hastening the collapse of the resistance movement's defences.

The man was rewarded for the fight against the ONLF and the abuses he committed against innocent people both in the open-roof prisons and ordinary prisons. He was promoted further and became the second-in-command of the Special Police Force. He became a powerful man and was one of the most brutal officers in the region. Many former prisoners mentioned his brutality and the abuses he inflicted on them in their testimonies, and in all the human rights reports published by rights groups, his name appeared at the top of the human rights violators' list.

The perpetrator fled the country after the overthrow of the regional administration in August 2018 and was one of 45 people indicted by the federal government for their role in the violence that took place on 4 August 2018 in the capital of the region, Jigjiga. He was arrested in December 2019 outside Ethiopia, and he is now in Ethiopian custody. The ONLF and the people he fought against, who now live peacefully in the Somali region, warmly welcomed his arrest. However, he has not been charged with the crimes he committed in the region against his own people, but only his role in the 4 August 2018 violence in which some churches were burned, some victims—predominately highlanders—lost their lives and a huge number of the city's properties destroyed. As a result, the indigenous people of the region have neither won a total victory nor expect justice to be achieved by the arrest of the perpetrator. In other words, to imprison him and charge him merely for his role in the violence, which resulted from the overthrow of the regime's man in Jigjiga that took place on 4 August 2018, is a slap in the face of the human rights abuse victims and indirectly justifies the human rights violations committed by perpetrators like him on behalf of the Ethiopian regime against Somalis in the Somali region.

Collective punishment, the other element in the new strategy, was also a decisive factor in weakening the military capabilities of the ONLF. The federal forces began their collective punishment strategy as part of the wider crackdown. However, the effects of the punishment on militants were limited until the Special Police Force joined the security forces and took over the leadership role in the implementation of the strategy. By increasing the intensity and widening the scope of the harsh collective punishment, the Special Police Force not only succeeded in destroying the defence lines of the ONLF but also in dismantling the military capabilities of the organisation.

The general punishment in the form of murder, harassment, imprisonment, terror and rape scared the public and forced them to run away from the resistance. In addition to that, the defectors of the ONLF, who led the Special Police Force operations against the ONLF and the collective punishments, knew many support networks of the rebel movements, and those supporters were especially targeted. The human rights abuse against the public dried up a vital source of income for the movement and destroyed its support base in terms of manpower.

The resistance movement depended on the material and moral support of the people it was fighting for. They had no source of income other than donations from the region's diaspora communities worldwide and the handouts they received from locals, mainly in the form of livestock or harvested crops. As part of the implementation of collective punishment, Ethiopian forces began to confiscate harvested crops and livestock and, very often, would arrest the owners of those properties for allegedly feeding members of the resistance movement.

The trade blockade, which was another measure of the collective punishments, adversely affected the resistance movement's military strength by restricting their movements and severely disrupting their supply lines both externally and internally. Just like Ethiopia, the Somali state is a landlocked region, and the inhabitants are heavily dependent on Somali ports for food supplies and other consumer goods. The trade blockade that Ethiopia imposed on the region, combined with the disruption of all other livelihoods as a result of the collective punishments, destroyed the trade sector and led to persistent hunger. Since the people they depended on to live were starved, the resistance movement starved, too.

The indigenisation of the war also reduced the motivation for the liberation war. As the conflicting parties became two local forces, the battle appeared to be an ugly civil war, and as a result, many people left the resistance movement. They withdrew from the liberation war because they felt that it had lost its purpose since it led to the killing of those it was supposed to liberate. The collective punishments severely reduced the resistance capabilities of die-hard militants and their supporters, who continued the liberation struggle, despite the extremely difficult situation. All in all, the new strategies worked for Ethiopia, at least in the short run, by defeating the ONLF militarily. However, that military victory and the subsequent peace understanding will most likely be temporary if the root causes of the conflict remain unresolved.

5

The Scramble for Natural Resources

The quest for the natural resources of the Ogaden/Somali state by foreigners began before the annexation of the region by Ethiopia. As mentioned in an earlier section, Haile Selassie, the Ethiopian Emperor, used the Somali state's natural resources as a bargaining chip in 1945 when persuading the US government to help him with the reoccupation of the region. He promised the US government that he would give American oil companies exploration rights over the natural resources of the region in exchange for the US's backing of Ethiopia's reoccupation efforts of the Somali region. At the time, the British government was administering both Ethiopia and the Somali Ogaden region and was planning to reunite the Somali territories. The British plan, which Haile Selassie lobbied against, failed because of the opposition of other big powers (including Russia, France, the US and Italy) to it.

The American oil companies began large-scale fossil fuel explorations after Ethiopia's reoccupation of the region in the 1940s and 1950s, following an understanding between the Ethiopian Emperor and the US president. The deal between Haile Selassie and Franklin D. Roosevelt in Cairo in 1945 over the reoccupation of the region and the subsequent exploration of its natural resources indicated that there was prior knowledge of oil and gas fields in the region. Reports from reliable sources showed that an American company, called Standard Oil, made explorations in the region in 1915 before the completion of the first Ethiopian occupation of the Somali region. The exploration took place in areas that were under Ethiopian occupation.

The documented history of the region shows that the scramble for natural resources began in earnest with the 1945 Cairo understanding and has continued unabated to this day. Sinclair Oil Corporation, a US oil company, took the lead and was later joined by other US companies such as Tenneco Oil Exploration. The American companies started their exploration efforts in the 1940s and continued their work until 1974 when they were expelled by the new regime. Tenneco discovered the Calub and Hilala gas fields in 1973 and 1974, respectively. The Soviet Petroleum Exploration Expedition (SPEE) took over the exploration work after the regime change in Ethiopia in 1974. SPEE made further discoveries of extensive gas reserves in Calub and Hilala in the 1980s, which were estimated at 118 billion cubic meters. The Soviet Union made huge discoveries of gas reserves in the Ogaden Basin and drilled a large number of gas wells, some of which were ready for production before their operations were ended. The Soviet oil company left the country after the overthrow of the Derg regime in 1991, which was led by Mengistu Haile Mariam. The EPRDF regime, which came to power in 1991, gave exploration rights to many companies from different continents, including ZPEB International of China, PETRONAS of Malaysia, GAIL (India) Limited, Lundin Energy of Sweden and Si-Tech International Limited (SIL) of Jordan. POLY-GCL Petroleum Group Holdings Limited, a Chinese company, currently holds the main contract of oil and gas exploration rights, and it has also discovered large new reserves of natural gas. These are estimated to be between 7 and 8 trillion cubic feet.

The quest for the Somali state's natural gas and oil reserves was one of the main causes of the annexation of the region and the main reason for the continuation of the occupation, which in turn became the chief cause of all miseries in the Somali region. The natural bounty was supposed to bring prosperity to the indigenous people of the land in which it was found. However, so far, it has only been the source of their suffering. In the following sections, we will examine the menace that originated from the scramble for the natural resources of the Somali region.

5.1 The Absence of Rightful Owners

The region's indigenous inhabitants have never been part of the agreements over their natural resources, which successive Ethiopian governments have been making with other governments and companies from all over the world. They have been absent from all phases of the decision-making process regarding their resources, and they have been deliberately ignored by successive Ethiopian regimes.

As mentioned earlier, the quest for Somali natural resources was the main reason the US government backed Ethiopia's reoccupation efforts, and the scramble started before the full annexation of the Somali region by Ethiopia. The other superpower that replaced the US, namely, the Soviet Union, came to the defence of the occupation after the Somalis liberated over 90 per cent of their land in the 1970s. The Soviet Union helped Ethiopia with their reoccupation of the Somali region in the 1970s just as the US did in the 1940s. Likewise, the Soviet Union's oil companies replaced the US companies after they helped Ethiopia with the restoration of the occupation. Whether the pursuit of the Ogaden's natural resources was the main reason for helping Ethiopia in its reoccupation efforts or not, the Soviet Union was given gas and oil exploration rights in the Somali region as a reward for their support.

Ethiopia made exploration and extraction contracts with many companies from different parts of the world between 1991 and 2007, but nearly all of those contracts were cancelled shortly after the signing of the agreements for security reasons. The companies withdrew after they realised the opposition to the project from the local people, which was expressed both in political and military terms. In other words, they pulled out because Ethiopia was not able to provide those companies with a safe environment in which to conduct their business. As a result, the scramble project lost direction and needed urgent rescue. Ethiopia neither had the technological know-how to extract gas and oil nor the security capabilities to guard the wide area of the project. Therefore, she sought external help to bridge these technological and security gaps.

Ethiopia saw China, a rising superpower, as the right place to seek help. China had already undertaken a project of this type in a similar situation security-wise; the neighbouring country of Sudan was in a state of civil war when Chinese companies produced oil there and built pipelines to transport the oil from the south to the north. The late Ethiopian prime minister Meles Zenawi paid a visit to China in 2012, and during that visit, the Chinese government pledged to help Ethiopia with its economic programme in exchange for the takeover of gas and oil exploration and extraction rights in the Somali region. Following the agreement between the two countries, the Chinese government established a company to carry out the agreed oil and gas projects. The POLY-GCL Petroleum and Natural Gas Investments Limited Ethiopian Branch, which is controlled and financed primarily by the government of China, was formed to help Ethiopia in the exploration, development and production of petroleum and natural gas in the Ogaden Basin.

POLY-GCL Petroleum Investment Limited is a joint venture of the Chinese government-owned China Poly Group Corporation and the Hong Kong-based Golden Concord Holdings Limited. The company has invested in the development and production of petroleum and natural gas in the Ogaden Basin, and the project is financed by the China Development Bank, which is owned by the government of China.

The Chinese company signed a contract agreement with the government of Ethiopia on 16 November 2013 to explore and develop a large area in the Ogaden Basin. The company acquired 10 exploration and development blocks in the areas of Calub, Hilala and Dohar with a cumulative total area of 117,151 square kilometres. The two governments of Ethiopia and Djibouti and the Chinese company also decided in subsequent agreements to develop gas fields. According to the agreed plan, POLY-GCL would construct a gas pipeline from the gas fields to a port in Djibouti, where it would build a gas treatment plant. The gas treatment plant would convert the gas into Liquefied Natural Gas (LNG), and the company planned to export the LNG to China.

The current prime minister of Ethiopia was a member of the government that had made the deals with POLY-GCL and Djibouti regarding the Somali state's natural resources, and his government approved the existing agreements regarding that issue. A few months after he came into power, the new Ethiopian prime minister was asked about the sharing formula of the revenue from the natural gas in the Somali state. He replied in vague terms that the natural resources belonged to all Ethiopians irrespective of where they were found and added that the government's plan was to allocate 5–10 per cent of the revenue from the natural resources for the development of the places where the natural resources were found. He said that this 5–10 per cent allocation to resource-producing places was customary in many African countries. His statement sparked outrage in the Somali region and immediately instigated a campaign spearheaded by the regional administration to get clarification from the federal government on that burning issue. Whether it was in response to the Somali demand or not, the federal government passed a new law in the upper chamber of parliament in June 2019, stating for the first time how the federal government and regional states would share the income from natural resources. The law will be effective from the 2013 Ethiopian calendar (2020–2021).

The new law on natural resource income sharing outlines how the revenue from the resources, which in this case consists of profit oil, taxes and royalties, should be distributed amongst the tiers of the government. The regional state where the resource is found gets 50 per cent of the revenue, the federal government takes 25 per cent and the other regional states share the remaining 25 per cent amongst themselves. Of the 25 per cent that the federal government gets, it distributes this to the regional states through a budgetary subsidy mechanism, and the region where the resource is found receives its share from that portion of the revenue. The law also assigns 10 per cent out of the 50 per cent of the resource-producing region to the vicinity where the natural resource is extracted as compensation for the environmental and economic damages related to the extraction.

Although the law is framed in general terms and is about natural resources found anywhere in Ethiopia, the available natural resource that everybody had in mind when parliament was passing this law was the natural gas found in the Somali region. The move was welcomed cautiously by the people in the Somali region.

The Somali public welcomed the law because it explicitly stated their future share from the revenue of their resources, and for the first time, they saw a public representative from the region, including the state president and state assembly chairman, taking part in the deliberations of that important law. Both the law and the representation of the region during the discussions were historic events that had not been seen before in the history of the Somali state's natural resources.

Despite the good news, the mood of the people was not celebratory because of the history of the scramble and the present situation on the ground. They have been excluded on the ground where the natural gas is being extracted just as they were absent from the decision-making processes for the deals that were made about their natural resources in the past. The local people and their representatives have no access to the exploration and extraction sites, let alone take part in the work of the project. Since the new federal government endorsed the agreements that the previous government made with POLY-GCL and Djibouti, which disregarded the voices and interests of the Somali region and has not changed the practice of excluding the resource's owners from the ongoing activities in the gas reserve areas, the mere passing of a general law outlining the sharing formula of the natural resources in the country will not change the justifiable scepticism of the people in the Somali region.

The problem with the Ethiopian government is not its laws but its practices. The discrepancies between the laws enshrined in the Ethiopian constitution and the practices of the government have been enormous. The constitution is a professionally written document that emphasises, amongst many other things, individual and ethnic rights. But in practice, these rights do not exist. Whether the new law regarding the sharing formula of the natural resources will be practised as it is written or follow the path of other ignored laws remains to be seen. As for the citizens of the Somali state, only a real change on the ground will change their sceptical views about the intentions of the federal government and its associates regarding the distribution of the income from the natural resources of the Somali people.

5.2 The Unlawful Scramble for Natural Resources

As mentioned earlier in this book, the scramble for Somali natural resources began before the occupation of the Somali region. In fact, the annexation of the Somali region was the means to realise the primary goal of obtaining its natural resources. After the annexation of the region by Ethiopia, the constant crackdown has been the means to maintain the occupation. As was the primary aim of the occupation, the scramble for natural resources by foreigners continued throughout the period of the occupation, although it has not as yet been successful in terms of utilisation because of the resistance from the sole owners of the resources.

The illegality of the occupation from an international legalistic viewpoint is examined in detail in chapter 12 of part I, and thus it is not necessary to repeat here, but the reader is strongly recommended to read that chapter to understand this perspective. In brief, the Somali region was neither under the rule of any power nor was it available for acquisition as being 'terra nullius', that is, open territory to be freely taken over by anyone prior to the Ethiopian occupation. The application of legal practices regarding decolonisation also shows that the Somali region possesses all the qualifications to regain its independence.

One need not make extensive references to international law and judicial practices here to prove the illegality of the scramble for the resources of other nations. It is both straightforward and common sense upon which all human beings agree: the idea of occupying a piece of land to loot its resources is like taking someone as a hostage to rob their property. As hostage-taking cannot legitimise the ensuing robbery of the property of the captive, so occupation cannot give the occupier property rights of the occupied land. The occupier has no right to use the resources of the occupied territory, let alone invite third parties to share those resources.

Not only was the original idea of the scramble unlawful, but the method of achieving it was also entirely illegal. Aside from the illegality of the occupation in the first place, the gross human rights violations committed by the successive Ethiopian regimes examined in previous chapters also put the legitimacy of their rule over the territory into question. Collective punishments, blockades, extrajudicial killings, starvation, illegal imprisonments, massacres, displacement, property confiscation, rape and more, which are all prohibited by international laws, were the crackdown measures used by successive Ethiopian regimes to maintain the occupation, and thereby undertake the scramble for the natural resources that belonged to the human rights abuse victims. The practice of such human rights violations by any state in a territory undermines its sovereign rights over that territory.

So far, the successive Ethiopian regimes have tried to get the Somali region's resources at the expense of their rightful owners; that is the grabbing of the land and its resources without its local stakeholders. However, reality shows that they can never eliminate the true stakeholders and that the land and its inhabitants are inseparable. Coercion is not a solution to the problem nor does a military victory legitimise the robbery of other people's resources.

The past dark history proved that military force and human rights violations, which the successive Ethiopian regimes used to maintain the occupation and the subsequent scramble for natural resources, led to destruction and hopelessness, which in turn led to confrontation and armed resistance—the result was a further increase in human suffering on both sides. A military approach is not beneficial to any side, and the denial of that reality will only prolong the suffering of the people, increase the destruction of the economy and the environment and lead to the continuation of unnecessary bloodshed. It is important to take lessons from that vicious circle of violence and counter-violence and alleviate the ensuing sufferings of people on both sides.

A change of attitude is needed first and foremost. Ethiopia should confront reality and address the problem head-on by looking at its root causes and seeking a just solution to this man-made tragedy. In doing so, it must admit its misconducts and replace its disastrous military approach with a peaceful one. Unless it admits its illegal activities in the region and takes corrective measures, the madness will continue and there will not be a winner at the end. It is never too late to find a peaceful solution with a win-win outcome. The illegal scramble project should be terminated, and a dialogue with the inhabitants of the region regarding their resources and future political status must begin. The best way to tackle the issue is to replace dictation with dialogue, force with cooperation and threat with encouragement.

Furthermore, the government is very keen to extract the natural gas of the state, but it should show that it also cares about the people and their well-being by reaching out to those who are still suffering from the unhealed wounds inflicted on them by the government and also those who live on top of the gas fields before extracting the gas from the fields under their feet.

Despite the reformist government currently in power and the recent law passed by the federal parliament on the sharing formula of the income from natural resources, the situation on the ground regarding the uprooting of the population living in the Ogaden Basin and the indigenous people's absence from the natural gas projects has not changed. In addition to that, the inhabitants of the Basin are suffering from an unknown disease that originated from the exploration of the gas fields, which is killing them in large numbers.

5.3 The Brutal Uprooting of Gas Field Owners

In addition to the general crackdown, the Ethiopian government embarked on an uprooting campaign in the Ogaden Basin, which involved the killing of people and their livestock, the abduction and expulsion of locals, village burning, the confiscation of land, and the setting up of large exclusion zones. The campaign was part of the main scramble project for that region's natural resources, and it was intended to get rid of the owners of the gas fields from the Basin before the extraction of the gas. The area of the Ogaden Basin is about 350,000 square kilometres and crude oil and natural reserves can be found in different parts of the Basin. The Ethiopian government was ethnically cleansing Somalis from all areas around the existing and potential oil and gas extraction sites.

The horrific ethnic cleansing, which has been going on for the last two decades in the Ogaden Basin, is not a hidden matter. It has been reported by independent observers including international human rights and relief organisations. There were thriving towns and villages in the Ogaden Basin before foreign companies and their Ethiopian army escorts arrived. The local people used to live there like any other place in the region as farmers, herders and traders. After the arrival of the exploiters, many villages were burned by the Ethiopian army and the inhabitants were either killed or driven from their land. Additionally, their properties were either confiscated or destroyed.

The Ethiopian army closed off a large area of pastureland where herders used to graze their livestock and set up exclusion zones of 30, 50, and 60 kilometres. These closures have created many problems for herders and their livestock. Apart from the loss of grazing land, the lives of both people and animals have come under threat because of the killing of any livestock or human seen in the area by the army.

No matter how hard herders try to prevent their livestock from entering closed-off zones, the animals, who do not understand exclusion zones, frequently attempt to move in the direction of the closed-off areas due to overgrazing in other areas, especially during the dry seasons, or because of their habit of going to familiar places. Whenever the animals go near exclusion zones, the army shoots them on sight, and the herders dare not retrieve them from the danger zones or they will be killed, too. Some animals die from shooting, while others are eaten by predatory animals after fleeing in different directions.

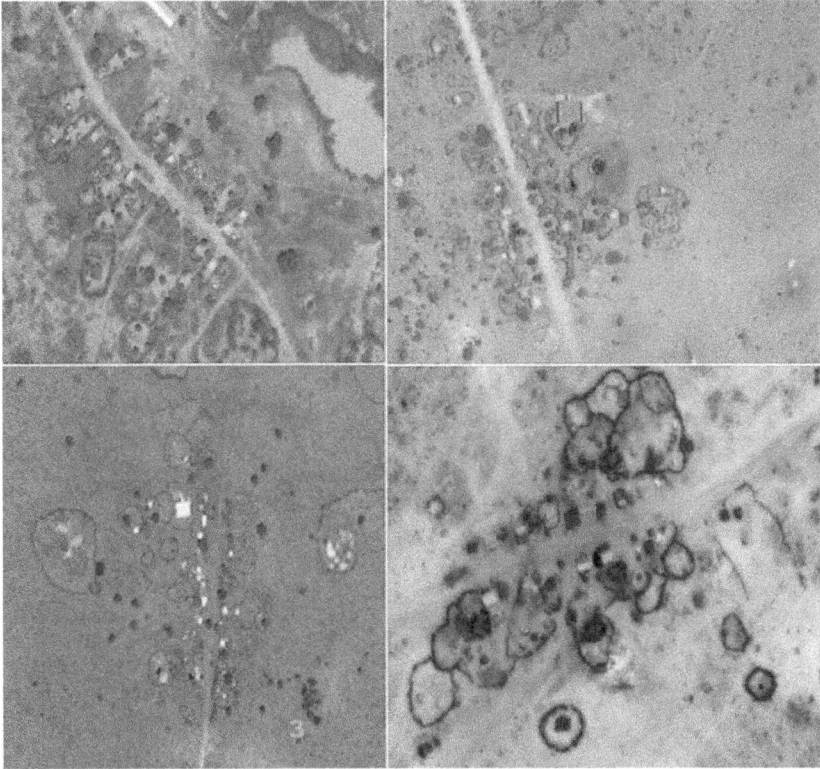

Image 5.1: The villages of Dameerey, Lasoole, Qamuuda, and Labiga after being burned down

The number of missing people amongst the pastoralist community has grown rapidly since the intensification of the exploration, not only in the nearby exclusion zones but also in places far away from the zones. Very often, livestock animals become lost and their owners go in search of them. Unfortunately, many of them never return. Government soldiers often kill herders looking for their lost animals on sight, wherever they find them, and they justify the murder by labelling them as informers of the resistance movement. Bullet wounds are seen on most of the bodies found. The people who are not accounted for are either taken by the government to unknown destinations or their bodies are eaten by predatory animals after their murder.

All the reports published by local and international human rights groups such as the OHRC and the HRW showed a strong correlation between natural resource exploitation activities and village burning, mass killing and displacement. Most of the villages that were burned were close to areas where well drilling and the exploration/extraction of natural gas took place. As you can see from the satellite image below, the destroyed villages of Dameerey, Lasoole, Qamuuda and Labiga are all near exploration sites. Labiga is very close to the Chinese gas extraction site in Abole, which the ONLF forces stormed in 2007. Lasoole and Qamuuda are located near the Calub reserve extraction sites.

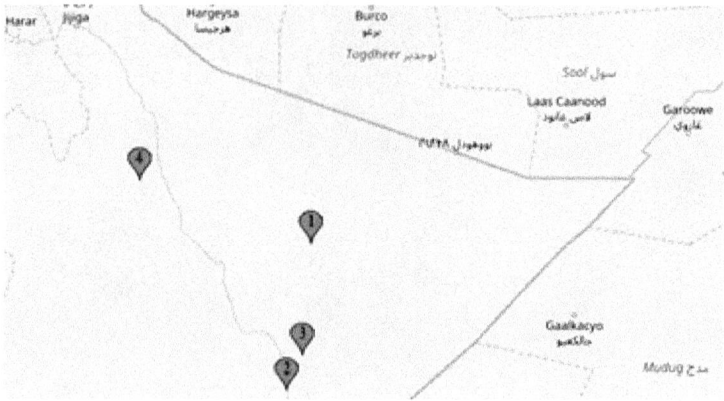

Image 5.2: The locations of Dameerey (1), Lasoole (2), Qamuuda (3), and Labiga (4)

5.4 The Economic Consequences of the Scramble

So far, the Somali region has not seen any economic benefit from the ongoing crude oil and natural gas projects in their state. However, the negative economic impact resulting from the uprooting of the locals is enormous. Farmers and herders have been taken from their lands, which they depend on for everything. Because of the removal from their ancestral land, they have lost both home and livelihood. After the villages they lived in were burned, they were forcibly evicted from their land, thereby making them homeless and displaced in their own country. The loss of agricultural land meant a complete loss of livelihood for these farmers, and the pastoral community's means of living was severely weakened and became unsustainable because of the grazing land they were driven from.

With the elimination of the villages and the expulsion of locals from their land, the Ethiopian government wiped out the capital, properties and sources of income of the local community in the Ogaden Basin. The lack of any compensation from the government for the economic tragedy it created also made the subsequent social and economic devastations permanent.

As a result of the village burning and evictions, farmers lost their productive land, the home they lived in and most of the property they owned. In addition to that, they did not find peace in the places they were expelled to because of the general crackdown that made everywhere in the region unsafe, and in such circumstances, restarting a new life became impossible. They become destitute refugees, dependent on food donations, and most of them have been living in feeding centres run by NGOs.

These exclusion zones combined with the general crackdown and blockades prevented local pastoralists from keeping their animals in their ancestral land, finding alternative pastureland or selling them. Some of the herders tried to change their way of living by selling their livestock, but they failed to do that due to government restrictions. The markets for livestock, which were mainly in neighbouring countries, became out of reach for local herders because of the blockade. The combined punishments made their livelihood unsustainable and prevented them from finding alternative sources of income.

The overall negative impacts of the scramble for the natural resources of the region on the pastoral and farming communities are huge. The scramble uprooted them from their ancestral land, destroyed their livelihood and reduced their population because of the killing, abductions and ensuing hunger. In short, they became a destitute, displaced and scared community unable to re-establish the livelihoods that were taken from them and had little hope of a better future.

5.5 The Environmental Impact of the Scramble

Usually, when the army completes Somali ethnic cleansing through killing, displacement and the burning of villages, the foreign oil companies begin the destruction of the environment bit by bit, starting with the cutting down of trees and removing of grassy pastures and ending the clearing work by creating empty spaces to conduct exploration and extraction activities of crude oil and natural gas. The consequent deforestation and subsequent exploitation and extraction destroy the habitat and turn large green areas into permanent deserts. Images 6–8 show the clearing process and the resulting deforestation.

Apart from obvious deforestation, much of the environmental

damage is not documented by the locals because of their exclusion from the project. The construction of the planned 749-kilometre pipeline from the extraction sites to Djibouti will certainly lead to further deforestation. Both the extraction points and the pipeline pose potential environmental risks such as fuel spills on the ground and other environmental degradations, including soil erosion, water contamination and air pollution.

A responsible and caring government would have made collaborative assessments and arrangements with the locals to deal with all of the existing and potential environmental stresses before undertaking a project of this type and magnitude. Unfortunately, the primary goal of the Ethiopian government and its partners in the scramble project is to extract the natural gas and crude oil at any cost. Therefore, environmental assessments, livelihood assessments and the impact on health are not part of their agenda.

This is a profoundly serious issue that will affect the lives and livelihoods of present and future generations. Therefore, it cannot be left to irresponsible agents, whose main aim is to deplete the natural resources and who do not care about the environment or the rightful owners of the natural resources. The status quo must change before things get out of hand. A change in attitude and prompt action on the ground are needed first and foremost. The government's lack of interest in the environment and the lives and well-being of the primary stakeholders and the latter's absence from the project must end.

Image 5.3: Land clearing

Image 5.4: Seismic Vibrator Trucks being assembled and in action

Image 5.5: A gas well site

5.6 The Health Repercussions of the Scramble

A mysterious and deadly disease linked to the scramble is killing many people in the Ogaden Basin every day. It first appeared in 2014 around the Calub sites in the Shilabo district and gradually spread to other areas of the Ogaden Basin. The number of people affected by the disease is increasing, and according to locals, around 2,000 inhabitants have been killed since the outbreak of the disease.

The symptoms of the disease include a swollen body, yellow or green eyes and palms, bleeding from the mouth and nose, falling teeth and hair, insomnia and fever. Inhabitants have also reported unprecedented miscarriages from pregnancy, birth defects, cancer and psychological problems that were not seen in the area before the disease.

The outbreak of the illness coincided with the Chinese company's takeover of the exploration sites. The Chinese company POL-GCL, which is partly owned by the Chinese government, admitted spilling toxic materials on the ground in one place near Calub, though they claimed this to be an accidental transport-related incident. The locals suspect a much wider and deliberate dumping of dangerous chemical waste in waterways and on the ground.

Because of the totalitarian regime in Ethiopia and in particular the restriction of independent media in the region, the disease was hidden from the world until February 2020, when the British newspaper The Guardian published an article about the sickness. International media has widely reported on it since then, but the Ethiopian government has denied the existence of the illness, and as a result, it has not responded to the disaster in an effective manner. It has not allowed an independent investigation to get to the bottom of the causes of the disaster, and it has not taken appropriate steps to alleviate the suffering of the affected people or allowed others to help them. Instead, it initially denied the existence of the disease and thereafter sent an investigation team consisting of government officials headed by the Ministry of Mines. As expected, the team's findings confirmed the pre-stated position of the government on the matter.

6

The Resistance's Narrowing External Paths

Since the imposition of the scorched-earth policy in 2007, the paths to the resistance movements were getting narrower. The government believed that the resistance movements could not live without the support of the population—just as fish cannot live without water—and, therefore, decided to punish the population collectively to cut the lifeline of the rebels.

To cut the lifeline of the resistance, it imposed a crackdown on the region, as detailed in earlier chapters. Meanwhile, abroad, it began a hunting campaign against the resistance members and their supporters living outside the region as well as their families at home. The collective punishments against the population and especially the supporters of the rebel movements are detailed in previous chapters. Here, the focus is on the dissidents in the diaspora and their families at home and the hunting of key resistance movement operatives outside the official borders of Ethiopia.

6.1 The Pressure from Home

In addition to the general collective punishment against the population in the region, the families of resistance members at home and their supporters in the diaspora were targeted to force the diaspora communities to cease their support for the resistance. The families at home were told to persuade their relatives not only to stop their anti-government activities but also to switch sides or face consequences. The families of the dissidents in the diaspora were treated like hostages, and the abuses perpetrated by the regime against them included imprisonment, torture, the confiscation of property and sometimes killing.

Under torture, victims were often forced to talk to their relatives and inform them of their ordeal and what they needed to do to free them. Sometimes, the communication between victims and their relatives took place in the form of telephone calls, but very often the victims were filmed on video in which they pleaded for help from their relatives to save their life and property by accepting the demand of the government. Many of those videos were shown on mass media and social networks, and the concerned groups/individuals were expected to respond in similar ways by using the media or presenting themselves to the authorities in person.

This new form of punishment, which was devised by the regional administration and headed by Abdi Mohamed Omar, brought a new dilemma to Somali Ogaden diaspora communities worldwide. They went there mainly as refugees fleeing from persecution at home, and they largely supported the struggle for freedom to end the repression and human rights violations in their country. On the one hand, it was difficult for them to ignore their parent's plea for help or for their actions to become a reason for the torture and killing of their families; however, on the other hand, accepting the demand of the government by breaking their ties with the rebel movements was contrary to what they stood for.

The majority opted for the hard choice of ignoring the plea from their relatives for two reasons. Firstly, they saw the punishment of their relatives as part of the sacrifice that every citizen must pay for the freedom struggle, and secondly, they were not convinced that the punishment of their relatives would end after they stopped supporting the resistance. On the latter point, they were proved right by the response given to those who opted to appease the regime because of the pleas of their relatives.

Some could not bear the torture and suffering of their parents, sisters and brothers and decided to end their support for the resistance movements or, at least, publicly declared to do so. However, a declaration of breaking ties with the rebel movements was not enough for the government. Despite ending their support for the resistance, the punishment against the relatives continued unabated, and the Ethiopian regime demanded even more from the relatives, including taking part in the fight against the rebels as a condition for the end of the torture. The regime made it clear that notification of government loyalty was not enough to release their relatives and insisted that they undertake concrete supportive roles as individuals and groups.

To counterbalance the activities of the dissidents abroad, the government decided to establish pro-government community organisations everywhere the resistance movement had support organisations. To help the government, these community organisations were to represent the government in various locations in general terms. The concrete activities that the government wanted the community organisations to do for it in the diaspora included establishing spy networks, propaganda networks and fundraising networks.

Following a series of visits paid by the former regional president Abdi Mohamed Omar and other officials to the diaspora communities, such community organisations were set up in Europe, North America, the Middle East and East Africa. Some of these community organisations became functional and, in collaboration with Ethiopia's diplomatic missions, took part in both the punishments of the relatives of the resistance movement at home and in exporting the terror of the Ethiopian state abroad.

6.2 The Export of State Terror

To ensure the total surrender of the population in the Somali region, the regime in Addis Ababa decided to widen its scope and geographical coverage of the crackdown. As detailed in the preceding chapters, the dehumanising collective punishment, the blockade and the uprooting that took place inside the region transformed it into a huge prison and made its inhabitants destitute inmates. However, that was not enough for the Ethiopian regime. The scorched-earth policy aimed to eliminate the resistant capabilities of present and future generations of people in the Somali region, and to achieve that goal, no aspect of society in the Somali region was to be spared in the regime's view. To complete its intended geographical coverage of the crackdown, the government extended the terror campaign to the diaspora communities—the only section of society that had escaped the persecution in the first phase.

Both the leaders of the rebel movements and many of their powerful support networks were based in the diaspora, and those forces become the target of the new state terror. The extended arm of the Ethiopian government reached many parts of the Horn of Africa region and carried out terror operations, including assassination, kidnapping and imprisonment, and the regime had some success in that mission as its operations on the ground showed. Making use of its diplomatic, intelligence and military bases in the Horn of Africa region, the regime eliminated some resistance leaders and kidnapped others. It also forced the various regional administrations in Somalia and the weak central government in Mogadishu to extradite anyone who was wanted by the EPRDF regime.

The martyrs of the resistance who were killed by the regime beyond the borders of Ethiopia included Abdirazaq Tibaa and Kamas Dhabar Jibarte who were murdered in 2011 in Ifo, a refugee camp in northeastern Kenya. The same forces assassinated Ilyas Sheikh Ali Siyad in Kismayo,

Somalia, in 2008; Abdi Abdullahi Sayyid in Nairobi, Kenya, in June 2011; Bashir Arte Bakidh in Somalia; Abdullahi Irad in Mogadishu, Somalia, in 1999; and Sheikh Mohamed Dubad, in Garissa, Kenya, in 2011. They also killed Khadar Ismail and Mohamed Hassan Abdi in Garissa in 2014.

Cases of the kidnapping and extradition of dissidents from the Somali state, which took place during the reign of the EPRDF, were many, but three cases that were widely reported in the press would suffice to shed light on those issues. The rendition of Bashir Ahmed Makhtal, the extradition of Abdikarim Sheikh Muse (Qalbidhgah) and the kidnapping of Sulub Abdi Ahmed and Ali Ahmed Hussein clearly show the intensity of the hunt and some of the methods the regime used to achieve its intended aims to export state terror.

6.2.1 The Rendition of Bashir Ahmed Makhtal

Bashir Ahmed Makhtal fled from Somalia on 31 December 2006 because of the fighting that was taking place between the invading Ethiopian army and the Council of Islamic Courts (CIC) and went to Kenya. The air space of Somalia was closed at that time because of the war, and for that reason, he travelled to the Kenyan border to acquire a visa and enter the country from there. Bashir was a naturalised Canadian citizen, and he was travelling with his Canadian passport. Immigration officials retained his passport after he submitted it for a visa application and took him into custody afterwards. They told him that he could not leave until the security agency had screened him. He was held in Garissa for six days before being transferred to Nairobi, where he was detained until his rendition. The security screening committee in Garissa told him after a week of his arrest that they did not find anything wrong with him security-wise, but they added that their seniors in Nairobi had requested him to be transferred to Nairobi to officially release him there.

While in Nairobi detention, Bashir was interrogated by both Kenyan and Ethiopian security officers. As soon as he saw the Ethiopian security agents, he became suspicious. The Ethiopian agents questioned him, undertook an intensive look at his physical appearance and asked him whether they could photograph him. From the agents' behaviour, Bashir realised the danger he was facing and contacted the Canadian Embassy in Nairobi, which was only one block from the police station where he was being held, and urged it to intervene. However, the embassy did nothing other than writing letters of concern to the Kenyan Foreign Ministry, which the Kenyan authority ignored. Bashir's relatives, who were alarmed by the involvement of Ethiopian security agents and worried about his safety, immediately filed his case at the Attorney

General's Office. The office set the date for the case hearing on 22 January 2007. However, the government of Kenya, which was determined to transfer his custody to Ethiopia, pre-empted that hearing by deporting him on 20 January to Somalia, which was under Ethiopian occupation at the time.

Bashir refused to board the plane to Mogadishu and requested to be deported to Canada instead. Because of his resistance to the forced deportation, he was savagely beaten by Kenyan security forces, and as a result of the assault, his shoulders were dismembered. Handcuffed and in pain, he was taken from Nairobi to Mogadishu by Ethiopian officials, and after being detained for two days in Mogadishu, he was blindfolded and flown on a military plane to Ethiopia on 22 January 2007. Before he was forcibly removed from the airport in Nairobi, he managed to inform his family of his situation. However, from that point, his whereabouts were not known until two years later when he appeared in a court in Ethiopia.

He was first taken to a military base in Debra Zeit, a town located 48 kilometres southeast of Addis Ababa, where he was held until his transfer to the infamous Maekelawi prison in Addis Ababa. He was held in solitary confinement in Maekelawi prison for two years, and during that period, he did not see anybody other than the prison guards and interrogating officers. He spent nine more years in another prison called Kaliti Prison.

Although he was subjected to daily enhanced interrogation and constant torture, which included sleep deprivation and confinement in a dark, cold underground cell, Bashir was not charged with any crime in the first year of his imprisonment. He was from a family with high standing in the Somali region, and the Ethiopian government believed that winning him over would change the direction of the freedom struggle and would enable it to defeat the resistance movements. Throughout that year, the Ethiopian authorities tried to get him on board and become part of the system, not by persuasion but by threat and punishment—an offer he constantly declined. Disappointed by his refusal to work with them and join their oppressive system, they eventually began to invent a criminal case to charge him with.

The case they built against the victim had multiple terrorism charges, including the accusation of being a leading member of the outlawed ONLF and a collaborator of the CIC in Somalia. The Ethiopian regime had labelled the ONLF as an internal terror organisation aiming to disrupt the peace and dismantle the Ethiopian state, and it accused Bashir of being the military and diplomatic coordinator of the organisation in the Horn of Africa. Furthermore, the regime accused him of arming the Somali CIC, which it had branded as a terrorist organisation and saw as one of its most dangerous external opponents.

In court, no proof of the charges against him was presented. Nevertheless, the court proceeded with the prosecution. His trial began in a military court; however, after 10 months, the case was transferred to a civilian court following an intervention from the government of Canada. The prosecutor demanded the death penalty for the accused. But after a lengthy trial, which was widely condemned by human rights organisations and the victim's lawyers as a travesty of justice, and which took nearly two years, the court eventually sentenced Bashir to life imprisonment in August 2009.

The punishment was also extended to his family. Nearly all of his extended family who were in the Somali region at the time were arrested. Some of them were given long sentences, but most of them were imprisoned without any charge. His elder brother, Garaad Hassan Ahmed Makhtal, who was a prominent traditional leader, was imprisoned in Jail Ogaden and died in 2009 of the injuries that he sustained from the severe torture he received.

Despite many years of lobbying by the Canadian government and Bashir's family to either release him or transfer him to a Canadian prison, Ethiopia refused both requests. The civil unrest in Ethiopia and the subsequent change of the head of the government, however, forced the regime to make some positive changes regarding the human rights situation, which led to the release of Bashir and many other political prisoners. After nearly 12 years in prison, Bashir was released from his confinement on 18 April 2018 and returned to Canada 2 days later. As a result of the pressure from people who had voiced their anger in public demonstrations and general strikes, the Ethiopian government to some extent waived some of its harsh practices and accepted some of the people's demands, such as the release of political prisoners and the free expression of political views.

Taking advantage of the relatively newfound peace in the Somali region, Bashir returned to his country of birth in 2019 to end his exile and assume the traditional leadership that his family held. Inheriting his forefathers' title, Bashir became a Garaad—a title given to traditional leaders of certain areas. We are not writing the biography of Bashir here: his rendition was part of the general hunt for the resistance movements, which is our primary focus. However, the striking resemblance between Bashir's rendition and that of his grandfather, Garaad Makhtal Dahir, in 1949 deserves special attention.

Bashir was targeted partly because of the history of his grandfather who fought European and Ethiopian imperial forces during the 1940s and 1960s. Garaad Makhtal Dahir was arrested in Mogadishu, Somalia, on 22 January 1949 by the British governor there, who rendered him to Ethiopia at the request of Haile Selassie, the Ethiopian Emperor. Like his grandson, Garaad Makhtal was imprisoned in Maekelawi prison and released nearly 12 years later. The charges against the two men were remarkably similar, and although Bashir received life imprisonment and his grandfather was sentenced to death, the prosecution demanded the death penalty for both men.

6.2.2 The Abduction of Peace Negotiators

Two high-ranking ONLF officials, Sulub Abdi Ahmed and Ali Ahmed Hussein, were abducted in Nairobi by Ethiopian security agents on 26 January 2014 with the help of the Kenyan police and security agency. The two officials had been invited by the Kenyan government for peace negotiations and were staying in Nairobi to attend a proposed third round of peace talks between the ONLF and the Ethiopian government as negotiators.

While leaving a restaurant in the centre of Nairobi after lunch, the two officials were grabbed by six men who had emerged from two cars. They were taken to a police station where they were identified and questioned by joint Kenyan and Ethiopian security agents before being driven to the border between the two countries. The ONLF officials had attempted to resist the public arrest but were overpowered when the kidnappers got help from the misinformed crowd. One of the abductors showed the gathering crowd his police ID and requested they help arrest the men, whom he described as terrorists, and added that they had come to bomb the city of Nairobi. Despite the chaos at the beginning of the arrest, the operation was well coordinated by the agencies of the two countries, and the vehicles in which the captive men were carried were not stopped at the border.

The families of the abductees and their colleagues became suspicious after the men went missing and their mobile phones were switched off, and they reported the missing men to the Kenyan police. The police told them that they would investigate the case and promised to provide information about their whereabouts as soon as they got any. Sources from the Somali regional administration indicated several days later that the two men were in Ethiopian hands. But the federal government of Ethiopia did not confirm this, and they denied any knowledge of the abduction and whereabouts of the two men.

The kidnapping of the peace negotiators was not only a blow to the peace negotiations, but it also cast a shadow over the neutrality and credibility of the Kenyan government, which was hosting the peace negotiations. Kenya was not only the venue for the negotiations but also the facilitator of the peace talks. Therefore, the Kenyan agency's participation in the abduction was not compatible with its role as a peace broker.

The Ethiopian government's abduction of the officials did not surprise those who knew the regime. The EPRDF regime often used the so-called peace negotiations it held from time to time with various rebel movements in the country as a means of getting information about its opponents, which it wanted to eliminate. The Ethiopian regime had carried out similar acts when it killed three ONLF negotiators and seized two others while holding bilateral talks with the regime inside the Somali region in 1998. It murdered a leading ONLF official in Nairobi in 2011, and it killed and wounded several ONLF members in other parts of Kenya. The Ethiopian government also hunted the ONLF and other Ethiopian rebel groups in other neighbouring countries, such as Yemen, Somalia and Sudan, killing some and abducting others.

Embarrassed by the damage the abduction had brought to the image of the country and the reputation of the government as an honest broker, the Kenyan government distanced itself from the abduction and took some face-saving measures both internally and externally. The government arrested two police officers—an inspector and a constable attached to the Nairobi CID—in connection with the abduction of the two ONLF officials and charged them. The officers were Police Chief Inspector Painito Bera Ngangai and Constable James Ngaparini Sipiti, and they faced various charges, including espionage on behalf of Ethiopia's intelligence services, though they pleaded not guilty. Externally, the government began diplomatic activities to free the two men and demanded the Ethiopian government to bring back the peace negotiators.

The Ethiopian response to the abduction was both confusing and misleading. The Somali regional administration claimed that the two abductees had come home willingly to negotiate with the Ethiopian government and that they would be talking to the press themselves to clarify their situation. However, Shimelis Kemal, the federal minister of communications, contradicted that statement by saying that his government was not aware of the alleged abduction of the ONLF officials. Another statement by Dina Mufti of the Ministry of Foreign Affairs also claimed that the Ethiopian government was not aware of the whereabouts of the alleged abductees or of any abduction that had taken place.

Despite the contradicting responses from Ethiopian officials regarding the kidnapping, the two men were held in a prison on the outskirts of Addis Ababa. In the beginning, they were held together in one place, but afterwards, they were separated as an interrogation tactic. The men sustained injuries at the time of being apprehended and were tortured in jail. Under both torture and threat, they were asked to switch sides and refute the abduction by declaring they had come willingly to Ethiopia. Although they were questioned separately, the two men responded negatively to the demand of abandoning the freedom struggle, despite the government's strong pressure that they do so. The ONLF, the organisation to which the two men belonged, also indicated that they would not return to the peace negotiations until the two men were freed.

For its part, the Kenyan government exerted diplomatic pressure on Ethiopia to return the two men to Nairobi and got some help from western diplomats based in Kenya in that effort. The peace negotiation between the Ethiopian government and the ONLF, which the Kenyan government was hosting, was a positive development and deserved the support of the international community; the way in which Ethiopia had tried to derail the peace process was in sharp contrast to international norms. The abduction of the peace negotiators was simply not acceptable to the ONLF, the Kenyan government or the international community, and there was no other way to rectify that blunder other than by bringing the peace negotiators back.

Ethiopia tried to cover the abduction saga up by coercing the abductees into confessing to a change of heart and voluntary home return but failed in that attempt after they blankly refused to do so. Eventually, she realised the failure of her deception and that her rough actions were counterproductive to her interests; nevertheless, she dragged her feet due to her totalitarian mentality of not giving in to her opponents, even when that might lead to her harm. She also hoped that western governments would once again tolerate her blunder and silence the Kenyan government.

However, both Kenya—Ethiopia's main ally in the region—and the international community representatives based in Nairobi felt that Ethiopia had gone too far this time and that she should mend her diplomatic relations with her closest friend and the west's most reliable ally in the region. Ethiopia had requested the Kenyan government to facilitate the talks and the abduction had taken place at the city of the venue of the peace talks and inside a friendly sovereign country that had taken Ethiopia's request seriously. Additionally, Kenya had initiated the facilitation of the peace process aimed at ending the Ogaden conflict, which has been the primary source of instability and the armed conflicts in the Horn of Africa region.

Despite many attempts by the EPRDF regime in Addis Ababa to thwart the effort to free the abductees and get away with its gross violation of the norms in international relations, Kenya and her friends stood fast, and Ethiopia was eventually forced to comply with the demands of the country and the international community and return the peace negotiators. After 14 months, on 1 June 2015, the Ethiopian authorities released the 2 abducted ONLF officials, Sulub Abdi Ahmed and Ali Ahmed Hussein, from prison and took them to the border between Kenya and Ethiopia. They were set free in the border town of Moyale, and from there, they travelled to Nairobi.

6.2.3 The Extradition of Abdikarim Sheikh Muse

Abdikarim Sheikh Muse, also known as Qalbidhagah (which translates to 'stone heart' in English), was rendered to Ethiopia by the Somali government led by Mohamed Abdullahi Mohamed (Farmajo) on 28 August 2017. He was first arrested in a hotel in Galkayo in central Somalia by a local militia belonging to the National Intelligence and Security Agency (NISA). He was then taken to Mogadishu by NISA after three days and stayed for another three days in prison before being handed over to the Ethiopian authorities based in Mogadishu.

In chains, the Ethiopian army transported him on a military plane from Mogadishu to Addis Ababa, via Baidoa in Somalia and Godey in the Ethiopian-administered Somali state. He was put in prison in Addis Ababa under the supervision of the Ethiopian security agency. The former Somali regional president, Abdi Mohamed Omar, who visited the prisoner in jail, requested the federal government to transfer him to Jigjiga. The motive of the regional president's jail transfer was to create some propaganda films about the prisoner and force him to renounce the cause he was fighting for—a humiliation that Qalbidhagah could not accept. Because of the high publicity of the case, the federal administration did not force the prisoner when he declined the jail transfer.

When Qalbidhagah was taken to Mogadishu, most Somali people, including him, saw it as a good sign. This was because of the new president in power who had been elected on the patriotism platform, and whom Abdikarim himself campaigned for during the election, and also because of the symbolic importance of Mogadishu as the seat of the government and the centre of the greater Somalia dream. But those hopes were soon dashed when the news of the rendition circulated on the streets of the capital and social media. Some senior parliamentarians went to the office of the president to get to the bottom of the case and persuade the government to reverse its plan in the event of a handover decision. The government told the lawmakers that the man was going to Ethiopia voluntarily and that they were merely assisting him in his request to be facilitated.

The public did not believe that Qalbidhagah was going there of his own free will, and as soon as the extradition was confirmed by the Ethiopian regime, the public reacted swiftly. Spontaneously, the Somali people in the Horn of Africa and elsewhere in the world expressed their anger in unprecedented unity, condemning the illegal rendition in the strongest possible terms and demanding the return of Abdikarim from the Ethiopian jail.

The government did not expect a negative reaction of this magnitude from the public, and because of its inability to explain its outrageous actions, it did not respond to the public's demand for clarification for some weeks. The extradition was confirmed by the Ethiopian communication minister, but the questions of who authorised the extradition, on what grounds and how the decision was made were still unanswered. The Somali government declined to answer those important questions and, as a result, speculations regarding the burning issue of the handover continued for weeks. On 6 September 2017, nearly three weeks after the arrest took place, the cabinet met. After the meeting, the information minister read a statement not only confirming the illegal handover of Qalbidhagah but also defending it. In the statement, the government changed its earlier version of voluntary repatriation by admitting that it had forcibly handed him over to Ethiopia. It justified the extradition on the grounds of terrorism combat agreements with the country. It described the man as a dangerous terrorist who was planning to attack Ethiopia from Somalia and who was a collaborator of Al-Shabab. It also branded the ONLF, the organisation to which the man belonged, as terrorists. The government's press statement also cited existing extradition treaties between Ethiopia and Somalia regarding what it called the terrorist organisations of Al-Shabab and the ONLF.

The government underestimated the public's outrage again as its press release did not calm the emotions of the stunned Somali people. On the contrary, the press statement fuelled public anger. Rendering a citizen, a freedom fighter and a former Somali army officer to the hostile country he was fighting against was not acceptable. The facilitation of the presidential palace (Villa Somalia) to hand over one of its citizens to their archenemy was not perceivable. And the entrapment of defenders of the republic by a government that they were defending was not logically comprehensible.

Abdikarim Sheikh Muse was not the first person to be rendered to Ethiopia by Somali authorities, but all the other renditions were made by regional leaders and warlords under the control of the Ethiopian government. The extradition of Abdikarim, however, was carried out by an elected government, on the orders of the head of the state and inside the capital city, which used to be the centre for Somali nationalism, and that was what made this extradition a special one and sparked such extraordinary public outcry.

Since the collapse of the central government in 1991, Ethiopia had been in control of the politics in Somalia both directly and indirectly. And the country had already suffered the mother of all humiliations: when Ethiopia occupied Mogadishu in December 2006, the Ethiopian army made the defence ministry and other symbolically important places their bases and the presidential palace became home to their political mission. Despite swallowing that humiliation on the grounds that it was a military defeat, the handing over of one of its citizens from the presidential palace to their archenemy was incomprehensible to the Somali public.

On the streets and in the media, people showed their dismay at that dreadful extradition and demanded the resignation of the government. They also demanded lawmakers to rise to the challenge and take responsibility by removing what they called a puppet government that was acting as an agent for the enemy and reinstall a government by the people for the people. The people's voice was clear, and most lawmakers shared the moral outrage of the public, though some of them still supported the government.

The outrageous actions of the government and the subsequent public uproar paralysed the functioning of the government and put the parliament in a dilemma. On the one hand, the country could not afford to lose the nascent government emerging from the ashes of over two decades of anarchy, and on the other hand, there must be consequences for the compromise of the country's sovereignty and the entrapment of its citizens for the enemy. Eventually, the leadership of the House of the People proposed to set up a commission of lawmakers to inquire into the case and come up with recommendations, and the members of the house voted for the establishment of that commission on 13 September 2017. A committee consisting of 15 senior members of parliament from both the opposition and the government were selected to review the case and return their findings to the house of parliament.

The committee's main task was to examine the validity of the governments claims regarding the justification of the rendition on the grounds of the label of terrorism and the so-called extradition agreements between Somalia and Ethiopia. The government alleged that Abdikarim Sheikh Muse was a collaborator of Al-Shabab and a leading member of the ONLF, which it labelled a terrorist organisation. It also claimed the existence of extradition agreements that it signed with Ethiopia in 2015 and 2016 in which the two countries recognised both Al-Shabab and the ONLF as terrorist organisations and agreed to cooperate in the fight against them.

The parliamentary committee began its investigation with a review of the agreements that the government claimed were the basis for the extradition. Omar Abdirashid, the prime minister of the time, denied the signing of any such agreement with Ethiopia. The Somali region in Ethiopia and the Galmudug region of Somalia signed security agreements following clashes between the militias of the two neighbouring regions in the border area. Two of the three signatories of the so-called security agreements between the two regions also repudiated the government's claim of an extradition agreement with the federal government of Ethiopia, calling it a fabrication to justify its illegal rendition. Premier Omar Abdirashid rightly pointed out that any agreement between the two countries would require the approval of both governments and parliaments and such things did not take place. As Abdikarim Hussein Guled, the former president of the Galmudug region and a signatory of the so-called security agreements between the Galmudug region of Somalia and the regional authorities in the Somali state in Ethiopia, testified, the agreements were only security cooperation arrangements that had been made by the two neighbouring regions following border clashes.

On the accusation of labelling the ONLF a terrorist organisation and its alleged sabotage activities directed into Ethiopia from Somalia, the committee did not find any evidence confirming those claims. The organisation neither had operational bases in Somalia nor did it make any attacks from Somalia to Ethiopia. Apart from Ethiopia, no country in the world recognised the ONLF as a terror organisation, and at the time, the organisation had offices in over 60 countries. In addition to this, Al-Shabab refuted the government's allegation of a collaboration between Qalbidhagah and Al-Shabab and denied any links between the two.

The 15-member committee, which was set up in mid-September, probed into the circumstances under which the extradition happened and examined the previous so-called security agreement between Somalia and Ethiopia in relation to the matter. The commission reported its findings to parliament on 18 November 2017. The findings of the report, which was backed by 152 out of the 161 members who attended parliament's deliberation of the case, were clear on the verdict of the extradition and the legitimacy of the ONLF, but not on who was responsible for the rendition.

The commission declared that the extradition was illegal and that the ONLF was a liberation front and not a terrorist organisation. The committee not only confirmed the lack of an extradition agreement between the two countries but also questioned the execution method of the extradition. In the event of any wrongdoing, Qalbidhagah should have been tried in Somali court, and even if there were valid extradition treaties between the two countries regarding ONLF members, the extradition should not have taken place before a proper judicial process had been completed. With a total disregard of its own judicial system, and in defiance of national and international human rights laws and covenants on the protection of prisoners, the Somali government hastily handed its own citizen to the archenemy of the Somali people on the behest of the Ethiopian government. As there were no extradition treaties between the two countries and standard extradition procedures had not been followed, it was practically rendition and not extradition.

On the question of who was responsible for the handover, the committee's findings were vague. It blamed NISA for misleading the government about the case and hiding it from the justice department. The agency is part of the government, and clearly, the highest responsibility of government departments lies with the prime minister and the president. Therefore, the highest political authorities could not escape the blame. The fact that parliament was unwilling to bring down the nascent government for fear of a return to anarchy could be a contributing factor to its unclear judgement on the matter. Blaming the security agency for fabricating and providing wrong information to the political leaders of the country has been viewed by critics as a face-saving alibi for the government.

Following the parliamentary report, which blamed NISA for the extradition, the head of the agency Abdullahi Mohamed Ali (aka Sanbaloolshe) was sacked, but the government survived. Although the head of the agency admitted in interviews he gave after he left office that he misled the public on the matter, he insisted that both the president and the prime minister had approved the extradition with full knowledge of the circumstances. However, to save face, the government made him the scapegoat and sacked him.

With the sacking of the head of the security agency, the government expected the issue to go away, but it was too big to disappear. Despite the government's vain attempt to put the issue behind it, the political fallout from the blunder continued. The main reason behind Farmajo's election victory was the image of patriotism he obtained during the six months (2010–2011) he had held the premiership. Farmajo refused to compromise on the disputes he had with the international community based in Mogadishu, and he lost his position largely because of that confrontation. From that point, Farmajo presented himself as a nationalist politician who could oppose foreign intervention and could sacrifice his position for the sake of restoring the nation's past glory, and that patriotism image, which he achieved to some extent despite his lack of charisma, became his biggest political credential, and it was the most important factor that enabled him to beat his opponents in the February 2017 election.

The handover of Qalbidhagah replaced the patriotism image of the president with that of a traitor, and the government's popularity dropped to the lowest level. Additionally, the president was neither a talented orator nor a distinguished intellectual, and his government experience was limited. The political, economic, and security challenges of the country were enormous, and the nascent government had lost its moral authority because of the rendition. Decisive actions were needed to restore public trust and to tackle the huge problems the country was facing. But the government did not take the bold steps needed to overcome the difficult situation and rescue the nation.

In vain, the public waited for an apology from their government on the issue of the rendition, but the taciturn leader dragged its feet even though it had accepted the parliament's verdict of illegality regarding the extradition case. Because of the government's indecisiveness, the Qalbidhagah saga continued to dominate the debate of the nation, despite the government's efforts to shelve it.

The case of Qalbidhagah, which never disappeared from the headlines, took a new turn when Ethiopia changed the head of its government and Prime Minister Abiy Ahmed Ali replaced Hailemariam Desalegn on 2 April 2018. The new Ethiopian prime minister introduced sweeping reforms beginning with, amongst other things, the release of political prisoners and the lifting of the ban on the outlawed armed opposition, which included the ONLF.

The Somali government feared the release of Qalbidhagah would bring it down and, as a result, began a campaign against his release. The

Farmajo government dispatched Somali officials to Addis Ababa to persuade the authority there not to free him. The Somali officials contacted the Tigray security officials who were holding the prisoner and requested them to hold him or liquidate him if they could not keep him there. Despite the huge efforts, the Somali government and their Tigray collaborators failed to further harm the prisoner because of the rapid change in the political landscape of Ethiopia and the quick collapse of the Tigray-dominated government.

At the request of the Somali government, Tigray security officials hid Abdikarim Sheikh Muse from the new government, and the prisoner having noticed the new drama around him began to contact the new authorities with the help of his relatives and friends. Eventually, the new government found him and released him. Abdikarim regained his freedom on 28 June 2018 and met the new prime minister of Ethiopia after his release. He was seen walking on the streets of Addis Ababa as a free man and talking with his friends who were sharing the happy moment with him on 30 June 2018. In a press conference he held on 1 July 2028, he thanked the Ethiopian prime minister for his release and showed his gratitude to the Somali people for their support. He called for Somali unity and forgiveness and for solidarity between the Somalis and the Oromos.

It is ironic that Abdikarim Sheikh Muse was rendered to the enemy he was fighting against for almost all his adult life by the nation he fought for, and that the enemy saved him from humiliation, imprisonment and possible assassination. When Abdi Mohamed Omar wanted to take him to Jigjiga to humiliate him, the Tigray security officers saved him from the regional president's dehumanisation plan. Again, Abiy Ahmed Ali rescued him from captivity and an alleged assassination attempt by the TPLF and Somali government officials. The aim behind the rendition and the subsequent dehumanisation plan was to appease the Ethiopian regime, but it is not clear whether the unexpected sudden protection of Abdikarim Sheikh Muse by Ethiopia was a sincere human gesture or a sinister action to humiliate the quislings in Jigjiga and Mogadishu.

The extradition of Abdikarim Sheikh Muse resulted in, on the one hand, a happy ending for the Somali nation in that the brave patriots who stood for the right thing at the right moment emerged victoriously, and their hero Qalbidhagah returned as a free man without harm. Additionally, the enemy collaborators lost both the trust of their people and the support of the enemy they were appeasing. On the other hand, it left a dark mark on the history of the nation, because of the authorisation of the handover by Villa Somalia and its occupant, namely, the president.

Not only did the rendition leave a dark mark on the history of the nation, but it also tarnished the reputation of the government of Somalia. The government failed the nation miserably regarding this case two times: taking the rendition decision was a betrayal and then not taking corrective measures in the aftermath of the fiasco was another failure. It was reported from a source in the cabinet that only two ministers abstained, one voted against the press statement of the cabinet and no one resigned because of the betrayal of the nation. Although they did not resign or publicly show their opposition to the extradition, the stand of the three ministers regarding the matter deserves some recognition in proportion to the use of their capabilities. The two ministers Abdi Farah Said (Juxa) and Mohamed Abdullahi Salat (Omaar) used silence as a show of support, which was the very least they could do to show their dissatisfaction with the decision. Mariam Qassim Ahmed was the only minister who opposed the betrayal and used all her capabilities to stop it by voting against it. Therefore, she is the only one deserving of recognition, though only to some extent because she did not resign and did not take a public standpoint regarding the issue at the right time.

As none of the ministers resigned over the rendition of Abdikarim Sheikh Muse, the cabinet as a whole should bear the responsibility of the fiasco, and it will be an incident that the presidency of Mohamed Abdullahi Mohamed (Farmajo) will be most remembered for. Noticeably, the blunder has overshadowed the achievements of that government.

7

The Ethiopian Unrest

The Ethiopian unrest, which began in earnest in 2015, was led by the Oromo and Amhara ethnic groups. The two nationalities were united in their opposition to the regime and made somewhat coordinated uprisings against it by demanding the reform of the system; however, their motives and grievances differed. The Oromo's grievances go back to the 19th century when Oromia was incorporated into the Ethiopian Empire forcibly by the Abyssinian kings of Johannes IV and Menelik II and faced subsequent oppression and marginalisation. In comparison, the Amhara discontent began in 1991 after they lost power to the Tigray People's Liberation Front (TPLF). In addition to its takeover, the TPLF further reduced the sphere of influence of the Amhara hegemony through the introduction of a federal system, which gave the ethnic-based federated states self-rule rights, and thus confined the hegemony to the Amhara region. The acquisition into Tigray of some districts claimed by the Amhara also further reduced their territory and thereby the scope of their power.

The two nations were united in their opposition to the Tigray-dominated EPRDF regime. However, due to their differing backgrounds, where the Amhara ruled the Oromos, and the historical antagonism between the two, they did not see eye to eye on how to reform the system. The Amhara wanted the restoration of the old system of government, which they led, and the abolishment of ethnic-based federalism. In comparison, the Oromo pressed for more devolution and representation, proportional to the size of the ethnic population.

7.1 The Oromo Uprising

Although the Addis Ababa master plan and government interference in the administration of Islamic affairs were the two immediate causes that triggered the Oromo uprising, the historical roots of their discontent go beyond the recent land grab and religious disputes. The uprising of the Oromo people was about the oppression imposed on them by both the Amhara-led successive governments that ruled Ethiopia from the middle of the 19th century up until the overthrow of Mengistu Haile Mariam in

1991 and the Tigray-led EPRDF regime that replaced them. The Oromo discontent accumulated during the reign of successive oppressive regimes, and the list of their grievances is long.

The government announced that they would extend the borders of the capital for developmental reasons and wanted to take some surrounding farmland areas for that purpose; however, the owners of the land did not believe the government's plan to be genuine. The government had already taken land from indigenous farmers in other parts of Oromia and elsewhere and leased them to foreign investors and their Tigray associates. Thus, the Oromo people saw the master plan as another land expropriation plan intended to dispossess them further.

The Muslims accused the government generally of intervening in the running of the internal affairs of their religion and, in particular, the election of the leaders of the Islamic Affairs Council of Ethiopia. They also claimed that the government was promoting the teaching of a sect from Lebanon with Ethiopian roots. The sect, known as Ahbash, was founded in the 1930s in Lebanon by Abdullah Ibn Al-Habashi, who was an Ethiopian scholar exiled by Haile Selassie. The protesters claimed the government was forcing them to accept the sect's teachings as a way of containing what it saw as the growing radicalisation of Ethiopian Muslims.

Although the government denied the alleged interference or the promotion of the Ahbash sect, its actions showed the contrary. Ahbash training courses titled 'Training Religious Tolerance', which were backed by the government and given by clerics from Beirut, were held in all the major cities and were attended by several hundred religious leaders from all regions. The curriculum of the only Islamic university in the country, namely, the Awolia Institute, was also reorganised and some of the teachers were dismissed. Independent observers such as the US Embassy confirmed some degree of government interference in the affairs of the Islamic religion and the promotion of the Ahbash sect.

The protesters also condemned the government's handpicking of the members of the Islamic Affairs Council and its dictation of the running of the affairs of the Islamic religion. In other words, they wanted to choose their religious leaders and administer the affairs of their religion freely.

Most of the Oromos are Muslims, and they also make up the majority of Muslims in Ethiopia. They led the fight against the government's interference in religious matters. The religious riots began in Addis Ababa long before the land protest, and the combination of the two uprisings generated general unrest in Oromia. Both grievances had historical roots and they reminded the Oromo people of the forced Christianisation they had faced, which was undertaken by the Abyssinian kings, and the expropriation of their land by the feudal system of the Amhara after the annexation of Oromia.

The Oromos make up over 30 per cent of Ethiopia's population of over 100 million people. Although they are the largest ethnic group, the Oromos have long complained about chronic marginalisation and the dispossession of their land, and those grievances came to the surface when the protest began. In other words, accumulated frustration over the centuries from these marginalised and dispossessed people led to the uprising.

The first thing King Johannes IV and his successor Menelik II did when they annexed Oromia in the 19th century was to Christianise them. The Oromo Muslims were given three months to renounce their religion or lose their jobs, whereas the pagans were forced to join Christianity immediately. Mohamed Ali, the father of King Lij Iyasu, was one of those forced to change their religion. To keep his position as chief of the Oromos in the Wallo province, he converted to Christianity and changed his name to Ras Makael. From that point, marginalisation and the forced change of identity and culture continued. Getting a job as an Oromo in the state during the long Amhara rule was not easy; therefore, many of them changed their name and religion and imitated the Amhara people to join the system of government. The culture and identity of the Oromo people were stigmatised, making them invisible within mainstream perspectives, despite being the largest ethnicity.

In the rural areas, the Oromos used to pay tribute to the Amhara feudal chiefs, and very often, those chiefs or the bureaucracy that replaced them represented the government. Those government agents frequently took the farmlands from the Oromos on the grounds of tribute by default, forcing the real owners of the land to work for them in the confiscated lands. The Mengistu-led government, which overthrew Haile Selassie, abolished the feudal system and introduced a corporative system in which collective ownership of the land was promoted. But this change did not return the confiscated lands to the original owners and did not give the farmers property rights over their farmland.

The anti-government protests of the Oromo people began in April 2014 in several cities across Oromia as a reaction to the leasing of farmlands to foreign companies and the proposed border extension of the capital. Ambo was the epicentre of the uprising, and the widely reported protests were started by Ambo University students. The government responded swiftly and heavy-handedly. It described the demonstrators as anti-peace elements and used overwhelming force against the peaceful demonstration, killing at least 47 protesters.

In November 2015, the anti-government demonstrations returned with full force in Ginci, which is a small town about 50 miles west of Addis Ababa. As usual, the Ethiopian government responded violently using disproportionate force. They fired live bullets at the crowd, killing over 40 people and imprisoning several hundred. To the disappointment of the regime, however, the crackdown ignited deep-seated anger and hardened the protestors' stance. The protesters began to demand a radical and systemic change of government.

The uprising spread across Oromia in a short period, and the next wave of anti-government demonstrations took place in August 2016. The protests reached a turning point that month when hundreds of thousands of people marched in more than 200 towns and cities across Oromia. As the protests grew in magnitude and strength, the government resorted to more violence to disperse them. About 150 killings and numerous injuries were reported from the August protests. The total number of people killed between November 2015 and August 2016 was about 400. Thousands of people, including the opposition and community leaders, were also imprisoned and some of them were charged with terrorism.

Human rights organisations and local groups reported nearly 300 killings from the venue of a festival that took place on 2 October 2016. The fatal incident occurred when a cultural festival attended by an estimated two million people turned into an anti-government protest. The annual Irreechaa festival, which was attended by Oromos from all walks of life to celebrate life and nature, was held in Bishoftu. The anti-government protest began peacefully, but because of the forceful reaction from the security forces, the event was not only disrupted but led to many casualties, including death and injury. The police used tear gas, rubber bullets and baton charges to disperse protestors, and as a result of direct hits by the police, some protesters died. Additionally, in the ensuing panic, some people died in a stampede and others drowned in a nearby lake.

The protest that began in the student camps under the pretext of the proposed Addis Ababa master plan, and the limited demand to cancel that plan, became the people's uprising and had far-reaching goals. They demanded the government to stop the violence against the Oromos, to free the Oromo people and other political prisoners, to end the discrimination and persecution of the Oromo people, to end military rule in Oromia and allow genuine self-rule and to reform the whole political system of Ethiopia. Parents and people from all walks of life joined the students in various locations, and even the local militia and police in some districts deserted the government and defended protesters against the attacks of the federal riot police and federal army.

Believing that it could still contain the uprising, the government declared a state of emergency on 9 October 2016, giving security forces and the army new sweeping powers. The security apparatus was already extensive and permeated all social structure levels, including individual households.

As part of the restrictive measures that the government imposed, mobile internet was blocked, social and mass media was either restricted or banned and all political activities were controlled. To quell the unrest, the government carried out mass arrests, and it admitted to the imprisonment of tens of thousands of people under the state of emergency laws.

Despite the crackdown, protests continued both inside Ethiopia and beyond Ethiopian borders. Oromos all over the world took to the streets in support of their people at home and used every opportunity to showcase their plight everywhere, including sporting events. Feyisa Lilesa, an ethnic Oromo marathon runner who won the silver medal at the 2016 Rio Olympics, drew the world's attention to the Oromo plight when he took the protest to the world stage. As he crossed the finishing line, he crossed his hands above his head. The signal was an anti-government gesture used by Oromo protesters.

The protesters not only grew in number after the huge influx of people joining, but they were also strengthened by non-violent resistance tactics, which they adopted and which included general strikes, sit-ins and food boycotts. Eventually, it became clear to the ruling elites that the uprising was unstoppable and that it could no longer be business as usual for them. However, the regime did not react decisively to this new reality. Instead of opening a dialogue with the protesters, whom it could not eliminate by force, it blamed the problem on foreign governments and outlawed opposition groups and, as a result, refused to talk to the protesters.

The government's lack of resolve and negative attitude further fuelled the conflict and led to more protests in Oromia and other regions of the country—the second biggest of which was the Amhara uprising. The Oromo uprising encouraged their Amhara neighbours who saw it as an opportunity to topple the government and joined them in the uprising. In the following section, we will review the Amhara protests and their effects on the Ethiopian unrest.

7.2 The Amhara Protest

From the formation of the present Ethiopian state until the overthrow of Mengistu in 1991, the country was ruled by the Amhara people, who dominated the political, cultural and economic sectors and controlled nearly every aspect of life in the country. They made their language the only official language, dominated not only the political system but also the civil service, the leadership of the army and the administration of the provinces. Using their position as rulers, they settled nearly everywhere in Ethiopia and displaced or marginalised the indigenous people of the lands they settled in. After the takeover by the TPLF-dominated EPRDF regime, the Amhara hegemony lost many privileges they used to enjoy, and their sphere of influence subsequently diminished when the ethnic-based federal system was introduced.

The Amhara hegemony was replaced by the Tigrayans after the regime change in 1991; they lost their political, economic and military position to the new Tigray-led ruling elite. The introduction of the ethnic-based federal system also forced the Amhara settlers to leave the other provinces and return to their original land. From there, the main discontent of the Amhara regarding the system began. The incorporation of the districts of Welkait, Humera, Tsegede, Tselemte and Ray-Akobo into the Tigray region further angered the Amhara people, who considered them to be part of the Amhara state. The rigging of the 2005 election by the government and the subsequent crackdown on the opposition increased that sentiment of discontent. Most of the political leaders that were affected by the 2005 crackdown were of Amhara descent, and their public political activities ceased until the Oromo protests erupted.

Encouraged by the Oromo uprising, the Amhara people started their own revolt against the government. However, unlike the Oromos, the other nations in Ethiopia did not sympathise with the Amhara protesters because of their perceived chauvinism, their oppression of other nationalities during their reign of power and their opposition to ethnic federalism. Despite the long list of grievances against the Amhara rulers, the Oromos forged an alliance with the Amhara protesters to strengthen the rebellion and eventually defeat the oppressive common enemy.

The Amhara protest began in full force in 2016 and appeared well organised. It started with anti-government demonstrations on the streets of the main cities, and despite the blockade of the internet, protesters were able to report their confrontations with the government to the world through social media and satellite channels. They also developed new forms of protests such as the so-called sit-in protests when the army began to kill protesters. For days, and sometimes a whole week, the protesters refused to open shops or go to work, bringing the cities to a standstill.

Gradually, the Oromo and Amhara ethnic groups coordinated their protests and staged simultaneous demonstrations in both states. The cooperation between the groups stretched the hands of the security forces and made them unable to respond to all the simultaneous demonstrations that were taking place in all major cities across the Oromo and Amhara states.

The cooperation between the Oromo and Amhara protesters was gradually reflected on a political level within the ruling EPRDF regime. New voices that were sympathetic to the protesters from an Oromo and Amhara background emerged from within the regime. In the beginning, the new critical voices did not challenge the system openly but wanted to calm the situation by accepting some of the reform demands of the protesters. The Tigray-led hardliners, however, did not want to compromise and instead contemplated another plan (the incitement of ethnic conflicts) to silence the protesters.

7.3 State-Instigated Ethnic Conflicts

Ethiopia is a country that comprises over 80 nationalities with distinctive languages and cultures living mainly in separate territories and brought and held together by the force of the state. Most of these nationalities are not Ethiopian by choice, and when and if the opportunity arises, they will probably leave the unwanted union. In addition to that, the ethnic-based federal system, which the TPLF-led government introduced, to some extent unveiled Ethiopia's artificial nationhood and recognised the different nationalities in the country, which were treated as one nationality in the past.

To weaken the opposition and crush the uprising, the EPRDF regime decided to instigate conflicts amongst the different nationalities using ethnic division and existing land and political disputes. Oromia, which was the epicentre of the uprising, has borders with many other nationalities, and to divert the attention from the uprising there, it created conflicts between the Oromos and nearly all their neighbours, such as the Afars, the Southern Nations, the Amharas and the Somalis. Similarly, the government fuelled the land disputes between the Amhara and other neighbouring states such as Benishangul-Gumuz and Oromia. As a result, many of the Amhara people were evicted from other regions such as the Benishangul-Gumuz and Oromia states.

For brevity and the purposes of topical relevance, we will only mention the conflict between the Oromos and the Somalis here. That conflict was not only the largest in terms of engagement and destructive consequences, but it adversely affected the efforts of the two nationalities to end the oppression and defeat the common enemy. It did so by partially diverting the former's uprising from its original purpose and by undermining the latter's struggle for freedom, which is the topic of this book.

7.3.1 The Oromo-Somali Clashes

The Oromo and Somali regions share a long common border of more than 1,400 kilometres, which divides the two administrative regions but not entirely the two nationalities who inhabit them. The unfinished border demarcation between the two ethnic groups does not reflect the real ethnic makeup of the territories of the two states, and mixed communities live on both sides of the border. Despite territorial competition and conflicts over natural resources, the two ethnic communities have lived side by side for centuries in the border areas and have been relatively integrated both socially and economically. They have intermarried, shared religion and culture and there are no language problems as the mixed Cushitic communities speak both the Somali and Oromo languages.

The Somali and Oromo regions have a similar history in that they were both forcibly incorporated into Ethiopia by the Abyssinians and oppressed by successive Ethiopian regimes. Economically, the two communities are interdependent, and politically, they have cooperated on numerous occasions in the past.

Oromia has been relying on the Somalis and their coastal cities for trade within the Horn of Africa region and the outside world. It sends its agricultural products, including chat and coffee—the two most yielding hard currency and export earning crops in Ethiopia—to the Somali regions to be consumed there or shipped further to the rest of the world. Currently, the Somalis send consumer goods to Oromia's markets and are keen to widen their supply base further.

The main reasons Lij Iyasu, the first Ethiopian leader with an Oromo background, was overthrown were his friendship with the Somalis in general and his contact with the Somali resistance hero Sayyid Mohamed Abdille Hassan. The European colonial powers feared that the cooperation between Iyasu and Sayyid might lead to the rise of a Cushitic power, which might change the balance of power in the Horn in favour of the Muslims and, therefore, threaten Abyssinia and their colonies in the Horn. In addition to that, Somalia used to be a base for the Oromo liberation movements, and the Somali government led by Mohamed Siyad Barre supported these organisations with arms and training and hosted a huge number of Oromo refugees in Somalia.

Apart from small, isolated local clashes over disputes relating to shared resources such as water wells and grazing land, there were no major conflicts involving large communities across the two regions before 1991. The scale and method of the organisation of the conflict in that year were new. The war was politically motivated and directed by one side, namely, the Oromo nationalist organisations such as the OLF and the OPDO, and the victims on the other side were mainly unarmed civilians. Many Somalis were killed and driven from their homes by these organisations and their supporters, and the new EPRDF government, of which the Oromos were one of four nationalities who formed it but the Somalis were not part of, somehow appeared to back the Oromo position on that conflict.

The 1991 attack on the Somalis was a political war and analysts blamed both of the Oromo organisations—the OLF and the OPDO— and the TPLF. The Tigrayans, who were ascending to power by violent means, were not in full control of the country at the time, and because of the history of the long struggle in the Somali region, they were expecting resistance. Thus, for the TPLF, the creation of the Oromo-Somali conflict was a pre-emptive measure against a possible uprising in that region. For the Oromo organisations, it was an opportunity to grab disputed districts before the border demarcations of the upcoming ethnic-based federated states.

Unlike the OPDO, the OLF was not part of the government but was in alliance with it, and the two pledged to work together. The cooperation between the two parties ended in 1992 when the OLF announced it would not be able to work with the government because of friction between the two Oromo organisations and the participation of the OPDO in the government. The disagreement between the OLF and the government eventually led to military clashes. The Oromo assault on the Somalis ceased after the OLF fell out with the government, and the forces of that organisation were dislodged by the government army from the territory it controlled at the time.

Although the attacks ceased after the defeat of the OLF in 1992, the conflict remained unresolved. Because of dozens of disputed places, the widespread pastoralist livelihoods of both communities and the frequent border crossings of the pastoralists in search of pastureland for their animals, it is difficult to clearly demarcate the boundaries of the two regions on ethnic bases. The Oromos complain that the Somali pastoralists are always on the move in search of pastureland and push the Oromos westwards. The Somalis also claim that both the Oromo and the Amhara people took advantage of the huge outflux of Somali refugees from the Somali region after the 1977–78 war, and during the EPRDF crackdown on the Somali people, by settling in the places they left. Both claims are valid to some extent. On the one hand, it is true that the green grassland on the Oromo side of the border attracted more livestock from the semi-desert Somali side and that some Somali pastoralists moved westwards beyond the border areas and deep into proper Oromia before the conflict began. On the other hand, it is also true that the Somalis had been losing land to the Oromos since the 1977–78 Ogaden war. Because of their proximity, they quickly filled the vacuum caused by the outflux of refugees in places such as Dire Dawa, Moyale and Negele.

In some parts of the border areas, such as Moyale and Tuliguled, clashes between the two communities have been more frequent than in the rest of the region and unorganised sporadic clashes would occur even during the time of relative peace. In 2012 and 2013, the Somali tribe of Garre and the Oromo tribe of Borane fought over disputed land in Moyale and its surrounding areas. Dozens of people were killed in those clashes, which started on the Ethiopian side. The fighting spilt over to the Kenyan side afterwards. Tuliguled is comparable to Moyale in terms of the frequency of conflicts. However, because of the disputed identity of the Jarsa and the politicisation of that conflict, the Tuliguled issue is more complex than that of Moyale and needs special deliberation. The prolonged conflict between the Gari and Jarsa communities, the location of the conflict area and its proximity to Jigjiga, the seat of the Somali regional state government, the removal of Jena'sani from the Somali regional administration and its incorporation into Oromia and the role of regional states, as well as the federal government, regarding the conflict all need to be investigated properly by the appropriate authorities.

Federal government initiatives to resolve the land disputes did not lead to peace settlements because of insincerity and the bias tendency that was often in favour of the Oromos. For example, in a disputed referendum that was held in 2004 to decide on the regional belonging of more than 420 kebeles (that is, neighbourhood associations), which are the smallest units of local government in Ethiopia, the government declared that Oromia had won 80 per cent of them.

Despite sporadic clashes from time to time, the organised clashes that ended in 1992 did not resume until the end of 2016. Although each regional government blamed armed groups from the other side for restarting the war, there are strong indications that the federal government was behind the recent conflict that erupted in December 2016. The EPRDF regime established local paramilitary militias known as the Special Police Force in both the Somali and Oromo regions to fight the ONLF in the Somali state and the OLF in Oromia, respectively. It again used the same militias to instigate the war between the two nations, by pushing them into the conflict and encouraging each one of them to fight on behalf of its nationality against the other.

As we mentioned earlier, some Oromo and Amhara leaders within the regime softened their position towards the protesters and the regional president of Oromia, Lemma Megersa, was one of those leaders who backed some of the protesters' demands. On the other hand, the Somali regional leader, Abdi Mohamed Omar, was a ruthless hardliner who had already cracked down on his own people and wanted to take similar action against protesters in the Amhara and Oromo regions. He made his stand on the matter public, and his anti-uprising views were known to the anti-government protesters in the Oromo and Amhara states.

To instigate the war between the two neighbouring ethnic groups, the federal government ordered the Special Police Force in the Somali region to help the federal anti-riot forces in parts of Oromia. When the news of the participation of the Somali militia in the fight against the Oromo demonstrators reached the protesters, some Oromo mobs turned against their Somali neighbours in retaliation. The Somali Special Police Force responded to the mob attacks on the unarmed innocent civilians with direct attacks around the border areas as well as inside Oromia. The Oromo militia retaliated by also attacking the Somalis inside the Somali state and around the border areas. As the government had planned, from there the conflict continued, and it fuelled the war further by encouraging each one of them to directly or indirectly punish the other party.

The paramilitary militias of both regional governments actively engaged in the war, and the regional administrations and the federal government were heavily involved in the bloodbath. But the Oromo leaders did not blame the Tigray generals who had orchestrated the war and then fanned it. Instead, they blamed the Somali regional president, Abdi Mohamed Omar, and his Special Police Force for instigating the war and presented the Oromos as victims of Somali aggression.

The federal government occasionally brought the two conflicting parties together to make peace as it claimed. However, critics argued that the government wanted to perpetuate the conflict for short-term political gains and the so-called peace plans were merely intended to cover up the real intentions and actions of the government. They further claimed that the strong federal army could have stopped the bloodbath and brought the communal violence under control in a short period had the government intervened.

Whatever the root cause, the latest clashes between the Oromos and the Somalis were large and very deadly, and their consequences were enormous. They resulted in a large number of killings and injuries, destroyed the economy and livelihoods of hundreds of thousands and made civilians internal refugees.

7.3.2 Casualties of the Conflict

A lot of people were killed and many more were injured since the conflict began. However, the exact number of human casualties is not known. Because of the lack of official registration of the rural communities and the fact that many of the places where the killing took place were not accessible due to topographic barriers or war-related reasons, many people were not accounted for. Therefore, it was not possible to know the exact number of people killed or injured. Most estimates put the number of people killed in the thousands, though the estimated figures vary slightly.

On average, the people who were reported killed in places where information about the number of casualties was available put the death toll in the hundreds. For example, in the December 2016 clashes in the Negele Borana areas, over 200 people were reported to have been killed, and in the same areas, hundreds more were killed in the February and March 2017 fighting, which saw the local militias from two regions taking part. The number of Somali civilians killed in the September 2017 clashes in Awaday, Oromia, was about 30. In December 2017, over 60 people of whom about 32 were Somali civilians were killed in the Hawi Gudina and Daro Lebu districts of the Oromo region. On 15 December 2017, several hundred Somali civilians were killed by the Oromo militia in Balbalayte and Awaday, and in July 2018, Oromo's militias killed 50 Somalis around the Moyale area. The number of injured people in these clashes are estimated to be in the thousands.

Despite the signing of a peace deal between the two regional governments in April 2017, the clashes continued until 2019. The incidents mentioned above, and the many others that took place between 2016 and 2019, indicate that the number of people killed or injured was in the thousands. In addition to that, the non-human casualties, which included the loss of homes and livelihoods, were enormous. Millions of people from both sides were forced to flee from their lands, leaving behind their homes, farms, livestock or whatever they owned.

The most obvious impact of the ethnic fighting was displacement. Millions of people were displaced from all sides and managing this problem became a nightmare for the federal and regional administrations. In the following section, we will outline the challenging issues related to this.

7.3.3 Conflict-Related Displacements

Over three million people were reported to have been internally displaced in Ethiopia of which several hundred thousand people were Somalis. Some of the displaced Somali people fled to Somalia and Kenya, but most of them are in different places within the Somali region. Many of them are in camps in the border areas and get assistance from the government and NGOs. Others live in the towns and villages amongst their communities and are often dependent on relatives. Of those hosted by the authorities, most of them are in the Dire Dawa, Liban and Faafan zones. The camps in Qoloji in the Faafan zone have the largest concentration of internally displaced people. Over 80,000 internally displaced people live in Qolaji alone.

The problem of displacement has been one of the most difficult issues for the government at all levels because of the multidimensional challenges that are involved. The roots of the displacement crisis were the interdependent economic, political and security issues. Apart from the political factor, the competition over resources is the main source of conflict. The problem began primarily with disputes over scarce resources, and because of the lack of a political mechanism to resolve these economic issues, some people resorted to force to obtain shared resources at the expense of others. These attempts were then resisted by the other parties and led to clashes, which in turn made it a security issue.

One resolution to the problem required fixing all three elements. The displaced people lost all their properties, homes and livelihoods and needed economic assistance to restart their devastated livelihoods. Some of them were traders and sought assistance to establish themselves in the urban areas. Others were farmers or pastoralists who needed both fertile land and farming equipment or pastureland and livestock.

But before all that, they wanted secure places where they could live, farm or keep their livestock. Either the places they had fled from were to be pacified and returned or new places should be found for them, and coping with that predicament was difficult. There were no empty lands as the places they had vacated were overtaken by newcomers, and in many cases, the new occupants of these places claimed to be the rightful owners who were taking back their ancestral land. Similarly, resettling them into new lands was not an easy job as every place was claimed by someone, and because of their different livelihoods, they required diverse and appropriate places to be accommodated, which could not be found in one location.

Solving the economic and security problems outlined above required determination and a political mechanism to deal with these issues. The core issue was how to secure the land and create environments that were conducive to a peaceful way of life and establish the means to live. In other words, it was imperative to create peace, which was a prerequisite for living, and viable economic activities by designing durable policies and establishing political institutions to formulate and execute them. A durable political solution needed time to be formulated and put into practice, and the internal displacement crisis required an urgent solution, and that seemingly unavoidable debate of how to go about the problem (whether to find a proper long-term solution or implement temporary hasty measures) led to a delay, which exacerbated the crisis further.

In addition to that, the federal government lost the trust of the conflicting sides. It was perceived either as the cause behind the conflict or at least responsible for prolonging it. Furthermore, because of the involvement of the different regional administrations who were part of the ethnic conflict that took place and the interdependency of the horizontal and vertical layers of those government components, as well as the internal conflicts associated with them, the government not only lost its credibility regarding the issue but its hands were somewhat tied.

The changing leadership of the federal government did not quickly restore the lost trust in the government. The new prime minister's peace gestures and assurances were received with scepticism in his first visit to Jigjiga. This was because of his Oromo background, the antagonism between the Oromo and Somali regional leaders at the time and the view of bias in favour of the Oromos, which the Somalis held about the central government's handling of the conflict. We will revisit this in chapter 12 to examine the effects of the change of the regional and federal governments on the issue.

8

The Reform in Ethiopia

After nearly three years of peaceful mass anti-government protests spearheaded by the Oromos and aided by the Amhara people, the EPRDF regime finally bowed down to the pressure of the uprising and began serious discussions on how to embark on the inevitable political reform demanded by the people. In a preliminary internal debate within the ruling EPRDF party, a difference of opinions soon emerged, with some members of the government demanding real change and others resisting the shake-up of the system. The division of the government was also a reflection of the ethnic standoff in the country where the Oromo and Amhara leaders, whose people led the uprising, were more receptive to their demands, while the Tigray group was not willing to make any real changes to the status quo.

At the time, the country was led by a prime minister from a minority ethnic group who presided over a government that was practically run by the security services and the army and under the leadership of people mainly from Tigray. Despite the high position he held during the EPRDF regime, his ethnic background restricted his political power and made him an outsider. On the one hand, the Tigrayans who had led the country since 1991 were not willing to relinquish power, and on the other hand, the Oromo and Amhara protesters could not accept the continuation of Tigray's domination. Given the uprising, which had reached a point of no return, and its growing support within the ruling party, a reform of the system was inevitable. However, the prime minister could not deliver the required reform mainly because of the opposition from the Tigray hardliners who controlled the army and security agencies and thereby practically ruled the country. As a result of his powerlessness and the need for an urgent resolution to the political crisis, Prime Minister Hailemariam Desalegn resigned on 15 February 2018, paving the way for a successor who could end the stalemate and deliver the reform.

8.1 Change of the Regime Head

As soon as Hailemariam Desalegn resigned, the campaign to fill the position he had vacated began. The Tigray party wanted a continuation of their rule, but the Amhara and Oromo parties, along with their mass anti-government protesters, wanted to end the disproportional power of the Tigray. The Amhara and the Oromo ethnic groups in total make about 60 per cent of the Ethiopian population, whereas the Tigray comprise about 6 per cent. The Oromos, who are the largest nationality in the country, led the uprising to change the oppressive and underrepresented regime in power. It was neither acceptable for the Oromos to be ruled by the Tigray minority any longer nor to restore the oppressive Amhara dynasty that had marginalised them and made them serfs. The Amhara people, who were determined to get rid of the TPLF's rule, knew that they could not topple the Tigray government alone, and they were aware of the aspirations of the Oromos. Therefore, they saw the inevitability of an Oromo-led government.

The Oromo People's Democratic Organisation (OPDO) met a week after the resignation of the prime minister to choose a chairman for the OPDO and a premier candidate. Abiy Ahmed Ali, who was the vice-chairman of that party, was the person the OPDO selected and put forward to become the leader of the EPRDF and subsequently the prime minister of the country. By the end of March 2018, the EPRDF council met and elected Abiy Ahmed Ali as their leader. The four parties in the EPRDF coalition (TPLF, OPDO, ANDM and SEPDM) each had 45 votes. The candidate got 108 out of 180 votes, most of which were cast by the Amhara and Oromo groups and whose combined efforts largely swept him to that victory.

Abiy Ahmed Ali was sworn into parliament on 2 April 2018 as the prime minister of Ethiopia, becoming the first Oromo to hold the premiership of the country, though he is not the first Oromo to lead the country. Lij Iyasu who replaced Menelik II and was the son of his daughter was also an Oromo. The two men shared the Amhara link: the mothers of both men were Amhara and they converted to their mothers' religion of Christianity. But they differed in how they achieved and exercised the leadership of the country. Iyasu was the heir to the throne by birth, and because of his young age, a regent ran the country on his behalf for the first year of his roughly four-year reign (1913–1916). Abiy Ahmed sought power and achieved it through the efforts of the Oromo people, who united in their uprising and propelled Abiy into power. The Oromo protesters demanded a regime change, and his nomination was the answer to their demand.

The new prime minister was also different from his predecessor in that he was not an outsider to the system. Indeed, it is not an exaggeration to say that he was brought up by the system. He was an army officer whose main area of work was the intelligence and security services, and he had not seen any other regime for the entirety of his working life. He also had the backing of the two largest ethnic groups, namely, the Amhara and Oromo nations, whose anti-government protests propelled him to the premiership. Although the Tigray held the highest positions in the army and the main government departments, most of the middle- and lower-ranking army officers as well as the civil service had Oromo and Amhara backgrounds.

Despite the obvious advantages Abiy Ahmed had over his predecessor in terms of public backing, he did not inherit an easy job, and initially, his manoeuvrability within the system was extremely limited. In a speech before parliament on 30 November 2020, the prime minister described the difficulties he faced at the beginning of his premiership. He said that the TPLF, which was alone in having full control of the country in all matters, had given him a hard time from the outset. For instance, they did not allow him to bring his security staff to his office or residence, and because of the TPLF security officials that ran the premier office, he felt like a prisoner in his own office. The powerful anti-reform forces within the regime did not wish him to succeed and so began to contemplate ways of frustrating his reform efforts. He added that the things they wanted to derail from the reform were, amongst other things, the instigation of communal violence amongst the different ethnic groups, the obstruction of justice, the assassination of the reformists and the looting of the country's monetary reserves, which the TPLF had exclusive control over.

On the other hand, the protesters wanted to see tangible and rapid progress towards democratisation and respect for the rule of law. The main dilemma for the new prime minister was how to strike a balance between the people's demand for a shake-up of the system to liberate the country from the repressive regime and restore freedom versus the hardliner's view of preserving the system at any cost to maintain the status quo or, as they put it, to prevent anarchy.

There was a real danger of a collapse in authority if either side of the extremists won. In the case of the hardliners getting their way, the protesters would have increased their anti-government activities and the standoff would have resulted in a bloodbath and the eventual collapse of the central government. The other extreme possibility of removing the whole system, which was demanded by most of the dissidents, would have led to anarchy given the ethnic antagonism. Considerate decisions that accommodated both sides and bold and rapid steps to deal with the crisis before things got out of hand were needed, and seemingly, he understood that well, as his actions showed.

To consolidate his power, he used shock therapy tactics against the anti-reform forces by firing a series of controversial and anti-reform figures in key positions, who seemed untouchable, and replacing them with his own people. To calm the situation and give hope to the people, he admitted in parliament on 18 June 2018 that the regime had committed acts of terror against its own people and promised the Ethiopian people to end the human rights abuses of the regime. He further emphasised that torture, which the regime used extensively to extend its lifetime, was unlawful and that the era of state-sanctioned torture was over.

Although he tried to unite the country by trying to find a middle ground, satisfying all the expectations of every group was impossible. The anti-reform groups were shocked by the acceleration of the courageous reform policies that he introduced and the rapid steps he undertook to consolidate his power. In contrast, some of the protesters, particularly his own Oromo people, felt that he was not doing enough to reform the system. An attempt on his life was made on 23 June 2018 by extremists who were not happy with the pace of the reform. A bomb was thrown at the prime minister while he was addressing a rally in Addis Ababa's Meskel Square. 2 people were killed and more than 100 people were injured, but the prime minister was unharmed.

Although the system was not as radically reorganised as the opposition wished, Abiy Ahmed introduced sweeping reforms. These reforms included the release of political prisoners, the gradual opening of the media, the widening of the political space and the removal of some of the repressive laws that had been designed to silence the opposition and the media.

8.2 The Release of Political Prisoners

In January 2018, Hailemariam Desalegn announced that his government would release political prisoners and close the infamous Maekelawi prison and detention centre, but he did not give a timeline for the release of the prisoners or the closure of the prison. He said the move was designed to allow political dialogue and resolve the political crisis of the country.

The Ethiopian people and human rights advocacy groups cautiously welcomed the move, though they questioned the sincerity of his intentions and, for several reasons, remained sceptical of the announcement. In the English version of the statement, the prime minister promised the release of political prisoners. However, in the Amharic version that was broadcasted on the TV of the government, the pardoning of people who had committed crimes was mentioned. This double communique reminded citizens of Ethiopia's practice of simultaneously releasing and arresting dissidents to make sure that the prisons never become empty. It was also known that the Amhara and Oromo parties within the EPRDF coalition were critical of the government's suppression of their people and were demanding genuine self-rule and an end to the TPLF domination. Therefore, the move was seen by analysts as the result of an internal power struggle within the regime.

Despite the public scepticism of his promise, he set free hundreds of prisoners, including well-known opposition figures, within weeks and freed thousands of other prisoners before he resigned in February. Abiy Ahmed accelerated the release process of the prisoners that his predecessor had started. Thousands of dissidents, including opposition leaders, were set free from the federal prisons and other jails in all regional administrations other than the Somali state. A few days after taking office, the new prime minister closed the Maekelawi prison and detention centre.

The new prime minister went even further on the issue by addressing the root causes of political imprisonment: the repressive laws and the monopoly of political power by the ruling party. To hold on to power, the ruling EPRDF party had abused the justice system by introducing what it called anti-terror laws, which it used extensively against the opposition to silence them. He took rapid measures to close most of the infamous torture and detention centres and to amend some of the repressive laws, including the anti-terrorism proclamation under which most prisoners of conscience were detained.

To improve the human rights situation, the prison system was partially reorganised, removing not only some of the notorious human rights abusers from their positions but also showing more openness regarding the human rights abuses committed by the regime. The state TV made a documentary about the systematic torture that was practised by security services over the years inside the prisons, and between 6 and 9 September 2019, the government re-opened Maekewali prison to the public, which had been closed in 2018, and transformed into a gallery. For several days, it was visited and viewed by former inmates to help them overcome their trauma and also by the wider public so that they could see a glimpse of the brutal history of the place. The four-day opening of the prison was also part of the government's showcase of justice reform.

In addition to that, the approval of the Organisation of Civil Societies Proclamation and the repealing of the 2009 Charities and Societies Proclamation removed the restrictions on independent human rights reporting. This enabled both local and international human rights investigators to operate relatively freely and easily conduct investigations into human rights violations. Judges also became bolder in their judgements. Some of the former prisoners joined the system, and some of them are leading important human rights institutions. Daniel Bekele, who is the chairman of the Ethiopian Human Rights Commission, was a former prisoner.

Despite some positive steps being taken by the government in reforming the justice system, critics regard the changes as too small to overhaul the whole system. They point out that only parts of the anti-terror laws were amended and that the police and prison personnel still lack the necessary training concerning the limits of force and the protection of human rights. They also argue that the justice system is not fully independent and that there are still many detention centres run by the federal and regional administrations, where inmates are badly treated and lack access to medical and legal aid. When reports of the abuses from these detention centres appear in the media, the authorities often dismiss the administrators of the facilities, but often they do not charge them with any crime.

Due to the recent unrest in Oromia, the ensuing crackdown there and the ongoing conflict in Tigray, much of what has been achieved in the initial stages regarding the reform of the judicial system are now in reverse. Human rights abuse of all forms perpetrated by the government are widely reported across these regions, and the old repressive laws have been reintroduced in practical terms according to independent observers.

8.3 Easing the Restrictions on the Media

In addition to the release of prisoners, the government removed its restrictions on the media, the freedom of expression and political participation. The new administration also lifted the state of emergency that had been imposed after the resignation of Hailemariam Desalegn, though it has been reimposed in some parts of the country.

Ethiopia was one of the most censored countries in the world and its press lacked the basic freedom to conduct normal journalistic work. Journalists were a targeted group, and very often, they ended up in jail. After the introduction of the reform, they were freed from jail, and access to media outlets was restored. The government lifted its restrictions on internet access and mobile applications as well as its ban on hundreds of websites, which were introduced during the protests. Media outlets based abroad, such as the Ethiopian Satellite Television (ESAT) and Oromia Media Network (OMN) stations, returned home and reopened in Addis Ababa in June 2018. They operated freely in the country until the new Oromo uprising in 2020.

Some of the press freedoms gained at the start of the reform vanished due to the new Oromo unrest and conflict in Tigray. Despite the unprecedented freedoms that the Ethiopian press enjoyed at the beginning of the reform, even then journalists complained about the limited access to government officials and the lack of institutional guarantees and independent bodies to protect the press. Positive changes were introduced by the current regime to safeguard the freedom of the press, but as there are no independent institutions that protect them, the regime can change its mind and reverse the press reform. The political transformation is fragile and, at times of uncertainty, political information becomes more sensitive. Media has been a useful instrument for the government in holding on to power, and the more its grip on power is shaken the more it becomes one-way communication, whereby only the government sends out information to the public, and already, there are signs of returning to the former press restrictions.

The new law, criminalising hate and the incitement of ethnic violence, is seen by critics as a new version of the terror law intended to criminalise critical voices. The recent government crackdown of the opposition in Oromia, the shutting down of the internet and phone communications in many parts of that state and internet blocking across the whole country whenever the government undertakes security operations are worrying developments and signs of the old habits of the Ethiopian state returning.

To be fair, the new threat to the press is also coming from within the press. Some of the big private media outlets are owned or administrated by activists or politicians with special interests. The mixing of the two roles is problematic and sometimes dangerous, particularly when the opposition party is the government. To protect press freedom from internal and external threats and to further enhance it, appropriate regulations should be put in place.

8.4 Widening the Political Space

Many politicians were freed from jails and political parties were permitted to register and run for office. As part of the prime minister's new political drive to open up the political space, the government promised that it would ensure free and fair competition in the coming election, and that policy announcement was boosted by the nomination of a former prisoner to head the electoral board. Birtukan Mideksa, who was an opposition leader imprisoned by the EPRDF regime, is today the head of the National Electoral Board of Ethiopia (NEBE).

Mideksa is not the only woman who has been appointed to a high position in the new system. The prime minister is determined to promote gender equality and has already done a commendable job in that regard: the president of the country and half of the cabinet are women.

In June 2018, parliament lifted the ban on three-armed opposition organisations at the request of the government. The three-armed groups, the ONLF, the OLF and Ginbot 7, were in military confrontations with the EPRDF government, which declared them terrorists. All three organisations are now registered parties and are planning to contest the coming election.

When the three organisations returned home, they were welcomed by their supporters in large numbers in their respective regions. Unlike Ginbot 7, which was primarily fighting for the removal of the regime, the other two organisations were fighting to free their people from Abyssinian colonisers. Millions of people welcomed the OLF leader in Oromia and Addis Ababa. In his speech to the jubilant crowd in the capital, the OLF leader thanked them for the warm reception and told them that the struggle for the freedom of Oromia would continue peacefully. Similarly, the ONLF leader addressed a large rally held in Jigjiga to welcome the homecoming of the ONLF leadership. In his address, he told the crowd that the armed struggle would be replaced by a peaceful one, but the quest for the freedom of the Somali people would continue until they were victorious.

The legalisation of the three organisations, their home return and their participation in the political system was the most significant development and the biggest step towards the political opening of the country. The three organisations waged armed struggles in response to the repression of the government. The government responded with force against the armed resistance and harshly suppressed not only their supporters and sympathisers but also punished whole communities in some regions to deny them hiding places. The vicious circle of attacks and counterattacks led to catastrophic results in terms of human rights abuses and the disruption of livelihoods. Ending the war and talking about political problems instead of fighting over them was a noticeably big step in the right direction.

Taking advantage of the reforms and the new window of openness, many parties have registered to contest the election and make their own political impact. For its part, the government promised the establishment of a genuinely democratic system, and it also pledged to review and make the necessary changes to the laws and institutions to adapt to the new pluralistic political system. There is an overall optimism in the country driven from the top towards democracy, but in practice, the transformation of the political process is not going smoothly and is not in line with the rhetoric of the leaders. Many impediments are hindering or reducing the progression of the transformation, including mistrust, power struggles and the lack of a pluralistic political culture.

The ruling party that is leading the reform process is the same party that ruled the country since 1991, which repressed the people of the land. Furthermore, the party occupies 100 per cent of the parliamentary seats and practically monopolises the power of the state. Only the top leadership has been replaced, and recently, the name of the party has been changed from the EPRDF to the Ethiopian Prosperity Party (EPP). Despite the new, reform-friendly leadership and the rebranding of the ruling party, the repressive history of the party is very vivid in the memories of those it victimised, including many political parties. Therefore, both the public and the parties are sceptical of the rhetoric of the government regarding democratisation and respect for the rule of law. Besides that, the ruling EPP party lost the TPLF, which had dominated the EPRDF during the transformation process of the party after the TPLF refused to join the new party. The deep mistrust between the two parties led to an armed conflict in the Tigray between the EPP government and the TPLF.

Besides the conflict in Tigray, the power struggles between parties, within parties, between regional states and between the federal government and the regional states have been widely observed throughout the country. These power struggles involve constitutional issues, economic and natural resource-based issues, political positioning and policy-based issues and ethnic issues. In addition to that, the rules of the political game, in a legal sense, are not clear. Additionally, independent institutions to arbiter the constitutional, political and economic conflicts do not exist, and so far, the reform process has been moving at the behest of the prime minister.

Ethiopia has never seen a pluralistic system of government: throughout its history, it was either ruled by absolute monarchs or by military dictatorship regimes. Multi-party democracy was neither the system in which political behaviour was conducted nor were democratic values and political processes part of the political culture of Ethiopia. The lack of both a democratic culture and the experience of a multi-party system, as well as institutional and legal impediments, led to delays and possibly new conflicts resulting from a misinterpretation of the new ideas and the conflicting interests of the parties, as illustrated by the recent developments in Oromia.

The recent unrest in the Oromo state is a worrying development. Initially, it was a dispute between the government and the OLF over the terms of the peace agreement. The two sides accused each other of violating the terms of the peace accord, and the disagreement led to military clashes between the government army and OLF forces. Although the political confrontation continued, the government made a peace deal with the political wing of the OLF after it distanced itself from its former military wing (the OLFA). The clashes between the OLFA, the former military wing of the organisation, and the government did not cease. The bulk of supporters of the organisation disliked many of the government's policies, especially what they referred to as the ill-treatment of the OLF and the OFC, and they showed that dissatisfaction in protests. For its part, the government accused them of misusing their new freedom and, in response to the protests, resumed mass arrests of opposition activists. According to Amnesty International, the government arrested at least 75 members and supporters of the OLF in the last week of January 2020.

The conflict expanded recently to other opposition parties, and the government used some of the old tactics of the regime to contain the unrest. Supporters of the Oromo Federalist Congress (OFC) and security forces clashed in several cities. Internet and telephone shutdowns and widespread arrests were reported in some parts of Oromia by independent human rights organisations and other independent sources.

The trigger for the escalation of the new unrest was the claim of the prominent activist Jawar Mohamed and the sudden removal of his security guards by the government in October 2019. Following his complaint, the supporters of the activist staged anti-government rallies in the capital and many other cities of Oromia. In the ensuing unrest, hundreds of people were killed.

The announcement of Jawar Ahmed to contest the coming election and challenge Abiy Ahmed further strained the relationship between the prime minister and the activist. Jawar Ahmed played a leading role in the uprising that propelled Abiy Ahmed to power, and he is popular in Oromia, especially with youths. The two men have differing views on important issues such as the federal system and the so-called special interest of Oromia in the capital, and both have sizable followers within the ethnic group to which they belong.

The political unrest in Oromia intensified after the killing of the popular artist and activist Hachalu Handessa in June 2020. The government accused the OLF and the TPLF of killing him, but the Oromo public blamed the government for the murder of the musician and the widespread clampdown on protesters. The arrest of some popular Oromo leaders, including Bekele Gerba and Jawar Mohammed, as well as the heavy-handed response of the government to the waves of protests that followed the killing of the artist, exacerbated the situation and further fuelled the unrest.

Politics in the Oromo region are very polarised and contentious. The success or failure of the prime minister's handling of the volatile political situation in that state will have profound effects on his premiership. In other words, Oromia is a testing ground for the prime minister, which will either derail his ambition to rule the country or boost it because of his Oromo background and the challenges it poses in terms of its political weight as the most populous and largest region in Ethiopia and its internal conflicts.

Abuse of power and human rights violations have been the main characteristics of the Ethiopian regimes, and the recent development in Oromia indicates that the situation has fundamentally not changed. Despite the arrest of some EPRDF officials, nobody was charged on the accountability of past abuses, and though the government established a reconciliation commission in 2018, it has not taken meaningful steps in that regard. In addition to that, independent judicial and constitutional institutions do not exist. This means that the government is still in control of everything, and there are no proper checks and balances in the system of governance.

Given the country's history of intolerance towards dissent and the concentration of power in the hands of the government, the recent suppression of the opposition in Oromia was not unexpected. Unless the government devolve constitutional and judicial powers to independent institutions, accept accountability and respect the rule of law, the failure of the reform will not be totally unexpected.

8.5 Rapprochement with the Neighbours

The EPRDF regime was not only in conflict with its people but also with some of its neighbours. The relationship between Somalia and Ethiopia was tense and difficult because of the latter's constant breach of the former's sovereignty, and technically, Ethiopia was in a situation of war with Eritrea. To improve the country's reputation, the new prime minister made contacts with Eritrea and Somalia, offering Eritrea a peace settlement over the border dispute, which the two countries fought over between 1998 and 2000, and promising Somalia to end the interference in its internal affairs.

8.5.1 Eritrea

Initially, Eritrea gave a cool response to the rapprochement initiative of the new Ethiopian prime minister because Asmara did not expect a genuine offer from Addis Ababa, given the antagonism between the two regimes and the history of the bloody conflicts between the two countries. Before the 1998–2000 border war, Eritrea fought against Ethiopia to gain independence, and that armed struggle took over 30 years. Eritrea was liberated from Ethiopia in 1991 after a bloody war in which each nation suffered a heavy loss of life, and it officially became an independent nation in May 1993.

At a peace deal mediated by Algeria, which was attended by the UN, AU and the EU and signed on 12 December 2000, a Boundary Commission was established and the two countries agreed to abide by the ruling of the commission on the disputed border area. The commission reached a decision on the matter on 13 April 2002 and awarded the disputed area to Eritrea, but the government of Ethiopia reneged on its earlier promise of accepting the verdict of the commission.

The Eritrean president, Isaias Afwerki, dismissed the Ethiopian peace initiative as another deceptive lie at the beginning. However, after a series of meetings between Ethiopian and Eritrean officials and, in particular, after the Ethiopian government unilaterally endorsed the outcome of the Algiers agreement on 5 June 2018, it became clear that the Ethiopian move of ending the conflict by honouring the agreement she had signed with her neighbour was genuine. Finally, the Eritrean leader was convinced of the sincerity of the initiative of Abiy Ahmed Ali and jumped on the peace wagon from Addis Ababa to seize the unexpected opportunity. The peace signing ceremony that finalised the agreement took place in Asmara in July 2018.

In compliance with the ruling of the commission, Ethiopia eventually withdrew its federal forces from the disputed area, clearing the way for Eritrea to take it over. Following the peace agreement, the two countries resumed diplomatic relations, established telecommunication and transport links and committed to free trade and economic cooperation, although Eritrea closed the border crossing shortly after it was opened.

The rapprochement between the two countries ended the frozen war, and both governments benefited from it politically. Eritrea got the territory it claimed in a legal sense, and the peace deal helped her to return to the regional and international arenas. On a regional level, it restored diplomatic ties with Djibouti and Somalia, and the leaders of Ethiopia, Somalia and Eritrea have recently been talking about regional integration and the political rehabilitation of Eritrea into the Intergovernmental Authority on Development (IGAD). On the international stage, the United Nations' sanctions on Eritrea were lifted following the diplomatic restoration between Somalia and Eritrea. The Ethiopian armed opposition groups based in Asmara returned home after the Ethiopian government decriminalised them and reached peace agreements with them. However, the peace deal between the countries weakened the bargaining position of these opposition groups and indirectly forced them to hasten their return home.

Despite the mutually beneficial results on the political side, little has happened in terms of economic cooperation. It seems that Eritrea is not willing to open its borders because of internal politics. The totalitarian system there is afraid of losing its grip on power if it opens its doors.

In addition to that, an important regional actor is being excluded from the peace process. The Tigray state shares a border with Eritrea and claims the disputed border area has not backed the peace agreement and is not part of the equation of the new relationship between Asmara and Addis Ababa. Furthermore, the ousted Tigray state administration, which was at loggerheads with the federal government since Abiy Ahmed Ali took control, was deliberately postponing the actual demarcation on the ground to frustrate the agreement signed by the two countries. Thus, despite the cordial relationship at the top leadership level and the signing of the peace accord, everything else was on hold until the eruption of war in Tigray. Although the federal army defeated the TPLF forces and controls all the main urban areas in Tigray, and Eritrea can militarily take over the territory it has acquired legally, the TPLF has not been eliminated and the organisation does not recognise the territorial claim of Eritrea.

8.5.2 Somalia

The pace of further integration between Ethiopia and Eritrea depends mainly on Eritrea, whereas the new relationship between Somalia and Ethiopia is directed by Ethiopia, because of the former's inability to exercise the full power of sovereignty over its own territory. Since the collapse of the Somali central government in 1991, Ethiopia controlled

Somali politics through local warlords and regional administrations with which she interacted freely without the consent of the Somali federal government. The new relationship between the two governments is based on the vague understanding that Ethiopia ends its direct dealings with the regional governments and, in return, the Somali government looks after Ethiopia's interests in Somalia.

On the surface, things seem to be progressing in the right direction, whereby Ethiopia is no longer breaching the sovereignty of Somalia by only conducting business with the federal government, and reciprocally, Ethiopia is getting what she wants in Somalia as a single package instead of exhausting herself with the dealings of multiple and sometimes conflicting local administrations. However, it is more complex than it seems because of Ethiopia's ambition to get a strong foothold on the Somalia coast, the weak government in Somalia, whose main preoccupation is to gain control of the country with the help of Ethiopia, and the lack of a written agreement.

Ethiopia already annexed a Somali territory and used all possible measures to undermine and prevent the return of an effective central government in Somalia, and despite the rhetoric, Ethiopia has not shown a fundamental change in her relations with Somalia. Ethiopia tried to access the Somali coast through destabilisation, and she is still pursuing the same goal with a different tactic. She has bought a 19 per cent share of the Barbara Port and is aiming to gain control of other Somali ports. Unlike Ethiopia, the geopolitical strategies of Somalia are not clear, and besides that, the case of Qalbidhagah, as outlined in chapter 6, exposed the vulnerability of the Somali government and the irresistibility of Ethiopia's demands. Critics argue that the idea of seeking Ethiopian help to restore Somali unity is like asking a predator to take care of its prey.

The rapprochement with Eritrea enabled the Ethiopian leader to be awarded the 2019 Peace Nobel Prize for ending the no-war-no-peace situation, but the tacit rapprochement with Somalia is unlikely to earn him another prize or make a breakthrough towards real friendship, given the past dark history, the vagueness of the rapprochement and the conflicting signals from Addis Ababa.

The Reform in the Somali Region

The reform that began in earnest in Ethiopia after the change of the premier did not reach the Somali region in time. The region experienced its own uprising and resistance long before the rest of the country, and because of that, it was expected that the Somali region would be the first to see positive change. But unfortunately, it was the last place the reform reached.

Abiy Ahmed Ali arrived in Jigjiga on 8 April 2018, which was five days after he was sworn in as the Ethiopian prime minister. The prompt visit to the capital of the Somali region was not a random journey but an indication of the seriousness of the situation there. There were grave human rights violations, an ethnic war was ongoing between the Oromo region and the Somali state and the administration in the Somali region was the most brutal party of the Ethiopian regime, whose repressive policies had led to the uprising that swept him into power.

Given that the Somali region topped the list of regions in the country in terms of human rights abuses, insecurity and bad governance, and the fact that the prime minister was aware of the situation, one expected that he would not only embark on sweeping positive changes in the region as soon as he arrived but since he had made it his first destination, also kickstart the reforms of the country from there. However, despite his charm and nice style of talking, in which he informed the crowd of the wind of change that would be reaching them soon, he left the region having implemented no concrete changes or outlining any reform plan.

9.1 Reform Delay

The reform delay was caused by several interlinked events, which were largely created by regional and federal political actors with conflicting political interests. The refusal of the Somali regional administration to introduce reform, the ethnic conflicts between the Somalis and the Oromos, the crackdown and control of the region via anti-reform elements within the federal government were the main reasons for the delay of the reform.

The regional president who ruled the region with an iron fist was not prepared to accept the reform of the political system. He was determined to hang on to power and wanted to keep the repressive policies in place to preserve the status quo. He also signalled that he would resist any dictation from the new federal authorities regarding the reform changes that were needed.

Abdi Mohamed Omar indicated his opposition to the new wind of reform from Addis Ababa in speeches he held at public rallies, and through the creation of a vigilante group and mobilisation of the Special Police Force, he demonstrated his readiness to use force to defend his position. In short, he created a tense atmosphere and appeared to be confrontational.

In a meeting with the elders in May 2018, he told them that the prime minister had lied to them when he visited Jigjiga and that the Oromos were waging war against the Somalis. The vigilante group known as HEG0 was established in May, shortly after the meeting with the elders. It aimed to mobilise the public, spread the propaganda of the regional administration and defend the regional government. The vigilante group was also presented by the authorities as a civil defence force against Qeerroo, which was the Oromo youth organisation that spearheaded the anti-government protest in Oromia.

To show the strength of his power base and his determination to resist the demands of the reform, the regional administration increased the frequency of military parades and frequently sent the Special Police Force to the hot spots of ethnic clashes between the Oromos and Somalis. Also, the Special Police Force in the rural areas were brought to the capital and big cities to work as vigilantes in addition to the job that they were trained for. When in uniform, they acted as soldiers, and when in civilian clothes, they acted as vigilantes.

Furthermore, to pre-empt the possible rise of dissenting voices in the region because of the reform elsewhere in the country, the administration increased both its surveillance of the public and its human rights abuses. New informants were also sent to public and private places and the imprisonments of individuals were doubled, to enhance the monitoring and collective punishments of the communities.

In his first visit to the Somali region, the premier was accompanied by the Oromo regional leader, Lemma Megersa, and in a gesture of reconciliation, the two men were seen on stage holding hands with the Somali regional president standing in the middle. Because of the ethnic clashes between the Somalis and the Oromos, the prime minister did not want to appear to be siding with the Oromo regional leader, and for that reason, he dragged his feet in confronting Abdi Mohamed Omar.

On the other hand, the Somali regional president used the sensitivity of that issue as an excuse to block the reforms. He framed the demands of the reform from Addis Ababa as the Oromos interfering in the affairs of the Somali state channelled through the federal system. Abdi Mohamed Omar also had friends in the federal system who opposed the reform and backed his position.

The anti-reform forces in the federal government used the Somali region as the main battleground to defeat the new prime minister and his reform plan. In his speech before parliament on 30 November 2020, the prime minister said that the anti-reform forces were planning, as a last resort, to divide the country into pieces by declaring secession in Tigray and the Somali state. Additionally, they wanted to use the latter region as an experiment and start the operation there. He added that he knew of their plan and that the main aim of his visit to the region was to foil their operation. On security grounds, the security forces tried in vain to persuade the premier to cancel his visit, but he understood that they were not sincere regarding their security concerns and told them that their duty was to secure the place and not to scare him. In the beginning, the regional and federal anti-reform alliance expected to win the war quickly, but gradually, the going got tough for them. And as a result, they resorted to more violence and human rights abuses to pre-emptively quell the looming unrest.

In the meantime, the suffering of the Somali people became unbearable. As a result of the increased crackdown and the federal government's unwillingness to intervene, the political, social and human rights crises of the region reached an explosive point. The region has not seen peace since the EPRDF regime acceded to power and, as mentioned earlier, crackdowns, collective punishments and blockades were the constant policy instruments the government used to maintain its control of the region. As a result of these harsh policies and the subsequent suffering they caused, it was hard for the inhabitants to carry out an uprising, but they had no choice other than to raise their voices, despite the difficult circumstances.

9.2 Protests

As mentioned above, the region was in the hands of a ruthless gang, consisting of federal and regional agents, who were determined to crush any dissent. The region was officially headed by the regional president, but the real rulers were the TPLF leaders and military commanders from Tigray. The new federal government had full knowledge of the situation but was unable or unwilling to intervene because of the TPLF's opposition to do so, and the inhabitants did not have the means to remove the tyranny imposed on them.

Despite the difficult situation, the inhabitants had no choice but to rise to the challenge and strive for the salvation of the region and the release of their people from both confinement and the open-roof prions. In so doing, they organised themselves and formed protest networks both at home and in the diaspora under the banner of Dulmidiid (anti-injustice). The freedom campaigns began at home with the formation of underground protest networks. Additionally, in the diaspora, solidarity meetings and demonstrations were held in various places across Europe, Africa, Middle East and North America. In the beginning, the protest movements held freedom marches in the diaspora and organised their campaigns through social media. Gradually, the underground networks inside the region and the movements in the diaspora succeeded in staging coordinated protests inside and outside the region.

The protests at home were mainly organised by youth networks known as the Barbaarta, who were inspired by their counterparts in Oromia and were encouraged by the reforms that the prime minister began at the centre. The Barbaarta began their protests in Dire Dawa and the Siti zone sporadically, though the frequency and size of the protests gradually increased. These two places spearheaded the protest campaign to remove the repressive regional administration. The Faafan zone, which was the centre of the Dulmidiid's movements and the seat of the regional administration, held frequent protests in several places outside Jigjiga and protests in the other zones followed suit.

Although the protests were held in all zones, the biggest uprising took place in Dire Dawa, Siti, Faafan and Liban. These zones were in a better position to stage protests compared to other zones where the ONLF was based and where the severest crackdowns were taking place, such as Jarar, Qorahay, Dolo, Nogob, Afdheer and Shabelle. Protests were held in big cities, such as Wardheer, Godey, Dagahbur and Qabridaharre, but these cities did not join the uprising in the early stages, and the protests there were less frequent because of the extreme collective punishments and consequent suffering. In other words, the more severe the clampdown, the weaker the protests.

As expected, the regional administration reacted to the protests with full force. This included killing, torture and imprisonment aimed at the protesters and anyone who was suspected of aiding them. For example, in May 2018, security agents hanged a young woman called Taysir Omar Food in a police station in Qabridaharre. Taysir has gone to a grocery market to buy food, and from there, she was arrested and taken to a police station. She was murdered instantly for allegedly giving information to prominent family members in the Dulmidiid movement. The killing of Taysir shocked the region and ignited protests throughout the Somali state. She was one of many killed in the uprising and even though the method of her killing was widespread in the region, because of its timing during the height of the protests, she became a rallying symbol for the uprising.

After the protest reached a point of no return, a large delegation of intellectuals and traditional leaders left for Addis Ababa to talk to the federal government about their plight, and they were joined by representatives from diaspora communities worldwide. Although the joint delegates met senior government officials, they were unable to see the prime minister or get the backing of the government, despite their long stay in Addis Ababa. This was because of the opposition from federal government elements, primarily Tigray.

The Tigray officials in the federal system backed Abdi Mohamed Omar, and because of that, they resented the presence of the protesters who had mainly come to Addis Ababa to see his removal from power. They told the delegates to go back to Jigjiga and make peace with the administration there and warned them of the consequences if they did not return. To further discourage the defiant protesters and show the seriousness of their threat against the delegates, they kidnapped some of the activists on behalf of the Somali regional president. At the time, the TPLF still held a powerful position in the government and decided to defend the stance of the Somali regional president for economic and political reasons.

The TPLF had a vested economic interest in the region. The Tigray people were not only the real rulers of the region, but they were also the main beneficiaries of the region's income. All aspects of economic life were under their control. They had a big say in the shaping of the budget through the agencies and projects that they directly administrated such as the Special Police Force and all war-related activities. They would get a lion's share of the approved budget as contractors of the main projects in the region. They also controlled the export of high-yielding crops such as chat/qat and had a monopoly over the import of essential goods. In addition to that, the TPLF was running the gas fields projects in the Ogaden as a result of its dominance over the federal government and the TPLF-owned companies' partnerships with foreign contractors. In other words, the TPLF as both the government and contractor used to sit on both sides of the table and sign the contracts for both parties.

Generally, the TPLF opposed the reform, and due to the above-mentioned economic interests, it did not wish for a meaningful change to the political system and was totally against a regime change in the Somali region. Furthermore, it wanted to confront the new prime minister and for this showdown to take place in the Somali region. The proxy war between the TPLF and the OPDO, which the TPLF had planned and that Abdi Mohamed Omar was ready to execute, was framed as a resistance to the interference of the OPDO in the federal government and the internal affairs of the Somali region.

As a result of the internal power struggle within the federal government, the representatives of the Somali uprising failed to persuade the government to intervene and help them end the tyranny in their region. The bulk of the delegates returned disappointed from Addis Ababa after three months, but they did not go back to Jigjiga as demanded by the TPLF. Instead, they went to Dire Dawa, the epicentre of the uprising, and from there, they continued the campaign for the removal of the regional dictator.

A two-day conference was convened in Dire Dawa on 1 July 2018 to discuss the political crisis and draw up a political roadmap. The main topics under debate were a peaceful and orderly transition of power to the people and the political plans for the region after the regime change. Several hundred intellectuals, elders, politicians and diaspora representatives attended the conference. The Dulmidiid movement, the Barbaarta protest movement and the Somali Regional Alliance for Justice (SRAJ) were the main forces behind the organisation of the gathering. In the communique, which was issued at the end of the conference, the delegates declared that they no longer recognised the regional administration and that they would march towards Jigjiga to form a caretaker administration. They also urged citizens to remain calm and refrain from violence.

While the conference was going on in Dire Dawa, the brutal regional administration and its federal agent allies tried to disrupt the conference and contemplated further actions against the uprising. Using both the Special Police Force and federal agents, the dictator began to hunt prominent members of the uprising and attacked peaceful protesters, killing and injuring many of them. He also sent extra troops to the districts to deter potential protests and reinforced the security of the capital with extra troops and vigilantes.

Despite this show of force on the ground, on the political side, he spoke in a conflicting manner in the final weeks before his departure from power. On the one hand, he urged his followers to resist, and on the other hand, he displayed a reconciliatory tone in the interviews he gave. He praised the prime minister and his reforms and declared to support him. He further blamed the EPRDF for the mass atrocity of crimes committed under his jurisdiction. He claimed to have been a puppet who was merely executing the orders of the chief of the National Intelligence and Security Service (NISS), Getachew Assefa, in all the years he was in power and, for that reason, claimed that he was not responsible for the crimes his administration had committed.

The hypocrisy of this puppet increased because of the insecure position he put himself in. His TPLF allies urged him to resist and promised to back him until the bitter end, but that assurance of support was gradually fading, and he had already spoiled his relationship with the new prime minister because of his anti-Oromo propaganda. As he was unable to manoeuvre himself out of this political deadlock, the end of his nearly 10-year rule as president appeared inevitable.

9.3 Regional Regime Change

The ruthless dictator became more unpredictable as the going got tough and the collapse of his regime drew nearer. He was told by the federal government to hand over his power in exchange for amnesty from persecution. He accepted the offer but reneged on the understanding afterwards. While the dialogue was going on between Jigjiga and Addis Ababa over the political crisis, the already tense situation on the ground was growing more violent. The uprising got stronger, and the political environment became harsher because of the increased crackdown. The situation continued to deteriorate, and it spiralled out of control after the communication between the federal and regional governments broke down following the decline of summons to Addis Ababa by the regional ruler.

On 4 August 2018, the government sent federal troops to the capital of the Somali region to arrest its leader and secure it. As soon as they entered the city, they seized the buildings that housed the main governmental institutions, such as the parliament, the presidential palace, the administrative departments and the TV station.

As a result of the intervention, a planned meeting of the parliament was cancelled, and the president was put under house arrest. Two days later, he resigned and handed over his power to the former finance minister, Ahmed Abdi Mohamed. On 7 August 2018, he was flown on a helicopter to Addis Ababa, where he was formally arrested on 27 August 2018. The regional parliament had stripped him and six members of his government of their immunity one day earlier—before the arrest. The arrest took place at his home in the capital and, according to police, five Kalashnikov rifles and four pistols were found in the house.

In response to this, the cronies of the dictator gave orders to the Special Police Force, the vigilante groups and the supporters of the regional tyrants to resist the intervention and defend their leader. In the ensuing violence, the supporters of the dictator attacked the communities from other parts of Ethiopia that were living in Jigjiga. They went on the rampage, killing mainly non-Somali communities and looting and destroying business centres. Over 30 people were killed in the violence, and many businesses, government offices and churches were also set on fire in other cities, such as Dagahbur. Although the other Ethiopian communities had the largest share of lives lost in the carnage, Somalis were also killed, and they took the brunt of the economic devastation since it was their capital city that was destroyed.

The Somali public generally welcomed the overdue intervention that they had been requesting since the new prime minister's accession to power. But the dying regime resorted to violence, which caused havoc in the capital city, and because of the limited federal intervention, it succeeded in destroying most of the city within hours. The federal army secured the key institutions, but it did not have the mandate to take over the administration and was not large enough to secure the streets. As a result, the dying regime and its supporters had enough time to create carnage. The violence that began on 4 August 2018 continued until the tyrant was taken from the city.

After the army had restored the security of Jigjiga somewhat, the political transition work began with the summoning of the central committee of the ruling party, the Ethiopian Somali People's Democratic Party (ESPDP), to Addis Ababa. That party conference in the capital was the first phase of the process. The second phase of the process was the gathering of district administrators and traditional leaders in Addis Ababa and meeting with the head of the federal government.

In the first phase of the government formation process, the central committee of the ruling ESPDP party convened a two-week conference in Addis Ababa under the leadership of the Somali federal minister, Ahmed Shide. In the meeting, changes were made to some of the rules of the party: a new chairman to replace the arrested leader was elected, 11 members of the central committee lost their positions and the interim president Ahmed Abdi Mohamed also lost his position. The conference was concluded with the approval of a caretaker president on 22 August 2018 to head the Somali region until the elections scheduled for 2020 would be held. Although the central committee selected the new president after they admitted him to the party, in actual fact, he was appointed by the prime minister.

In the second stage of the process, the prime minister met with delegates of about several hundred people from all the districts on 24 August 2018. The representative of the people requested a comprehensive reform and a genuine change in governance from the prime minister. Additionally, they sought the protection of human rights and respect for the rule of law. While sitting between the newly appointed leader of the region, Mustafe Muhumed Omar, and the minister who represented the region in the federal government, Ahmed Shide, the prime minister addressed the gathering, promising them a genuine reform and a brighter future and answering some of their concerns.

One of the concerns that the delegates raised was the sharing formula of the income from natural resources, and they were both apprehensive and eager to hear his view on that issue because of an ill-perceived statement he made about it before the meeting. He used about 10 minutes of his 25-minute speech to clarify the earlier statement he had made about the share percentage of the revenue from the gas fields in the Ogaden Basin. In an interview that he had given while on a visit to the US, he said that it was customary in African oil-producing countries to give 5–10 per cent of the revenue to the place where the resource was found. He told the delegates that he meant the place to be the district where the gas wells were located and not the whole region. The new caretaker president also commented on the issue. He said that he was not aware of any existing regulations regarding the sharing formula of the revenue and added that it should be negotiated between the regional and federal authorities to reach a mutual agreement, and in a gesture of agreement, the prime minister nodded.

Following his nomination, the new caretaker president went to Jigjiga, the seat of his government, where he began the process of forming his cabinet. He had little time to select the members of the government because of the political crisis and the need to fill the vacuum left by the ousted regime. Fortunately, he managed to assemble a cabinet of well-educated people relatively quickly and most of them had higher degrees (that is, masters and PhDs). The list of his cabinet was presented on 2 September 2018.

In addition to the professionally qualified cabinet he had assembled, his educational and professional background was truly relevant to resolve the problems of the region that he had been selected to lead. As an agricultural economist, he had been working as an advisor to the United

Nations Humanitarian Coordinator for Somalia when he was chosen to head the region. He worked as a humanitarian officer with international organisations such as the United Nations and Save the Children across Africa and the Middle East. Before he left the region, he worked as a civil servant and as a politician. He headed educational intuitions and also served as the deputy minister of regional education. Pastoral and agropastoral livelihoods of which he is an expert are the dominant livelihoods in the Somali region.

Besides that, the new leader showed resilience in his campaign for the freedom of the inhabitants of the region and the ensuing confrontation with the oppressive regime. He also sacrificed a lot for that cause. The regional tyrant warned Mustafe Muhumed Omar of the consequences of the criticism of his government and told him that his family would pay the price unless he changed course. When Mustafe refused to bow down to his threats, the tyrant killed his brother Faisal Muhumed Omar in October 2016, and the rest of his family were either jailed or forced to flee the country. Their properties were also confiscated. But all that did not deter him from his campaign to remove the repressive regime. On the contrary, Mustafe resolutely increased his advocacy of human rights. His bold activism for the rights of his people and his steadfastness in the face of the threats and subsequent abuse of his family made him an exemplary figure and encouraged others to take a firm stand against injustice and establish the justice movement.

His professional background, coupled with his tireless campaign for the freedom, dignity and human rights of his people, indicated that he was well equipped to understand the problems of the region of which human rights abuses, insecurity, bad governance and poverty were the main issues of concern.

However, the crises in the region were enormous, the resources were limited, the man was an outsider to the system and his power was restricted by the patron-client relationship between the federal government and the regional government. As a result, his political manoeuvrability was limited, despite his understanding of the situation of the region, his awareness of the needs of the people and his eagerness to make and rapid positive changes to the state.

10

The Asmara Peace Agreement

The Ethiopian government and the ONLF signed a historic peace agreement in Asmara, Eritrea, on 21 October 2018. Workneh Gebeyehu, the minister of foreign affairs, and Mohammed Omar Osman, chairman of the ONLF, signed the agreement for the Ethiopian government and the ONLF, respectively. The two-round negotiations in Eritrea started in September. In the first round, which concluded on 18 September, the parties reached a common understanding of the peace process in general terms and how to proceed with the talks. The second phase concluded the negotiations with the signing of the peace accord.

The government delegation, which was led by the foreign minister, included Ahmed Shide, the finance minister representing the Somali region in the federal government, and Mustafe Muhumed Omer, president of the Somali state. Redwan Hussein, Ethiopia's ambassador to Eritrea also attended the meeting. The ONLF delegation was led by Chairman Mohamed Omar Osman and included the secretary-general, Abdirahman Sheikh Mahdi, and the foreign secretary, Ahmed Yassin Sheikh Ibrahim, and several senior members of the executive committee.

Despite its ambiguity and resemblance to a declaration, the peace agreement was historic in that it was the first agreement of its kind between an Ethiopian government and a liberation movement from the Somali region. The conflict, which began with Abyssinia's attempts to conquer parts of the Somali region in the 14th century and later became the main preoccupations of the two parties after the full takeover of the region by Ethiopia in the last century, never ended, though the level of clashes varied. Successive Ethiopian governments and consecutive liberation movements inherited the centuries-long conflict from one another, but they had not agreed to any peace deal before the one that was signed in Asmara.

The negotiations that led to the peace deal began in good stead, and for several reasons, there was far more optimism to reach a successful outcome compared to the earlier talks between the two parties. Prior to the start of the talks, the Ethiopian government lifted the ban on the ONLF and introduced a reform that led to the release of thousands of prisoners, eased the restriction on the media and political expression and a regime change occurred in the Somali state. A ceasefire was declared unilaterally by the ONLF and welcomed by the government, and delegates from the organisation arrived in the Somali region.

In the communique given after the signing of the peace agreement, the Ethiopian foreign minister said that the peace accord would end the decades-long conflict and would allow the ONLF to pursue its political activities inside the country peacefully. For his part, the chairman of the ONLF said that the positive political development in the country had encouraged them to sign the accord and declared that his organisation was ready to contribute to the reform and the development of the region.

The host country was not represented in the venue where the document was signed, although it was instrumental in the making of the deal and had separate talks with both parties. A third-party presence in a venue outside Ethiopia was one of the cornerstone preconditions of the ONLF for any peace deal with Ethiopia, which the Ethiopian governments always objected to. But they reluctantly accepted this during the Nairobi peace talks. The absence of the Eritrean government from the peace-signing venue in Asmara was something of an impediment between the two parties and their well-known positions (that is, the ONLF's insistence on having a third-party presence and being in a neutral country and Ethiopia's rejection of both of these conditions). But whether that was a compromise the two sides reached together or a unilateral Eritrean design is not clear.

10.1 The Road to Peace

The war was not the choice of the ONLF, and the organisation was pursuing its political engagements peacefully when war was imposed on it. A peaceful resolution to the conflict was the organisation's preferred option, and it indicated on numerous occasions its willingness to reach a negotiated settlement with the government of Ethiopia.

Even during the war, the ONLF maintained its commitment to a peaceful settlement to the conflict and declared its readiness to talk to the opposition. Taking advantage of that open-door policy of the organisation, the government initiated the first contact with the rebel group. The government approached the organisation directly and the first contact took place in the region. Unfortunately, the direct contacts between the two parties ended disastrously and worsened the situation because of the betrayal of the government.

The government was not sincere regarding the peace negotiations, which it initiated, and from its actions, it seemed that the initiative was merely a blackmail attempt intended to get intelligence information about the organisation and kidnap or assassinate the peace negotiators of the organisation. The ONLF ended the so-called direct peace talks when the government assassinated the organisation's negotiating team in 1998. Amongst the peace team members killed in that assassination were Sheikh Bashir and Deq Abdi Rasin.

From that time, the ONLF changed its approach to peace talks with the Ethiopian regime by introducing preconditions: future peace negotiations were to take place in a neutral country and in the presence of an international body. The ONLF stuck to that principle, and since adopting that clear standpoint, the organisation did not pay attention to any peace attempt that did not fulfil their preconditions until 2017. However, the Ethiopian regime did not cease its deceptive peace initiatives.

Disregarding the preconditions stated by the organisation, the government made several attempts to reach out to the ONLF in the old fashion using other sections of society. For example, in 2005, the Ethiopian government sent elders to Europe to talk to the ONLF about peace and act as mediators between the Ethiopian government and the resistance group. The elders met with both the diaspora communities and some of the leaders of the ONLF, but they returned home empty-handed after the ONLF made it clear to them that it would only negotiate with the Ethiopian government about the conflict on the terms of the ONLF's stated preconditions.

The positions of the two sides hardened after the Obole battle, and the Ethiopian government introduced scorched-earth policies in the region. Despite the crackdown, the prime minister of the time, Meles Zenawi, realised that without a political settlement, the war could not be ended and, as a result, began to contact the ONLF through intermediaries. He made contact with Kenyan President Mwai Kibaki and some politicians from the Somali region in Kenya asking them to facilitate peace talks with the ONLF.

The Kenyan government accepted the Ethiopian request and informed the ONLF of the Ethiopian peace offer. After the organisation gave a positive response to the peace initiative, the Kenyan government appointed a team led by the former defence minister and the Garissa senator, Mohamed Yusuf Haji, to facilitate the talks. The Kenyan officials received assistance from some international organisations to facilitate the peace negotiations. Amongst these organisations was Conciliation Resources, which provided technical support to the negotiating parties and the host country in terms of training, information gathering and the exchange of relevant experiences and lessons from conflict resolutions elsewhere.

Unfortunately, the Ethiopian prime minister who initiated the peace talks died in August 2012, which was weeks before the scheduled date for the start of the talks. He had requested the peace talks following the failure of the military option to eliminate the resistance. The history of his nearly 22-year tenure in office showed that he was not a man of peace, but because of his preferred option's lack of achievements and the pressure he was under at the time, he was forced to look for other methods to find a way out of this difficult situation. The pressure came from both the resistance and Ethiopia's foreign partners in the scramble for the resources of the Somali region.

The resistance movement maintained its military resistance at home and intensified its political activities abroad. Although the crackdown diminished the military capabilities of the ONLF, it maintained a military force capable to launch targeted attacks inside the region. In addition to that, almost every conference the prime minister attended nearly anywhere he travelled was disrupted or overshadowed by anti-government protests from the region's diaspora communities.

Besides that, he wanted to give the oil companies that had come to exploit the region's resources a security guarantee, which was not possible without a peace deal. Given the aforementioned reasons and the fact that he was the absolute ruler of the country, it was expected that he would take decisive action towards peace or at least take a clear standpoint in favour of a peaceful resolution.

The first round of talks between the two sides began on 6 September 2012 in Nairobi amid uncertainty about the Ethiopian position, which had been caused by the sudden death of the prime minister. In addition to the Kenyan government, some organisations were present at the opening ceremony. The Ethiopian delegation was led by the defence minister, Siraj Fegessa, and the ONLF team was headed by the foreign secretary, Abdirahman Sheikh Mahdi. The first round of talks was held from 6–7 September. In that initial round, the two parties agreed on the general principles of the proceedings and the date and the agenda for the next meeting.

In the second round, which took place from 15–17 October 2012, the Ethiopian delegation came up with preconditions: it wanted the peace talks to be held under the framework of the constitution and for a representative of the regional government to attend the negotiations. The change in the Ethiopian position was mainly the result of the participation of General Abraha Wolde Mariam, who was the head of the eastern command and who joined the negotiations in the second round. The general was not only a close friend of the Somali regional president, but he was an effective ruler of the region, and he was a representative of the anti-peace hardliners in the government. The second round of the talks ended in a deadlock after the government side made it clear that the negotiations could not continue unless the ONLF recognised the Ethiopian constitution as the basis for the talks, and the resistance movement refused to abide by the rules of the government. In their separate press releases, the two sides declared that the talks had been stalled. The two teams left the venue in total disagreement and went back to report to their respective superiors.

The talks were put on hold after the second round due to the disagreement over the constitution; Ethiopia wanted the talks to take place within its framework and the resistance organisation saw it as irrelevant to their cause. However, the peace process that began in Kenya in 2012 officially continued until 2018, though they were disrupted by the Ethiopian regime's kidnapping of some ONLF negotiators in 2014 and did not resume until 2018.

The other major disagreements centred on the participation of the regional administration and the approach to the peace talks. The ONLF presented itself as the sole representative of the region and wanted to be dealt with in that regard—a representation that the government did not recognise. Ethiopia's delegation, which consisted of high-ranking military and security officials, wanted to deal with the problem as a security issue, whereas the ONLF wanted to focus on the root causes of the conflict.

With the help of facilitators, the two sides agreed to talk again in Nairobi. But before the start of the third round, two ONLF peace negotiators who had arrived in Nairobi for the talks were abducted by Ethiopian security officials. As mentioned in chapter 6, Ethiopia kidnapped two members of the ONLF's negotiating team in January 2014. The abduction of the officials not only disrupted the negotiations, but it disappointed everyone involved in the Nairobi peace talks. In particular, it humiliated the host country and put a question mark on its credibility as an honest broker. Despite the resumption of the talks in Kenya in 2018, after nearly four years of interruption, the host country's role in the process had diminished since the abduction. The latest round in Nairobi was preceded by secret direct talks in Dubai, UAE, in which the two parties agreed to return to Nairobi to formalise the outcome of their undisclosed talks.

After a break of several years, the two parties met again in Nairobi in February 2018, but they did not make any breakthrough. According to the Kenyan facilitators, the last meeting was a follow up of the earlier direct talks between the two parties outside Kenya. Reliable sources from within the ONLF reported direct talks between officials from the Ethiopian government and the ONLF in Dubai in 2017. In that meeting, the Somali state president, Abdi Mohamed Omar, and two army generals from the government's side attended. The same sources indicated that the two sides came to an understanding on a number of issues of which the ONLF's acceptance of the full participation of the regional administration in future peace talks was the main concession the ONLF team made.

The Dubai talks created suspicion and led to quarrelling within the organisation because of their secret nature and the participation of the regional dictator who had overseen the genocide that took place in the region. For unknown reasons, the meeting was not disclosed by the leadership of the organisation even to the central committee, let alone to its grassroots members and the public until it was reported by independent observers, and the members of the organisation demanded an explanation from their leaders.

After the news of the meeting surfaced and circulated on social media, the organisation convened an executive committee meeting in Stockholm in January 2018 to calm the high-running emotions and clear up the rumours. A delegation from the Kenyan mediating team, which was headed by Mohamed Yusuf Haji, also visited the conference venue to discuss with the organisation's executive committee, which was meeting in Stockholm, about the peace process.

In the meeting, a heated debate was held in which the participants exchanged their views frankly. The Dubai meeting attendants were strongly criticised for breaking the negotiation principles of the organisation, for bypassing the official negotiating team and for secretly meeting with the regional tyrant, whereas the team justified its secret talks with the enemy on the grounds of the rapid changes in Ethiopia's political landscape and the need to take part in the shaping of that change. Eventually, the executive committee decided to continue the talks at the Nairobi peace venue to restore the unity and harmony of the organisation. The meeting also approved the concession made by the team in Dubai: the full participation of the regional administration in future talks.

The Nairobi talks resumed on 11 February 2018, and the Ethiopian delegation included the regional president, Abdi Mohamed Omar, and was headed by a TPLF general. The ONLF team was headed by Abdirahman Sheikh Mahdi, the organisation's foreign secretary. Also present in the meeting was Sheikh Ibrahim Mohamed Hussein, the former chairman of Al-Itihad/the UWSLF, although it was not clear in what capacity he attended. Just like the previous rounds, the 2018 meeting, which concluded the Nairobi-based peace process, ended in failure.

The Nairobi-based peace process broke down due to deception from the Ethiopian side. It is not clear whether the man who initiated the talks but did not live to see it through was genuine about them. However, it became crystal clear to everyone who had been following the process that his successor was not interested in peacemaking. Hailemariam Desalegn's administration was not only unprepared, but he also lacked the political capacity to make the kind of decisions needed to end a conflict as big as the Ogaden conflict. The main aim of the government was to divide the organisation, and to some extent, it had some success in that regard.

The Dubai talks and the abduction of the negotiators were part of a plot to destroy the organisation from within through infiltration and mistrust. The ONLF achieved some publicity from the Nairobi talks for the cause it was fighting for, and by presenting itself as a peacemaker, the resistance movement improved its image and reputation. However, the organisation emerged disunited as a result of the Ethiopian regime's deception and the fruitless talks.

The ONLF was stronger as an organisation when the talks started than at the time they ended due to the deceptive games of its enemy and, amongst other things, its inexperience in peace negotiations. However, in terms of the historical perspective of the struggle, the way the talks started was a milestone step forward. In the centuries-long struggle for freedom, it was the first time the two sides of the conflict met as equal parties and started negotiations on the terms of the oppressed. It was also the first time the international community had witnessed a peace dialogue between a resistance movement from the Somali region and Ethiopia. Presenting the cause in its right form in such a venue improved its overall image and the reputation of the organisation that was leading the struggle.

Although the Ethiopian government agreed to start the talks on the terms of the ONLF, it used dirty tactics to bypass the agreed principles. To undermine the ONLF's third-party principle, which the government had only officially accepted, the Ethiopian regime coordinated with its Kenyan ally the nomination of the Kenyan team. The entire team was from the Somali region in Kenya and was headed by an elder statesman who had roots in the Ogaden region. Despite representing the Kenyan government because of their ethnic background, the team resembled the elders from the Somali region in Ethiopia, whom the government used to send to the ONLF as mediators. In the first round, the Ethiopian delegation insisted that the Kenyan government act as a facilitator and not a mediator, and in the second round, its team included Mowlid Hayir, who was a representative of the regional government. The ONLF wanted Kenya to mediate and strongly objected to the participation of the regional government in the peace talks. It succeeded in blocking the representation of the regional administration, and the talks continued without the Somali regional administration representative. But eventually, it accepted the role of the Kenyan government as a facilitator. The Ethiopian government's precondition of holding the talks only under the framework of the constitution, its portrayal of the problem as a security issue and the abduction of the peace negotiators were also part of its tricks.

The regime's deceptive tactics, which the ONLF forcefully rejected in the initial stages, eventually worked for the Ethiopian regime in the final stages. Using the regional administration and influential individuals, the TPLF made unofficial contact with some ONLF executive members, which was headed by the organisation's foreign secretary, and persuaded them to meet the Ethiopian officials in an unofficial manner. Two TPLF generals, Sheikh Ibrahim Mohamed Hussein, former leader of the UWSLF, the regional president, Abdi Mohamed Omar, and four ONLF executive members attended the meeting. Not only was the meeting hidden from the public but the subjects of the talks were not disclosed.

Given the clear rules of the organisation regarding the conduct of peace negotiations, the Dubai meeting was a clear deviation from its agreed peace strategies. The make-up of the gathering was unusual, and the participation of Sheikh Ibrahim Mohamed Hussein was especially eye-catching. This type of contact was contrary to the negotiation principles of the organisation and that break in the rules not only gave the government superiority in the negotiating tactics, but it also disastrously shattered the organisation's unity and confidence.

When the talks resumed in Nairobi on 11 February 2018, the Tigray regime was in limbo, and the dying regime tried to prolong its power by making unofficial deals with the ONLF with the help of the regional administration. The talks were led by the generals who had attended the Dubai meeting. The TPLF generals were not necessarily coordinating with the other EPRDF parties, and their main aim was to boost the standing of their collapsing regime and erode the credibility of the ONLF by enticing the organisation into an illusive peace arrangement. The ONLF delegation did not have the full backing of the whole organisation because of the previous undisclosed talks in Dubai and the mistrust they had caused within the organisation. The talks ended in failure, but ironically, that failure was a sigh of relief to the majority of ONLF members because of their lack of trust in the process.

The Asmara peace agreement was not part of the Kenyan-led peace process. It was the result of a change of leadership in Ethiopia and the subsequent political reform and rapprochement with Eritrea. The lifting of the ban on the armed opposition and the opening of the political space in Ethiopia laid down the foundation for the peace deal, and the peace agreement between Eritrea and Ethiopia accelerated the process.

The reformist government of Abiy Ahmed Ali reversed the 2010 parliamentary decision, which added three organisations, including the ONLF, to their list of terrorist organisations. The government also allowed these organisations to operate in the country and peacefully pursue their goals, and thereby removed the need to take arms to achieve their political goals.

The peace treaty between Ethiopia and Eritrea made it difficult for Eritrea to host armed organisations opposing the new friendly government in Ethiopia. As a result, the Eritrean government put pressure on the ONLF and others it was hosting to reach a deal with the government as soon as possible.

10.2 The Peace Agreement

The main elements of the agreement were to end hostility, negotiate over disputed issues under the framework of the constitution and establish joint committees to further carve out the details and oversee the practical implementation of the peace accord.

The first point was straightforward as the two sides had already ceased the fighting, but the agreement as a whole was very vague. The agreement was about general principles and lacked detail in concrete matters and methods of implementation.

The main root cause of the conflict was the government's continued violations of human rights against the inhabitants of the Somali region, and the most contentious part of this human rights issue was the resistance organisation's primary demand for self-determination rights for the inhabitants of the region. The constitution provides guidelines on how to exercise the right to self-determination. It requires the party that seeks to exercise that right enshrined in the constitution to pursue its political objectives in a peaceful manner and, in return, obliges the government to respect and uphold the provisions of the constitution.

In the Asmara deal, the two parties agreed to abide by the constitution. However, the provisions of the constitution have requirements that are in some cases open for interpretation. Thus, the practical implementation of the right to self-determination detailed in article 39 is not as straightforward as it appears. Although the secession issue was not on the immediate agenda of the organisation when signing the document, and certainly the Ethiopian government is hesitant to talk about that right, let alone permit the practical exercise of it, the organisation was formed mainly to fight for that right. Therefore, sooner or later, it will have to raise the issue unless it changes its original goals.

However, before that primary issue, the less contentious and urgent problems needed to be addressed for the organisation to establish itself inside the country and for the two parties to build a working relationship. The practical implementation of the plan in logistical and financial terms and regulations relating to political participation in an organisational and individual capacity were carried out. With the help of the regional and federal governments, the organisation has moved out of exile and is registered and recognised as a political party.

Although many of the immediate practical works were implemented in terms of rehabilitating the organisation both socially and politically, there are still several outstanding issues that are of a long-term nature, including the use of natural resources, ethnic/regional power-sharing, income distribution, the devolution of power, and the big question of separation or coexistence. The proposed joint committees' main task was to deal with these outstanding issues. However, to this date, the joint committees, which were supposed to be operational by now, are not established, and that delay is not an encouraging sign. Although the outstanding issues are complex because of the need to coordinate with the other political players in the country, especially with the regional administration, which officially represents the region, the delay indicates the fragility of the agreement, which is also shown by the lack of a third-party body who could arbiter in the case of a disagreement or reneging of the agreement by one side.

10.3 The Homecoming of the ONLF

The military wing of the resistance movement and the bulk of the population that supported the organisation did not leave the region, but most of the top leaders of the organisation and the large diaspora community that backed it were in exile. Several hundred armed militants who were trained in Eritrea were also in that country.

Some of the leaders of the organisation arrived in the region before the signing ceremony of the peace deal to prepare for the homecoming of the organisation. But the ONLF army in Eritrea and the leaders of the organisation arrived in Jigjiga, the capital city of the region, in a well-coordinated and spectacular manner on 21 November and 2 December 2018, respectively.

Wearing their uniforms and waving the flags of their organisation, the newly trained militants landed in Jigjiga. Ethiopian Airlines' historic special direct flights from Asmara to Jigjiga were eye-catching. The colourful mixture of the two contrasting and contradictory flags, which were painted on the carrier, stitched onto the clothes of the crew and the uniforms of the militants and waved by the large jubilant crowd to welcome the militants at the airport, were symbolically striking and interesting to watch.

The two flags symbolised the Ethiopian state and the unborn state that the rebels were fighting for, and they harmoniously flew together. Many of the onlookers asked themselves whether what they were watching was real or if they were imagining it, and the question was appropriate given the history of the conflict and the incompatibility of the two flags. The marvellous journey, which combined the contrasting flags and their bearers, was unimaginable just a few months ago, and to many, it appeared a theatrical show. Given the vagueness of the Asmara agreement and the unreliability of the Ethiopian state, their concerns were genuine, but perhaps a break from the harsh reality was not a bad idea—at least to prepare themselves for the next battle ahead.

The spectacular arrival of the ONLF army was followed days later by a grand festival at the football stadium of Jigjiga, where the official welcoming ceremony of the ONLF took place. Large crowds from all provinces of the Somali state filled the stadium, waving and wearing the flags of the ONLF to celebrate the organisation's homecoming. Delegations from neighbouring countries also attended the well-organised event. The president of the Somali state, spokespersons of the distinguished guests and the leaders of the organisation addressed the tens of thousands of people who had gathered to witness the event.

The unprecedented peaceful atmosphere and the joyful celebratory mood were uplifting. A sentiment of victory oozed from the venue, as though the long war for the liberation of the land had already been won. However, the crowd was aware that was not the case, and the leaders of the resistance movement reminded them of that reality in their speeches. Overwhelmed by the happy moment and speaking in an emotional manner in which he was not used to talking, the organisation's chairman,

Mohamed Omar Osman, told the crowd that the unfished liberation work would continue, and the remaining part might be harder than the previous part.

The victory sentiment of returning home unvanquished not only delighted them but also encouraged them to continue the struggle. However, the starting point for the remaining struggle resembled the 1991 situation. That hard reality of restarting the struggle from square one did not make them enthusiastic, but the resilient public was used to setbacks and the unpredictability of the Ethiopian state and was not, therefore, downhearted.

11

The Honeymoon Period

The peace deal was preceded by a reform, which was the main factor behind the deal. The Ethiopians were released in large numbers from both the ordinary prisons and the large open-roof prisons, which the bulk of the population lived in as a result of the curtailment of their basic rights and of which the Somali region bore the brunt of the suffering. The agreement also came after torrential rainfall, which had not been seen in several years and which reached every corner of the Somali state.

The bounties of peace and rainwater are two things the Somali people most frequently ask their Lord for in their prayers. Water is the source of life, and the livelihoods of the pastoral and agropastoral Somali communities depend on rainwater. Peace is a precondition for the long-term sustainability of any livelihood. These two bounties, which are a fundamental source of prosperity, were missing for most of the recent decades.

The Somali region was in a state of war since it had been conquered by Ethiopia and had witnessed different types of armed conflicts on local, regional and international levels. Many countries from all the continents, including the biggest powers of the world, were directly or indirectly involved in the Ogaden conflict, which has been the main source of instability in the Horn. Successive generations of the Somali people in the Ogaden region did not see peace, which most of the human race take for granted. They longed for a conflict-free life, wondering whether they would ever see peace in their lifetime.

Due to environmental changes, droughts were very frequent in recent decades. Three to four seasons of rain failure were a common occurrence, especially in the last decade. The last drought, which took place from 2017–2018, was a severe one. Most livestock starved to death, including camels, which are considered to be the most drought-resistant animal, and farmlands were deserted as the result of the drought. As this sought-after bounty of rainwater was getting scarcer, the prayers of the people were getting louder and their desperation was becoming more apparent.

Despite the pessimism, the people's prayers for peace and rainwater were answered. By the first half of 2018, torrential rain fell heavily all over the region and peace gradually returned by the second half of that year. The combination of these two bounties that were prayed for by most inhabitants of the region was a dream come true. One does not understand the value of a thing until it is no longer there. The people of the region know the value of a peaceful and prosperous life. They are grateful to their Lord for granting them these much-desired bounties and are determined to maintain the peace and establish sustainable livelihoods.

11.1 Unprecedented Freedom

As detailed in the preceding chapters, the indigenous people in the Somali state were all living in one open-roof prison as the result of the collective punishment. These open-roof prisons also contained extraordinary state-administrated prisons that were used for individual confinement, which most of the people in the state had been imprisoned in at one time. The types of torture and other punishments used in those prisons were unparalleled as reported by independent human rights organisations and told by the inmates. A prisoner described the horrendous treatments there as something 'nobody has ever seen or ever heard the like of before and no human being could ever even imagine'.

While in that situation, a wind of political change that originated from the central highlands of Ethiopia blew in from the west. Political winds from the highlands, which were frequent, used to always bring bad news to the people of the Somali region. However, before the new wind arrived, news reached them that this wind would be different to anything they had seen before.

They waited for the wind with apprehension, not believing much of the positive news coming from Addis Ababa. Nevertheless, they did not give up hope. After a long wait, they realised that the change was real to some extent. They also understood that the reform would not reach them because of their exceptional situation, unless they fought for it.

After a relentless pursuit, eventually, the reform reached the Somali region and brought many changes that restored many fundamental rights to the people and alleviated some of their sufferings. The people were released from all types of prisons and the freedom of movement was returned as a basic right. The freedom of expression, which used to be unknown to successive generations, was also achieved. Since the introduction of the reform, free expression in terms of political views, religious practices, media, news and social communications became relatively easier.

Both the movement of goods and people had been extremely limited in the region due to the twin punitive policies of the blockade and crackdown, which had been imposed on the region simultaneously. The blockade, as well as trade monopoly, disappeared instantly with the collapse of the regime. Within a noticeably short period, the people returned from their hideouts in the Horn of Africa to their hometowns, and the shelves of shops were filled with consumer goods that came from the neighbouring Somali coastal cities, making the ghost cities lively places again.

With the return of the ONLF, the huge political barrier, both in terms of expression and political participation, was removed. The terrorist-labelled organisation became legal again, so its political views were no longer considered anti-peace or treacherous propaganda. The removal of that barrier not only removed the ruling party's monopoly of politics in the region but also impacted the shape of present and future political participation.

The media also became freer as a result of the regime change in the region. Despite the delay, regional TV (SRTV) lost its monopoly after the opening of a privately-owned TV station (Nabad TV) in 2020, and more privately-owned independent media outlets are expected to follow suit. Social media is perhaps the most widely used type of media because of its easy access on a mass scale. Although it is not free of problems and can be sometimes destructive, its advantages outweigh its problems.

Although the freedom of expression is not limitless, the contrast between the situation before and after the reform is huge. As all fundamental human rights were curtailed, the freedom of expression in any form was not possible to talk about, let alone exercise, under the previous regime. Certainly, freedom of expression is not without its problem today, and further improvements are needed in some areas. However, there are no major hindrances regarding the exercise of that right today in the Somali region. The limits of this newly found freedom are not properly regulated (if at all), and that is the main cause of the problems relating to that issue so far. The lack of clarity has led in some instances to different interpretations of those rights. And subsequent confrontations have occurred between some individuals or organisations, who accuse the authority of infringing on their rights, and the government, who blame them for overstepping their freedom rights.

All in all, freedom returned to the Somali state in all areas of life. In fact, the region is freer today than many other parts of Ethiopia. There are no political prisoners, and the infamous jails are closed. There are no restrictions on assemblies, the formations of political organisations, the expression of political views or the movements of people. Media has taken a pluralistic form, and the government is no longer the only actor in the political field, which is becoming more competitive. In short, freedom in all its forms is flourishing there.

11.2 Spontaneous Reconciliation

Through the creation of the Special Police Force and the substitution of that force for the federal army in the fight against the liberation movements and to carry out the collective punishment of the inhabitants, the Ethiopian regime succeeded in indigenising the conflict. The local militia carried out atrocities on behalf of the Ethiopian security forces, and the puppet regional administration was forced to take political responsibility for the human rights abuses committed by the Special Police Force on behalf of the Ethiopian regime.

As a result of the indigenisation of the conflict, Somali society not only lost cohesion but their struggle for freedom was also overshadowed by that tragic phenomenon. The civilian population had been victimised by the abuses perpetrated by the Somali regional state and its security forces as well as the Special Police Force's and the ONLF army's killing of one another.

The perpetrators and the victims belonged to the same community, sharing an ethnic identity, culture, religion and locality. And because of the many bonds that united them, they could not be separated. The fact that in many cases the abusers were also victims complicated the abuser-victim categorisation. Furthermore, both the abusers and their victims were too many to be tried in ordinary courts and there was no transitional justice system in place. Thus, the risk of infighting erupting because of the widespread grievances was not only real but very likely.

The combatants of the ONLF and the Special Police Force had been fighting for years, killing one another; now the former enemies were the new forces who were expected to secure the region together, a task that was not easy to coordinate, if not impossible, given the bloodshed between the two sides. They had been recruited and trained for opposite aims, and their outlook regarding the state and the people who live there had been framed by their recruiters along with the goals they were striving for, that is, an organisation of liberation and a coloniser they were liberating the land from, respectively.

Despite that difficult situation, there was no other way than try to get along with one another, at least until the dust settled. Fortunately, without prior planning, the people of the region instinctively put aside their grievances and differences and moved forward, concentrating on the practical issues instead. The new regional administration welcomed the ONLF and made well-coordinated preparations for their homecoming. In return, the ONLF supported the new government in its effort to re-establish the administration and fill the vacuum left by the ousted regime. The two sides also coordinated in merging the ONLF militants with the Special Police Force, and all sections of society showed a sense of responsibility and tolerance.

11.3 Relative Peace

As a result of the sense of responsibility and cooperation shown by nearly all sections of society, peace returned to the region. Although the remnants of the previous regime tried to obstruct the restoration of peace and are still dreaming of destabilising the security of the state, the region is enjoying unprecedented calm, and there are strong indications that it will be maintained, at least in the short run.

The regional government is using multidimensional approaches, not only to maintain security but to advance peace in the long term. Combinations of traditional and academic methods are being used by highly qualified people who are leading the security service department to complement the regular security apparatus. Some voluntary organisations are also supporting the efforts.

As mentioned above, the people of the region are tired of war. They know what it is like to live in a conflict zone, and they have tasted the fruits of war. They quickly grabbed hold of the chance for peace, which was their biggest dream, when the first opportunity arrived, and they are determined to preserve it.

Despite the concerted efforts to establish peace, and the determination of the administration and the people of the region to maintain it, the relative peace they have gained is very fragile and lacks the fundamentals to stay firm in the long term. To make it durable, extra work needs to be done, especially by the federal government, on the root causes of this centuries-long conflict.

The current peace is unparalleled in terms of its timeline and in comparison to the other regions of Ethiopia. Relative to past decades, there is a sense of peace now, which previous generations have not seen. The region is one of the most peaceful states in Ethiopia and one of the most harmonious regarding ethnic coexistence, and that unprecedented ranking is even recognised by the often-chauvinist highlanders who credit that remarkable achievement mostly to the region's new leader.

However, since the root causes of the conflict are not solved, the fundamentals for durable peace are not yet established. The people of the Somali state have shown their eagerness to hold on to that fragile sense of peace and their desire to make it permanent. However, without reciprocal commitments from the centre and the removal of the root causes of the conflict, it cannot last. The repetition of the dark and conflictual history can be avoided if Ethiopia responds positively to the peace efforts of the Somali state by changing both its attitude and policies. The totalitarian outlook of the central government, and its coercive oppressive policies that caused the conflict, must be replaced with open-minded cooperative attitudes and with solution-oriented policies presented in a peaceful manner.

12

The Crisis Management State Administration

The administration was born out of the preceding crises, which started with the gross violations of human rights and ended with the removal of the regional state president after a standoff with the federal government. The immediate work of the new caretaker administration, which emerged from the crises, was to manage the pressing issues resulting from the upheaval.

12.1 The Pressing Issues

Pressing issues of both a short-term and long-term nature became the main preoccupation of the new regional administration. They involved many problem areas relating to politics, security, administration, justice, social services, federal shares, natural resources, corruption, internal displacement and more. Despite huge economic and political constraints, prompt actions were needed to find rapid and appropriate solutions to these problems. An urgent issue that required immediate attention might also be a lasting one. Therefore, all of these pressing problems were not necessarily short-term issues and vice versa.

What makes a problem an urgent issue is politically debatable, but generally, the graveness of the problem and its effects on the lives of people, the functioning of the governing system and the well-being of society, as well as the indispensability of what is at stake, are good indicators of the level of its importance and urgency. In the following sections, we will highlight the problems relating to the pressing issues mentioned above as well as what, so far, has been achieved in dealing with these problems and the reasons for the failure of what has not been solved.

12.1.1 Political Reform

The many political problems that the new regional administration faced could be categorised into short-term problems, such as the management of daily life politics, and long-term problems, such as the question of self-rule. Whatever the classification, the politics of the region are shaped by the patron-client relationship between the federal government and the regional administration imposed by the centre and the desire of the region's inhabitants for genuine self-rule.

Although the region is constitutionally an autonomous entity, and the regional government is answerable to the people of the region through their regional representative assembly, in practice, the members of the assembly are not elected by the people but are nominated by the regional administration, which in turn is handpicked by the federal government. The federal authorities are solely responsible for the rules governing the conduct of politics in the country. The election, the political participation criteria, the composition of constituencies and the census are all under the jurisdiction of the federal institutions. The constitutional rules of this political game and the unwritten patron-client practice have reduced regional authorities to a subordinate role regarding political behaviour.

Like his predecessors, the acting president was appointed in August 2018 to lead the region until the next election, which was scheduled for August 2020. Because of the short-term appointment and the need to find solutions to the pressing issues that had resulted from the crises and constitutional limitations, the focus of the crises-born administration was to extinguish the burning fire first and foremost. Thus, the long-term perspectives of long-lasting issues are not the prime focus here, as they are nearly beyond the reach of a caretaker administration.

The main political problem that required a quick fix was the broken political system of the region, which needed reform to make it functional. Political problems of that magnitude need bold decisions, which in turn necessitate a strong mandate for the authority that undertakes such decisive measures. However, the man appointed to lead the politics of the region and, at the same time, reform it did not have the required mandate to do the job. He was an unelected outsider, who was not part of the political elite, and his unfamiliarity with the system and the patron-client relationship between Addis Ababa and Jigjiga were the main constraints that limited his manoeuvrability.

He was not a member of the regional assembly who had been appointed by the previous regime, and the political elite was all part of the old regime. The president brought with him political activists and civil servants that were part of the SRAJ and Dulmidiid networks, but his attempt to appoint them to government positions was blocked because of the foreign passports that most of them were holding. The political system that he was hoping to reform was practically in the hands of the anti-reform old guard. In other words, he was supposed to reform the old broken system using the same people who had broken it in the first place. The remnant of the old regime did not only oppose the reform, but from day one, they began to undermine the authority of the new government using their friends who were still in power in the federal system and the ruling regional party.

In addition to that, the man who appointed the regional leader was not in full control of the federal government and was struggling to consolidate his power. However, unlike the regional leader, the federal leader was part of the government machine before ascending to the highest position, and in that sense, he was in a better position to deal with his opponents. Unfortunately, the Machiavellian tactics that he used to strengthen his power and maintain it involved limiting the powers of the peripheries, and consequently, he was not ready to give the new Somali leader sweeping powers.

From that precarious position, the new caretaker president began to reform whatever he possibly could under the federal guidelines, starting with the ruling party, which was the only political reform the regional authority could initiate locally. He joined the party when he was appointed as a caretaker president and was made second-in-command. The party was led by a federal minister who, like the prime minister, was politically trained by the EPRDF regime and who was not keen to change the only system he knew and that had made him successful career-wise. The leadership of the party by a man with such a background added another bottleneck to his limited power, which further reduced his political manoeuvrability.

Walking a tightrope, the caretaker president started the reform with the restoration of the official name of the region. The Somali state, which is the official name of the region in the constitution, is now used instead of the Ethiopian Somali state. The original flag of the Somali state, which included a five-pointed star indicating the common heritage of the five Somali-inhabited parts of the Horn, was also restored. The reform of the party that followed also began with symbolic changes to its logo and name, changing its name from the ESPDP to the Somali Democratic Party (SDP). The structural form of the party was reorganised afterwards.

The previous regime added an 'E' denoting Ethiopia to the abbreviations of institutions in the region to emphasise the Ethiopian identity of the Somali inhabitants. Symbols that showed the Somali heritages were also removed from flags and logos. The new regional regime dropped the Ethiopian word and restored the heritage symbols, thus restoring the region's true image and Somali identity.

The move was enthusiastically welcomed by the Somali inhabitants, and the federal government did not object to it. Ethiopia consists of many different nations with distinct cultures. Preserving the different cultures and identities does not clash with the membership of the federal order, and therefore there was no need to suppress one's identity or imitate other cultures. Besides that, in other regions of the federal republic of Ethiopia, the word 'Ethiopian' does not precede their local names.

Before the convening of the official party conference in April 2019, preparatory meetings were held, and most of the work of the first part of the party reform, which concerned the structural changes of the organisation, was carried out in those meetings. But in the second part, there was a contest to fill those positions. The new president wanted to inject new blood into the party to accelerate the reform, whereas the old guard that was led by the chairman of the organisation and who feared the reform would affect their positions, wanted to minimise the change to the top leadership to preserve the status quo as much as possible.

The contest eventually turned into an open confrontation, which led to a coup attempt. With the assistance of some federal associates, the old guard of the party tried to oust the new regional leader by accusing him of undermining the security of the state and the unity of the Ethiopian people. For his part, the president and his supporters denounced them as anti-reform agents. The row and subsequent attempt to oust the president was widely reported in the media.

The caretaker president got the backing of the people, and that backing emboldened him further, making clear that the reform was more important to him than the position. Eventually, the prime minister intervened in the matter and called the president and the chairman of the party to his office on 26 January 2019 where he mediated them.

What the three men agreed upon was not disclosed, but the party conferences that was held afterwards ended successfully. The chairman retained his position, but the rest of the nine-member central committee were members of the president's cabinet, and the majority had been nominated by their regional bosses. The prime minister, who attended the closing ceremony of the party conference, was pleased with the outcome.

The ESPDP reincarnated itself into a new party after it put new people in charge, changed its symbols and rebranded itself as the SDP. Together, the ESPDP's regional government and the EPRDF's regime were responsible for the gross human rights abuses that took place in the region, and because of that history, the image of the ESPDP party was haunting. Getting rid of the name alone would not change the reputation of the party, but the reformers believed that it could contribute to the image-building process.

After the conference, the reformed SDP party presented itself as the champion of the people and the only inclusive party that could unite all sections of the Somali society. That self-projection was dismissed by its main competitor, the ONLF, as baseless. The ONLF and the ESPDP fought a bloody war, but the former was fighting on behalf of Somali inhabitants, while the latter was part of the Ethiopian regime. To compete for the leadership of the region, the two contesting parties began to position themselves before the election and the ruling party's image-building was part of that campaign.

While the reform and preparations for the election were going on in the Somali region, similar election preparations were underway in other parts of the country at the federal level. In Oromia, for example, the OPDO, the OLF and the OFC were competing for the leadership of that region. On the federal level, the EPRDF party began to disintegrate after the TPLF refused a reform package that included admitting to the ruling club the ruling regional parties that had not been included in the EPRDF arrangement. A new federal party called the EPP was formed to replace the dying EPRDF party, and the premier and his team wanted to bring all of the ruling parties under one umbrella. The periphery parties that were not part of the old federal party disliked being excluded from the ruling club and, as expected, seized the eagerly awaited opportunity that allowed them to be part of the club and joined it.

Like the other periphery parties, the SDP welcomed the new party and enthusiastically agreed to join it. However, the practical process of joining the new centre party disoriented the SDP to some extent. This was because of the new arrangement's ramifications for the image and standing of the SDP in the Somali region. Unlike the EPRDF arrangement, which was an amalgamation of independent parties, the EPP is a single party, which makes the regional parties branches of that party.

The SDP party spent a lot of time and effort to rebrand itself as the only credible Somali party representing the Somali region, and in building that brand, it removed the Ethiopian word from the party's name and the institutional symbols of the region. Suddenly, the party needed to rebrand itself as part of the EPP and change its name and symbols again. The membership of the new party, which represents the whole country, strengthened its political position nationwide, but the replacement of Somali symbols with Ethiopian ones removed its projected image as the representative of the Somali region both in symbolic and political terms.

For many years, the periphery parties campaigned for the participation of the political club at the centre, and certainly, they were happy with the new prime minister's invitation to not only join the centre party but also take part in the shaping of it. However, the offer was not priceless; the price was to get rid of their parties: a price they were not prepared for but that they had to pay. Had the SDP leadership known that their party would disappear this way, they would not have wasted huge amounts of time and effort to reshape it.

Because of their desire to be part of the centre politics and the patron-client system that binds the federal and regional authorities, the SDP had no choice but to follow the directions of the centre. In doing so, it had to dismantle itself to get a place in the EPP. The new party is still under construction, and the SDP is taking part in that building process with mixed feelings: it fears it might be swallowed by the big ethnic groups of the Amhara and Oromo and hopes to be not only visible at the federal level but a decisive part in the highest national decision-making body, too.

12.1.2 Security Issues

Security in the region remains a big issue, that is, the safety of civilian lives as well as their property and everything that is essential to their sustenance, such as food, water and energy. As the topic of the discussion is the administration's performance in the short period it ruled the region, the safety of civilian lives and property is the prime focus in this piece. The other aspects of the issue tend to be long term and beyond the examination period.

The previous regime was ousted in a violent manner by the federal army, and in that process, dozens of lives were lost and a lot of properties destroyed, particularly in the first few days of the upheaval. Although this fatal violence took place in several cities, the capital city of Jigjiga bore the brunt of the casualties both in terms of lives and material losses.

The federal army clashed with supporters of the ousted president, including segments of the Special Police Force, during the operation, and the security situation remained tense for the following few weeks mainly due to the unclear position of the Special Police Force. The disgraced president used to maintain his power largely through the loyal Special Police Force, which he had established, and there were fears that they might resist the removal of their leader and either fight in the cities or retreat to the rural areas to regroup and launch attacks from there.

After securing Jigjiga, federal forces moved southwards and took control of the main cities one after the other. They bypassed the Special Police Force, which was stationed in the cities, without any encounter breaking out between the two forces. The disoriented Special Police Force moved around for several weeks but gradually realised the irreversibility of the change, and the bulk of the force joined the process of restoring the security of the state.

However, die-hard supporters of the ousted president within the force, which included its top leaders, did not take part in the peacebuilding process. Instead, they decided to sabotage it and took prompt actions to prepare themselves for the next battle. Taking advantage of the precarious security situation and the concentration of the federal army's attention on wider security, they began to take as much of the money looted from the state and from the private sector as possible during this chaotic period. The money was transported on vehicles and taken to neighbouring Somali regions; from there it was sent to other destinations worldwide using money transfer systems. Some of that money was used on security sabotage actions afterwards.

The federal army and the federal police led the first phase of securing the region, but gradually their functions were overtaken by local forces, namely, the Special Police Force and the state police. The Special Police Force was not an ideal force to take over the security of the region; indeed, a new security apparatus would have been preferable because of the force's bloody history, poor human rights record, lack of proper training regarding the respect of the rule of law and due to the criminal elements within the organisation.

However, as there was no other alternative force that could replace the Special Police Force, the disreputable force became indispensable. Carefully, the regional authorities handed the executive responsibility of security to the ordinary police and the Special Police Force. Before the handover, the forces were briefly trained on the new security approach, which was based on respecting the rule of law and protecting human rights.

The reform of the forces is an ongoing process. The main aim of the reform is to turn those forces into professionals, and the way to achieve that is to give the existing force proper training, particularly regarding the rule of law and add new professionals to replace the unqualified members who are not fit for purpose. A new modern intelligence unit has also been established, which is expected to assist all the security forces in information gathering.

The Special Police Force, which is the biggest force, has undergone a huge transformation. Its role involves securing the borders of the region in coordination with the federal army as well as keeping the safety of both urban and rural life in coordination with the ordinary police and other local forces. Initially, it was established to kill and dehumanise the people of the region, and in fact, it excelled in the fulfilment of that original goal. The new instructions given by the new administration were to protect the very same people it used to abuse. Such a huge shift of purpose and behaviour will certainly not be easy to accomplish, but it is an inescapable reform given the lack of an alternative force and the necessity to fill the security gap.

As a result of the addition of several thousand newly trained soldiers, the force has increased in size. Due to training regarding new approaches that have led to changes not only in terms of tasks but also the mindset of the soldiers, as well as inputs by the new leadership, encouraging steps have been taken to make the army more professional. The change of the top leadership is the key to the positive changes that have taken place. The new head of the force General Mohamed Ahmed Mohamud was a professional officer in the federal army with regional expertise. He played a big part in the restoration of security during the chaotic weeks between August and September 2018 and was instrumental in reshaping the force following the end of the upheaval.

Despite the huge efforts made by the leadership of the organisation and the regional government in transforming the Special Police Force, further improvements are needed. There are many rotten members in the force who cannot serve the people because of their history of human rights violations or because of their inability to adjust to the new situation. In other words, what has been done so far regarding the cleansing of the force is not enough to sustain a healthy force in the long run. It must be cleaned up further until it attains an acceptable standard of professionalism.

Many of those who are not fit for purpose have mental problems and require rehabilitation, and most of them are criminals. Well-known criminals who took part in the killing and punishment of the people are still part of the leadership of the force, and that sad reality not only sends the wrong signal to victims, but it also spoils the reform efforts and undermines the justice system.

Human rights abuses were the means the force used to control citizens, and that subculture became a habit they could not get shake off in a short period. Unfortunately, many incidents of abuse by elements of the force are reported from across the region, which indicates that the atrocious soldiers are still overstepping their mandate. Besides that, there are rough elements within the force who have links with their former bosses and are still looking to disturb the peace from their exile retreats. Allegations of stirring up tribal conflicts and attempts to kill individuals linked to such rough elements have been reported in some places.

The above-mentioned misconduct problems of the force show that the control mechanisms are not good enough. Effective controls and a zero-tolerance policy should be implemented by the regional authorities to overcome the problem. The government was slow in the reform process of the force and that was understandable because of the need to prioritise the wider security concerns, but a substantial screening and a thorough clean-up are necessary to build a reputable force and the sooner the better.

In addition to the problems associated with the regular security forces, the previous administration also established local tribal militias in the districts. They are intended to fight the rebels in their immediate surroundings. These local militias very often take part in tribal conflicts and sometimes take actions contrary to public security and governance. They are more loyal to their clan relations than to the state, and at times of conflict, they take matters into their own hands. Such militias should not exist. This problem posed by the irregular militias highlights another loophole in the security sector that needs to be fixed urgently.

Given the crises from which the government emerged and the following political and security upheavals, the restoration and maintenance of the security of the region was a relief and, to many, an unexpected achievement of the new regional government. Still, a lot of work—of which a full cleansing of the security sector is the most important job—remains to achieve a sustainable security level in the long run. But overall, the administration made good progress in many areas of the security sector; the transformation of the sector began after the takeover of the leadership of the department by a highly qualified person, Hussein Hashi Kasim, who held a PhD degree in a relevant field.

12.1.3 Administrative Capacity Gaps

When the previous regional regime was ousted, the whole administration collapsed from the highest unit to the lowest unit, leaving a huge power vacuum throughout the region. After the formation of the regional government, the new state government began the work to install new administrations in all districts and zones. It was a heavy task to undertake because of the need to fill the vacuum in the shortest possible time to avoid anarchy and to also put the right people in the right place.

The new president nominated a team from each zone and instructed them to set up temporary administrations in the areas they represented. The teams faced some difficulties in finding the right people for two reasons. First, most of the people with administrative experience were part of the previous corrupt regime. Second, the previous governments used to send people to the districts without prior consultation. But this time the locals were given the opportunity to participate in the selection, and that meant more bargaining based on tribal balances and individual interests.

Although the two problems prolonged the process in some districts, most of the teams managed to establish working administrations in their districts within a short period. The new administrations comprised a combination of new people and a remnant of the old regime, though the latter was the dominant group in most of the zones. Because of the urgency to restore public services, the new administrations started work soon after the nomination without any training and before the introduction of a standardised code of conduct.

Similarly to the regional government, local administrations started their work by prioritising vital services, such as health, in the most populated areas and gradually increasing their cover capacity both geographically and in terms of services being offered. The local administrations were established in an emergency to fill the vacuum; however, most of them remained in their positions, apart from some individual replacements, following evaluations made by the state authorities.

The performance of the transitional administrations in the districts varied. Some of them failed to function properly because of problems related to the nomination process or because they did not provide adequate services in time and, as a result, did not gain public confidence. However, most of them succeeded in functioning to varying degrees; some of them made huge amounts of progress unexpectedly, both in terms of good governance and the provision of services.

Although the local administrations are generally functional and some of them performed well, there are prevalent problems, which have been widely reported from the districts, that stem from the establishment process and the lack of proper scrutiny. The nomination of local administrations by the regional government was to some extent indirect because of the use of nomination teams and the devolved system, whereby the locals select their administrators from within their district. This method of nominating and the poor scrutiny by the regional authorities are the chief causes of the administrative problems in the districts.

The hasty establishment of local governments was unavoidable given the urgent need for them; indeed, a thorough examination of candidates was also difficult if not impossible given the time constraint. Filling the administration gap was the main priority and, in so doing, some people who were not qualified for the job became amongst those selected. The reasons for this were a shortage of professionals, personal and interest connections or tribal balances.

Because of the local administrations' fragility, the regional government was expected to carry out further scrutiny of their work in addition to the regular follow up. But that is not the case as reported by reliable independent sources. As a result of the lack of proper checks or scrutiny, some local administrators have been abusing their power and are, in many places, acting like small kings.

12.1.4 Public Services

The public service departments resumed work following the restoration of the local administrations. The services returned against the backdrop of widespread impoverishment, high expectations and scarce resources. The war and the crackdown led to impoverishment, while the defeat of the brutal and abusive system gave people a sense of victory and made them hopeful of not only overcoming the deprivation but also of realising their dreams, including their primary goal of regaining self-rule and the subsequent reshaping of their future. Both human and capital resources were extremely limited; decades of destruction and suppression had hampered any investment into public services, leaving them undermanned and underequipped.

Public service departments required heavy investment to get them to the required level of capacity in which to provide services optimally in the long run. All public service departments including health, education, transport, water and sanitation were running under capacity due to inadequate planning, infrastructural underdevelopment, insufficiently qualified personnel and a lack of necessary technical tools. But before those long-term problems can be dealt with, urgent matters need to be tackled such as lifesaving services with whatever resources are available.

The staff of the public services sector are working in a challenging environment, even though they used to work under much harder conditions before the reform. However, because of the persistence of these difficult conditions, they have internalised most of the bottlenecks as part of their daily challenges. Following the regime change, the working environment and economic conditions for public service workers improved to some extent because of wage increases, better facilities, the addition of extra staff and the introduction of other work-related improvements. Thus, despite the huge obstacles that persist, they have resumed work in better conditions compared to the recent past.

Both the government and service personnel have input tremendously into public services and remarkable progress has been made. However, as all the services are not quantifiable, and there are too many to cover in a small section of this book, we will not examine all of them here. Instead, we will outline the investments in the main social services of health and education and the water and transport services; we will concentrate on the tangible things that have so far been approved as projects or have been allocated resources from the regional budget or other external sources, to get a broad picture of the development.

The investment made in the health sector, as detailed by the regional authorities, includes the construction of 3 new hospitals, the upgrading of 3 existing hospitals, the expansion of 5 hospitals and the construction of 30 health centres and 3 new blood banks. The projects of this sector have either been completed or their work is ongoing. About 5,500 health staff have been added to the workforce according to government sources. Other health-related improvements include the investment of 150 vehicles of which 130 are ambulances.

In the education sector, the regional government announced their approval of the construction of 450 schools. 11 of these schools are boarding schools and have been earmarked for the children of poor families and nomads. Nearly 80 of the schools are secondary schools, and 3 of them are technical academies. Some of the projects are completed, some are ongoing and some are approved but not yet started.

According to budgetary figures released by the regional government, water and transport were also a significant component of the regional budget expenditure. As part of the infrastructural development package intended to increase the service capacity, the state government invested 2 billion Ethiopian Birr into water projects. The construction of a 24-kilometre-long road is ongoing and has been completed in the main cities, and many cobblestone roads are under construction in 6 cities. Gravel roads stretching to about 1,100 kilometres have also been built or are under construction in the rural areas.

Other infrastructural investments include several light industries such as milk and honey. The regional Parliament House is under construction and so are regional administration offices for all of the 11 zones and 6 cities. Communal houses of between 40 and 50 units are also being built in each of the 11 zones except the capital.

12.1.5 Justice System Reform
Justice, which in broad terms is about fairness, is universally held as a value and practically appreciated. Essentially, it requires one to be fair not

only to mankind but to all beings. As a concept, justice is a useful guide to moral goodness, and its practical application to life is even more valuable. The concept of justice is based on religions, ethics and laws that may differ in their interpretations of fairness, and because of that, there are endless theories of justice with differing views on its conception and its applicability.

However, the differences in these interpretations are not based on the primary message of fairness but on the degree of fairness. In today's civilised world, there are international rules and covenants made by international bodies that are accepted by nearly all nations, which have been introduced to harmonise any differences and promote justice where there are some failings. Therefore, justice deniers can no longer hide behind the facade of differing views.

Despite its importance, and the commitments made by governments across the globe to be just, in many parts of the globe injustice is prevalent. Those deprived of justice such as the people of the Somali state understand its value more than those fortunate enough to experience it in their daily life, even if it is not a complete understanding. Justice for the Somali people living in the Somali state is absent as a concept, because of the centuries-long human rights violations. In other words, the synonyms of the word 'justice' are unknown to them, whereas its antonym of 'injustice' and the synonyms and related words of that term are there use in their vocabulary daily: abuse, mistreatment, human rights violation, suppression, repression, subjugation, confiscation, punishment, abduction, murder, assassination and more.

As detailed in earlier chapters, human rights violations were the norm in the Somali region rather than the exception. Suppression and human rights violations were persistent in the region throughout the period it was ruled by Ethiopia, but during the EPRDF regime, the abuse increased exponentially, and the collective punishment dehumanised the already downtrodden population, traumatising them to a degree.

Against that tragic backdrop, the new reformist government came to power. To begin with, the traumatised population required physical and psychological rehabilitation to alleviate their sufferings. But only a judicial remedy could give them permanent relief from their mental and physical pains.

Because of the pervasiveness of the atrocities and the insufficient capacity of normal courts to deal with the widespread abuse, some sort of transitional justice arrangement was needed. Although the regional government promised to prosecute anybody accused of committing a crime if requested by the victim, so far, it had not undertaken any comprehensive plan in that direction. The regional government understands the importance of justice to the reconciliation efforts and, therefore, wants to initiate some sort of legal settlement, whereby the victims get reparation and the abusers get punishment or forgiveness after an admission of guilt and remorse.

However, there are obstacles hampering government action towards such settlements that are of a regional and national nature—the perpetrators of human rights still hold some power and there are jurisdiction problems related to the federal abusers. They may require the involvement of international bodies. The main obstacles in the establishment of a transitional justice arrangement are limited resources, political conflicts, judicial jurisdiction problems and a lack of prioritisation of the issue by both federal and regional political actors.

The regional government neither has the economic resources nor the expertise to undertake a transitional justice arrangement. The setting up of such an arrangement requires expertise in the field, which does not exist in the region, and the implementation of the programme necessitates funding, which is not available. Reparation for the victims and the undertaking of the legal operation are contingent on the availability of funds, and therefore the economic bit is the key.

The perpetrators were federal and regional authorities. Judicially, the regional government does not have jurisdiction over the federal authorities, but the other way round is true. Therefore, without the consent and the backing of the federal government, a transitional justice arrangement involving all perpetrators is not possible.

Politically, it is even more difficult to initiate a comprehensive transitional justice arrangement because of its implications for the federal government. The remnants of the EPRDF regime are still the main stakeholders of the federal system, and any attempt to undermine their position or standing will be resisted by them with a big probability of the attempt backfiring. In addition to that, many of the TPLF perpetrators who led the atrocities are even beyond the reach of the federal government.

Even though the federal government established the Ethiopian Reconciliation Commission in February 2019 as part of Prime Minister Abiy's push for reconciliation and reform, there is no functioning federal policy framework to deal with past wrongs. In addition to that, the federal government's approach to the human rights abuses in the Somali state disregards the lives and rights of the Somali people, as shown by its actions. The only thing it did regarding the matter was the indictment of 45 individuals for allegedly instigating the violence in which predominantly non-Somalis were killed during the Jigjiga disturbances on 4 August 2018. Moreover, because of the war in Tigray, the unrest in Oromia, the COVID-19 pandemic problems, the preparation for the upcoming election and constitutional problems resulting from the deferred election, the human rights issue is not on the government's immediate agenda.

Political regional actors, such as the ONLF and the Somali Prosperity Party (SPP), do not see eye to eye on how to approach the problem. The ONLF often talks in vague terms about forgiveness and unity. The regional authorities accuse the organisation of hampering the efforts to act against the perpetrators, whereas the organisation accuses the regional government of hiring known criminals. Independent observers have indicated that there is some truth to both accusations. They also pointed out that the political parties in the region are preparing themselves for the election, and therefore the transitional justice issue has been shelved for the time being.

Due to the aforementioned reasons, comprehensive transitional justice involving all of the perpetrators seems remote for the time being, but at least locally it is necessary to make some sort of legal remedy to heal the wounds as much as possible and proceed with the reconciliation effort. Inaction prolongs the suffering, and further denials of justice would be a hindrance to reconciliation and will accordingly undermine the restoration of the cohesion and functioning of society.

To be fair, the obstacles to a transitional justice programme are understandably beyond the capacity of the regional government to overcome them alone. Nevertheless, they cannot be a justification for inaction, and the government is not blameless on the justice issue. There are many judicial matters that could be solved through the usual judicial system or could be corrected via political processes, but so far they are not undertaken.

There are well-known criminals in the security forces and there are confiscated proprieties still not returned or occupied by perpetrators with government connections. The hiring of criminals sends the wrong signals: on the one hand, it indirectly vindicates the perpetrators of the atrocities they committed, and on the other hand, it contradicts the government's stated policies on the issue. Thus, it further aggravates the sufferings of the victims and undermines its own credibility on the issue.

The policy of prosecuting human rights violators only on the request of the victim is itself critic worthy for two reasons. Firstly, most of the victims are too weak to reach government offices, let alone file a criminal case in courts against powerful criminals, and many others are too scared to confront their abusers. Secondly, keeping perpetrators with proven criminal records in government positions or leaving them to freely operate in the public domain is dangerous to the public and appears to validate injustice.

The president has persistently criticised others for not siding with victims, by allegedly failing to condemn the perpetrators, and courageously demanded from atrocious TPLF leaders to come to terms with their Somali victims, starting with apologies and remorse. His clear stance and brave advocacy for justice are praiseworthy, but they need to be backed by action on the ground from his government.

12.1.6 Equitable Federal Share

The Somali state is one of currently 10 federated states that make up the Federal Republic of Ethiopia. It is the second-largest in areal mass behind Oromia and the fourth biggest state, population-wise, after the Oromo state, the Amhara state and the Southern Nations. It has the biggest natural resources, and the revenue from its natural resources is expected to be the main source of the republic's income for decades to come. Potentially, the state has all the fundamentals for a prosperous life.

In reality, however, the state has so far been one of the poorest federated states; it has been at the centre of conflicts in the Horn, a torture centre for subdued inhabitants and its resources have been a magnet for invaders. These factors are the sources of its suffering and, more recently, its spread of disease. Its unsettled relations with Ethiopia have been of the master-subservient relationship type in practical terms, and its politics have been organised and directed by the master through the patron-client system.

With that situational picture of the state in mind, the new regional authorities appointed by the federal authorities began negotiations with the centre on shared matters of the federation, demanding a proportional share in representation, income distributions, infrastructural investment and more. They also demanded a negotiated law on the sharing formula for the revenue of natural resources.

On the question of representation, the Somali state has been underrepresented in the federal system. Given that it was the fourth most populous region, logically, it should get the fourth largest representation in federal parliament, but that is not the case. Today, the state is represented by 23 members of parliament in the House of the Peoples Representatives (HoPR). This is a disproportional representation, which puts it in the fifth position behind the smaller state of Tigray.

In a letter signed by the president of the Somali state, Mustafe

Mohumed Omar, on 10 December 2019 and addressed to the National Electoral Board of Ethiopia (NEBE) and the House of Federation (HoF), the regional leader asked for equitable representation in federal parliament. In his statement, which he based on the rules made by the HoF regarding equitable representation and the 1994 census carried out by the electoral board, the president stated that the right share of the region's parliamentary seats was 32. Using the constitutional rules on the matter, the president explained in detail the share calculation formula of parliamentary seats and requested the concerned authorities to make the necessary corrections before the next election scheduled for 2020 (which has been delayed to 2021).

In response to the growing demand for proportional representation in government, the prime minister has added a new ministerial position to the Somali list, making the total Somali representation two ministers and two vice ministers, and Adan Farah (former Somali state vice president) is now the speaker of the HoF. On the question of parliamentary seats, so far, the federal authorities have not given a public response to the request of the Somali state and even though there will not be any change to the issue before the election, the case is assumed to be under consideration. Fairness and transparency are not usually attributed to Ethiopian politics and the Somali state has been the chief recipient of all of the injustice in the republic. Therefore, an unjust response is not unlikely, but it will be remarkably interesting to watch how the reformist prime minister will justify a further denial of justice on the matter if that takes place.

The economic marginalisation is more severe than political discrimination and a simple observation is enough to see the difference between the Somali region and the rest of proper Ethiopia, in terms of development and standards of living. However, for those who are unable to visit the country or are not familiar with the situation, a quantitative description of the situation would have given them a better picture. And bearing in mind that information gap, we have tried to get as much economic data as possible. Unfortunately, we were unable to get figures for the budgets of the states over time, and for that reason, we could not make direct comparisons of income distributions based on that important indicator. However, we have some data on the distribution of external development investment, direct loans to small- and medium-sized enterprises (SMEs) and the federal government's distribution patterns of funds earmarked for job creation in urban areas.

From World Bank-funded projects, which has amounted to $14.2 billion since 2008, the Somali region got approval for 7 out of 648 projects (or 1 per cent). According to data published in 2017 by the Ethiopian Central Bank, the Somali region's share of direct loans to business was 1.6 per cent, which is a remarkable figure compared to the 38.9 per cent of the Amhara region. From the federal government's urban job creation programme, the Somali state's share of the total employment created through the scheme was 1.4 per cent. Oromia, the Southern Nations (SNNPR), Amhara and Tigray got 40.5 per cent, 17.3 per cent, 16 per cent and 14 per cent, respectively. As a result of the generous support they received, SMEs in other parts of Ethiopia grew rapidly, whereas the developmental growth of their counterparts in the Somali region stagnated. According to 2017 data, only 0.2 per cent of the SMEs were based in the Somali region. The Oromia share for SMEs was 31.1 per cent, the Tigray share was 25.1 per cent and 24.5 per cent of SMEs were based in the Amhara region.

This limed data gives is just the tip of the iceberg regarding the persistent marginalisation of the Somali region. This institutionalised discrimination is not compatible with nationhood and the degree of marginalisation is unbearable. Given the dire situation, a change is inevitable; however, strong resolve is needed to embark on sweeping changes that can make meaningful effects on the current sad condition. But in the meantime, the process of reversing institutionalised marginalisation must start, and any incremental step in the right direction will be welcomed.

On infrastructural investment, the president recently said in a TV interview, that the region was awarded seven top-class roads, which is a remarkable and unprecedented investment from the centre—the likes of which the region has not seen before. On 29 October 2020, the Ethiopian Road Authority (ERA) launched a 300-kilometre-long road construction project. The prime minister attended the launch ceremony, which was held in Godey. The president also mentioned in that interview the ongoing work of extending the electricity supply. Some cities already have 24-hour electricity, and according to the plan of the project, around 30 small towns and villages will receive electricity, too.

These investments announcements are good news, which no doubt will be appreciated by the inhabitants, and a good start and a big boost for the standing of the regional government. However, compared with the rest of Ethiopia, the Somali state is underdeveloped, and it will require much more investment to reach the average Ethiopian level of development.

12.1.7 Natural Resource Issues

As mentioned in chapter 5, in June 2019, parliament approved a law on the distribution of income from natural resources. According to the new regulation, the state where the resource is found gets 50 per cent of the revenue, whereas the other states in the federation get 25 per cent. The federal government distributes the remaining 25 per cent through the budgetary system and the resource-producing state gets its share. Although this law concerns all natural resources, the only available natural resource in Ethiopia is the Ogaden gas; thus, the law was introduced first and foremost for the revenue share of that resource.

The revenue income of which the state gets 50 per cent is Ethiopia's share of the net profit:

> The oil and gas company gets priority recuperate production cost as part of contractually stipulated cost recovery agreement. This means the company first deducts capital expenditure in acquisitions of machinery, plants, buildings, etc.; then deducts intangible exploration costs; then deducts interest payments on loans; then deducts administrative expenses and other technical fees as operations expenditures.[1]

And finally, whatever remains of the 'profit oil' is shared between the company and the Ethiopian government in a predetermined ratio of roughly 85:15. Therefore, the 50 per cent is not a share of gross production or even net profits, it is 50 per cent of the government's share of the profit.

But over time, the country's share of the profit will incrementally increase, and the company's share will go down reciprocally due to the dwindling of production costs. Costs associated with exploration, construction and some of the production will decrease gradually, and some of them will disappear entirely in the future. Therefore, royalty incomes will increase over time depending on the contract.

On paper, the region's percentage share of the country's net profit share regarding the natural resource is applaudable; however, the problem is in the implementation. The constitution (Article 40(3) and Article 89(5)) grants the state ownership of natural resources, and the Petroleum Proclamation (295/1986) grants the Minister for Mines and Energy full rights to regulate and administer them. As the sole owner of the resources, the federal government assumes full property rights. Without reference to the state government and the inhabitants of the

---

[1] Liban Farah, 'Laughing Hyenas: Red flags the new Somali regional president should be wary of', *Wardheer News*, August 31, 2018, https://wardheernews.com/laughing-hyenas-red-flags-the-new-somali-regional-president-should-be-wary-of/.

region, it regulates, administers and makes deals with the companies over exploration related matters as well as all revenue-related agreements.

The federal government's monopolisation of all aspects of the project (that is, regulation, administration and the issuing of licences to contractors), the untransparent system of the government, the lack of an independent watchdog institution to scrutinise the work and the exclusion of real stakeholders (that is, the Somali state and its people) from project-related activities are not encouraging signs. If the real owners of the resources are excluded from all the processes that lead to the profit-sharing process, how can they trust that the last stage will suddenly be transparent, inclusive and fair?

The people of the state and their government have so far been passive onlookers on the matter. When the federal government initiated the project, they were not given prior consultation on the future of their resources, and their protests over the misappropriation of their resources have often been ignored. The irresponsible behaviour of the federal government over the matter has already led to many problems. The current crises over the mysterious sickness in the districts around the exploration sites in the Ogaden Basin reveal the gravity of the situation. The symptoms of this tragedy, which are looming in the region, are a direct result of the irresponsible policies that were single-handedly pursued by the federal government.

People are dying in huge numbers over a sickness believed to have originated from toxic materials dumped on the ground by POLY-GCL—the Chinese company that holds the main contracts in the exploration areas. After international media widely reported the case earlier this year, the Ethiopian government sent an investigative team led by officials from the Ministry of Mines and Energy to investigate the alleged disease. Weeks later, the team made a report rebuking international media and denying the existence of the mystery disease.

This tragic case and the reaction of the government clearly portray the essence of the problem. In addition to its monopoly of the natural resource project, the government is also acting here as a court by investigating its own misdoings and acquitting itself of all allegations. The appropriate response to the crisis was to send an independent body of experts to the area to investigate, but instead, it sent those who caused the problem. In other words, the government's arrogant attitude and its negligent behaviour, as manifested here, are the chief causes of the problems in the region.

As mentioned in the preceding chapters, the people of the Somali region became familiar with the project when the removal from their ancestral land, the killing of their livestock and the burning of their villages began to make space for exploration activities. That horrible start is a stark reminder of the federal government's behaviour and an indication of what to expect at the last stage of revenue sharing. Given its deplorable activities on the ground and its persistent single-handed approach on the matter, the government does not appear to be trustworthy on the issue. But still, it can change that gloomy situation by taking some confidence-building measures, which include the establishment of an independent watchdog, the full participation of the people of the state in all the processes and by taking some steps towards transparency. Honouring the law on the resource revenue share, of course, is not a confidence-building measure but a make-or-break matter.

12.1.8 Corruption

Corruption can broadly be defined as the abuse of power to acquire economic benefits, political interests or both. Depending on the system of government and the type of corruption, it could be a hidden and illegal practice, a legal and widespread practice or a mix of the two. Economic corruption is illegal in nearly all societies and is easier to identify than political corruption because the latter is not illegal everywhere and does not always involve money.

In the Somali state, all types of corruption have been widespread, despite their illegal status. During the EPRDF regime, corruption was systemised and became the driving force behind all levels of government activity in the Somali state. The whole system was running on corruption, and the higher the administration ranking the higher the abuse of power and the embezzlement of budgetary funds and other public money.

The practice of corruption in the region was not only systemised during the EPRDF regime but it was also federalised, as its main recipients became the federal authorities within the region. The federal generals, who were the real rulers of the region, used to take their portion of the region's budget at source before it reached the region's account. The federal authorities also used to get preferential treatment in the distribution of contracts and were often awarded the biggest projects. In addition to that, they used to overbudget the institutions that were under their direct administration, such as the paramilitary militias, by manipulating their numbers, uniforms and equipment.

Since the regime change in the state, corruption is neither federalised nor systemised, but it did not disappear and is unlikely to be eliminated given the strong corruption culture in place and the lack of an administration that is strong enough to make revolutionary changes. The fact that it is no longer systemised due to the ending of the patron bribery practice and the efforts of the administration in restructuring the system of government and inputting most of the budget where it was intended is, nevertheless, commendable.

The new administration has made visible progress in reducing corruption by eliminating parts of it, especially the bribery of external actors. With the removal of TPLF generals from the region, the diversion of a portion of the budget to the generals at source ceased. The contracts that they used to get from the remaining budget and their trade monopoly on essential goods also ended with the fall of their regime.

The new system of government has a built-in control mechanism, which directly or indirectly prevents the systematisation of corruption. The system of government in the region is now very decentralised and to some extent transparent. Although elections have not yet been carried out since the regime change, preparations for a pluralistic system have gone far enough for the opposition to challenge the government; there is also a full devolution of power, whereby the local administrations are selected by the locals. Parliament also has specialised committees that to some extent scrutinise the projects. In such a system, corruption cannot be systemised; however, without strong scrutiny, it cannot be easily uncovered, let alone fought.

During the short period in which the regional government was in power, it made a documented number of investments into projects to do with infrastructure and public services. The huge investment in the social sector in which health and education got the lion's share was strikingly remarkable. The building of so many schools in so short a period was unexpected, and historical records could prove it as unparalleled.

The government has been in power for only a short period, and to conduct meaningful empirical analysis, one needs data over time, and for that reason, we cannot make a conclusive statement regarding the level of corruption. However, we know the federal part of the corruption, which was one of the biggest, if not the largest, is gone, and the huge investment in public services is a good indication of a budget being used for its intended purpose. In short, corruption has been reduced, and milestone steps have been taken in the right direction. But given widespread corruption practices and the lack of effective auditing, it is unlikely to go down drastically from the current level, let alone be eliminated entirely. Unless the authorities take proactive measures and sharpen their auditing work, the problem will not only continue but what has so far been achieved will not be sustainable.

12.1.9 Internal Displacement

As a result of the ethnic clashes between the Somalis and the Oromos in the border areas during 2016 and 2018, over a million people belonging to both nations were displaced, and most of those of Somali origin fled to the Somali region. The bulk of the displaced Somali people fled to the Dire Dawa, Liban and Faafan zones. Some of the displaced people returned home afterwards, but still, hundreds of them remain displaced. Qolaji, in the Faafan zone, is currently hosting the largest number of internally displaced people. The population of Qoloji is estimated between 80,000 and100,000 people.

The situation was very acute when the regional regime was deposed: the clashes were still going on, the daily influx of internally displaced people was big, there were no facilities and there was a power vacuum in the period between the deposition of the old administration and the formation of the new one. After the formation of the administration, the new regional government, in collaboration with aid agencies, began to act. They started with much-needed lifesaving relief: food, shelter, health, sanitation and more. In parallel with the relief efforts, it also started a dialogue with the Oromo regional administration and the federal government about how to end the conflict. Despite some sporadic clashes in the Liban and Dire Dawa areas, the regional and federal authorities succeeded in ending the fighting after a short period.

The hostility ended thanks to the Lord's permission and the joint efforts of the regional administrations and the federal government. Some of the displaced returned home, but the majority remain in camps and are unlikely to return to the places where they fled from, especially those who fled from the Oromia side of the border. Most of them have already indicated their determination to build new lives in their state of origin and are waiting for the next stage: a permeant settlement.

The government has started the next process of permanent settlement for internally displaced people, but the project requires huge funding, which the regional government alone cannot provide. Places to settle them and the resources required to implement a durable solution are the two main elements required to start the long-term settlement programme. The regional administration has already identified and designated some places for the new settlement; it is also in contact with aid donors and is expecting to get external help.

Although not life-threatening, the current living conditions of the internally displaced camps is not sustainable, and the sooner they close the better. But the preparation for durable solutions takes time; this is because the amount of money needed for such solutions is larger than what can be fetched from the accounts of the regional government. Additionally, the collection of external resources depends on other factors, which the regional government does not have control over.

The regional government cannot be blamed for something beyond its capacity; however, that does not give it a licence to take a back seat. It is solely responsible for its citizens' safety and well-being, and it should not wait until all the required bricks of the project are in place. In other words, it is imperative to take the initiative and start the work of implementing durable solutions and find the missing bricks while in action.

13

The Struggle after the Peace Agreement

In this section, we will review the current situation of the struggle and outline its future progression scenarios. The core issues under discussion are the immediate effects of the peace deal on the struggle, the role of freedom fighters as organisations and societies and the implication of the new peaceful approach on the struggle for freedom. The two conflicting parties have never tried to solve the conflict through peaceful means; thus, the new approach is a new phenomenon and uncharted territory for both sides with unpredictable outcomes.

There are several registered parties in the region today who all claim to be promoting the interests of the Somali people and representing sections, if not the whole, of society. However, aside from two, these parties are either new or do not have traceable track records showing their involvement in the struggle. For that reason, we will only examine the two main parties: first, the party with the many names, that is, the SPDP, ESPDP, SDP and SPP/EPP, which ruled the region since the mid-1990s, and second, the ONLF, because of their former role on the opposite side of the struggle and because of their influential position on that particular issue and within society.

Society as a whole has been part of the fight to regain freedom and end the occupation of its land. Successive generations inherited the struggle for freedom and self-determination from one another, and since the region's incorporation into Ethiopia, the dream for independence has been prevalent. Despite the long endeavour and the lack of achievement of its goal, the spirit of the struggle never died, and the resistance persisted with many ups and downs as well as occasional breaks for revitalisation. The issue here is whether there has been any change in the attitude of the people regarding the struggle and how the new approach might affect their dream of freedom.

13.1 The ONLF

The ONLF inherited the leadership of the struggle from the WSLF in the mid-1980s, and to this day, it is unchallenged in that role. The organisation signed a peace agreement with the government of Ethiopia after a bloody war. The main points of the vague agreement were to allow the ONLF to pursue its political goals in a peaceful manner and in accordance with the guidelines of the constitution, the rehabilitation of ONLF militants into society and the formation of a joint committee to deal with outstanding issues.

During the negotiations, due attention was not given to the root causes of the conflict, and the two sides did not agree on a clear roadmap for a solution to those issues or durable peace. The ambiguous peace agreement, the persistence of the root causes of the problem, the unpreparedness of the ONLF for the new situation and the apparent lack of interest from the Ethiopian government to create a meaningful resolution to the conflict were not encouraging signs.

The first two points of the agreement have been implemented: the organisation is now a recognised political party and the militant fighters of the organisation were given the choice to either join the Somali region's security forces or to take a specified amount of money and pursue civilian lives. Both options were taken by some of them, but most of them chose civilian life. The government reneged on its promise to establish a joint committee, and the so-called outstanding issues were never disclosed, though they are perceived to be issues of contention relating to the root causes of the conflict and the future shape of their relationship (that is, the continued membership of the republic or a separation), as well as the rules governing that relationship.

The region is now ruled and represented in the government by the SPP/EPP, and the ONLF is one of many opposition parties in the region. The ONLF might not have much leverage, but during the negotiations, it had the opportunity to enter into a dialogue with the government over all issues on behalf of the region, but that possibility is gone with its acceptance to abide by the constitution, which takes it away from being able to represent the region. As a political party, it can advocate for issues and fight for its objectives—and that is the option it opted for when signing the deal. However, the chaotic and harsh political environment it joined has hampered its ability to raise its voice as it wishes, and its position as a political underdog prevents it from making any considerable impact.

The postponement of the issues relating to the root causes during the negotiations, and the subsequent reneging by the government of the establishment of the committees that were supposed to address them, indicates the government's lack of resolve to tackle the core issues and the inability of the ONLF to actualise them and bring them to the table.

In other words, the government is unwilling to talk about the core issue of the region's future relationship with the federal republic, and the ONLF does not have any leverage that could force the government to change its position. Furthermore, the government has the upper hand here, and it is not willing to change the status quo. The ONLF must either accept that reality or officially break the partly broken agreement and take the blame for the consequences.

Given this stagnant process, it seems the ONLF is not in an ideal position to be in after all the sacrifices it made for the cause, but the blame for the lost momentum lies squarely with the organisation itself. The organisation showed skilful tactics on the battlefield and remarkable endurance in the long war and its dire consequences. However, due to a lack of preparation, internal problems and inexperience in peace negotiations, it neither handled the processes that led to the peace deal in a professional manner nor did it carry out impressive work after the peace agreement was implemented.

It was expected that the organisation would take an offensive position on the negotiating table, using its vast experience of the insurgency, but unexpectedly, it quickly found itself on the defensive side and appeared amateurish. It did not stick firmly to its long-held principles for a negotiated settlement during the negotiation period, and bit by bit, its enemy made inroads into the decision-making body of the organisation with the help of the regional administration, thereby influencing the organisation's decision processes at the source.

Internal sources from the organisation reported secret and informal contacts between the organisation and the government on a regional and federal level, but the most widely reported contact is the Dubai meeting that took place at the end of 2017. The Somali regional president, two TPLF generals, a private individual called Sheikh Ibrahim Mohamed Hussein (who had an undeclared role) and four members of the ONLF executive committee attended the meeting.

The meeting was a clear breach of the organisation's code of conduct regarding negotiations and showed for the first time the Ethiopian government's clear penetration into the organisation's policymaking processes. From that meeting emerged a saga known as the Dubai saga, which fragmented the organisation and still haunts it to this day. The saga, which began with that meeting, damaged the credibility of the peace process by exposing its unofficial hidden agenda and shattering the unity of the party by creating mistrust amongst its members. The Dubai saga not only caused new conflicts within the organisation but also renewed old differences that had previously been buried.

The majority of the members of the organisation suddenly felt betrayed by their leaders after news of the Dubai meeting broke, and they denounced the meeting as an outrageous act. As a result of the shockwaves that the blunder sent through the organisation, a central committee meeting was convened in Stockholm, Sweden, to cool down the explosive situation. The committee decided not to break off the peace negotiations but to take them back to Nairobi. The aim behind the move to restart the negotiations at the official venue and in an open manner was, first and foremost, to restore confidence in the peace process, but the negotiations that followed dealt a further blow to the credibility of the process.

The negotiations resumed in Nairobi on 11 February 2018 with nearly the same attendants as the Dubai meeting. The TPLF generals, the regional leader, the individual with the mystery role and four members of the ONLF, of whom two had attended the Dubai meeting, gathered at the negotiating venue to restart the negotiation from where they officially ended in Nairobi, but practically to conclude the tacit deal made in the Gulf state kingdom of UAE.

The photographs from the conference did not calm the critics; on the contrary, they confirmed their fears of a hijacked process. They followed the Nairobi meeting with apprehension and prayed for the talks to collapse out of fear that the worst would happen, that is, the betrayal of their just cause. The talks ended without agreement, and because of that outcome, the bulk of the members of the organisation felt relief.

The failure of the talks temporarily calmed nerves, but neither the Stockholm conference nor the failures of the Nairobi talks removed the mistrust within the organisation that originated from the Dubai saga and the internal old rivalry was renewed. Due to internal rivalry and mistrust, the organisation lost cohesion. The liberation front needed to restore unity by solving its internal conflicts and making peace amongst its factions before making peace with the enemy.

Before the Dubai saga, the organisation had other quarrels that were related to its historical evolution and saw the two opposing sides in a new feud. The secret talks in Dubai not only awoke old internal conflicts but also increased the level of mistrust and fuelled internal power struggles.

The ONLF is a movement that was practically established and maintained by self-appointed grassroots volunteers who were united by the dream of freedom and were living worldwide. The first generation of these grassroots volunteers were the remnants of the WSLF. While the name of the organisation was later changed, the members continued with the liberation work they had been undertaking. The change of the organisation took place under the ongoing struggle, where the members of the new organisation were already acting on the liberation of their land before the new organisational structure had been put into place.

Volunteers from the WSLF grassroots dominated by the Western Somali Youth Liberation Organisation (WSYLO) were instrumental in the establishment of the first working administration of the organisation. They also dominated the administration that emerged from the organisation's first general conference in Garigo'an in 1992. Despite the formation of the administration, which took the leadership of the organisation, the struggle continued in the way it began due to geographical limitations, limited resources and limited organisational capacity. Thus, the organisation remained a coalition of like-minded individuals, groups and organisations committed to liberation.

Before the election of the first administration, there were functioning organisations representing the struggle in many parts of the world—each one acting on its own. In many places across Europe, America, Asia and Africa, there were functioning organisations. The organisations in Sweden, Norway, Denmark, the UK, Germany and many other places in the world became the new bases and representative offices for the mother organisation.

The home-based volunteer members, who had established this organisation and the ready-made organisations that the ONLF inherited from the previous liberation movement, lifted the position of the organisation and accelerated its development. Largely due to their input, it became a large organisation within just months of the election of its first administration. With little input from the central administration, the organisation also found itself represented across half of the globe within a short period—a representation more than that of many independent nations.

Although the organisation would hardly have become a large organisation without the struggle-minded volunteers who waited patiently in the liberation fields and pursued the liberation work on its behalf, the inner workings of the organisations were affected by problems resulting from the self-mobilisation nature of its members and the loose connection amongst the different units of the organisation worldwide. On the one hand, these self-mobilised individuals and groups did not always follow the direction of the centre, and on the other hand, the central administration was in many instances behind the volunteers both in terms of action and thinking. Due to the lack of proper coordination and the divisions resulting from differences in opinion, location and more, eventually, internal conflicts and sometimes power struggles emerged.

This internal rivalry and resulting power struggle were vividly manifested in an open row amongst the leaders of the organisation in 2006, which led to the formation of a splinter group. The root cause of the disagreement was a power struggle between the young intelligentsia who demanded more influence in policymaking and in the participation of the leadership of the organisation and the old guard that was hesitant to open the door for them.

The young cadres were the main driving force of the organisation, but they had very little say in the running of the organisation. They saw the executive committee as an incompetent body that was hampering the progress of the struggle and wanted to reform it by changing its composition and renew it by taking positions in the top leadership. The leadership resisted the idea of putting new blood into the organisation and justified their opposition out of fear of being infiltrated by enemy agents and for the sake of minimising the risks of the struggle. In other words, they were not willing to give leadership roles to new people whose sincerity and loyalty had not yet been proven.

When Mohamed Omar Osman became the chairman of the organisation in 1998, he began to open the old guard club somewhat by gradually relaxing the strict practice of seniority. He began giving responsibilities and roles according to suitability and not necessarily according to seniority. Some senior executive members resented the new leader's method of distributing assignments out of fear of losing their positions of power to young activist cadres if the gates of the club were opened to them. These senior members openly opposed the leader over the issue and even tried to oust him, but the young intelligentsia rallied behind the chairman.

The standoff between the chairman and a group of senior executives became public in 2006. Allegations were exchanged between the two sides, not only within the circles of the organisation but also in the support community networks. The plot to oust the leader had failed due to the lack of sufficient support from within the organisation; however, the revolt continued. Attempts were made from both sides to contain the conflict, and eventually, a compromise was reached between the chairman and the rebellious leaders.

In the compromise, the chairman backed away from his initiative of expanding the ruling club and encouraging the cadres to take on leadership roles. For their part, the old guard, who were now opponents of the chairman, pledged to return as loyal members of the ruling club. The compromise disappointed the young intelligentsia who had wanted to reform the organisation from within. Two members of the executive group that rebelled also expressed their disappointment with the compromise and refused to accept it.

The two leaders who refused the compromise formed a splinter group afterwards. Mohamed Sirad Dolaal, who was a veteran of the WSLF movement, held a high position in the ONLF, and at the time, was the head of the research and policy department, and Salahuddin Ma'ow, who was the head of treasury of the organisation, refused to abide by the compromise and formed another faction. Mohamed Sirad Dolaal became the new leader of the ONLF splinter group, and Salahuddin Ma'ow became the second-in-command of the new ONLF group. Dolaal was killed in action in 2009 by Ethiopian security forces inside the Somali region. Ma'ow took over as leader of the group after Dolaal's death. The group returned to Ethiopia to make a peace deal with Ethiopia as they claimed they would in October 2010, but they disappeared from public politics after their return home.

After the compromise, the cadres were silenced, and the chairman tilted more towards the top leadership clique, whose power had increased substantially to the point of reducing the chairmanship to an almost ceremonial position. The success of the old guard over the young intelligentsia further widened the gap between the two groups. Some of the cadres chose to abandon the organisation and find an alternative way of continuing the struggle, while others simply retreated and waited for the eventual reform of the organisation. However, the majority stayed and remained in their positions for the sake of the unity of the organisation and the struggle.

Although the young intelligentsia was disappointed, the organisation moved forwards in a vigorous manner, despite the differences, and the struggle maintained its tempo for two reasons. First, the region was experiencing a devastating crackdown that had spared no one and that required a united response from the organisation and the whole of society. Second, the organisation was led by a highly regarded chairman who gave the unity of the party the highest priority and whom the cadres were not prepared to disappoint.

Alarmed by the ongoing scorched-earth policy underway in their region and worried about its consequences for their people, the freedom fighters of the region (both individuals and organisations) tightened their belt and moved forward, putting their differences aside and concentrating on the larger issue of rescuing their people from the collective punishment and dehumanising violence that had been unleashed in the region. Given the gravity of the situation at home, it was not the right time for an internal feud, and they understood that.

The people of the Somali region reacted forcefully to the atrocities that the Ethiopian regime was committing in the region at the time. In their capacity as human rights activists, politicians and lawyers, the diaspora community made an extra effort to draw the attention of the world—especially the UN—powerful countries and member states, such as the US and the European Union, and international media to the plight of their people. In addition to that, the Ethiopian government was confronted by freedom fighters on world forums to the point that the Ethiopian prime minister had to use back doors to avoid the noisy opponents who would wait for him in front of conference venues in the west to protest the human rights violations of his atrocious regime.

In response to the strong resistance shown by the people of the region, especially in the international arenas, and the failure of the scorched-earth policies to eliminate the ONLF, in 2012 the Ethiopian prime minister announced his willingness to talk to the ONLF to find a peaceful resolution to the problem. The ONLF responded positively, and the two sides agreed on the date and venue of the talks. Although the man who initiated the talks died weeks before the start of the first meeting in Nairobi, the peace process began on 6 September 2012.

Despite the devastation of the Somali region due to the crackdown that began in 2007 and the ensuing weakening of the ONLF army and its support base at home, the organisation's peace negotiators entered the peace venue with their heads held high. The talks came as a result of the resilient resistance at the request of its enemy and started on the preconditions of the ONLF. From that strong position, the organisation entered into the negotiations that had begun in Nairobi. As detailed in chapter 10, the talks continued at that venue intermittently until 2018. Unlike the optimism of the first phase of the negotiations, the organisation emerged from the last round of talks divided and weak because of the Dubai saga, which we detailed above.

Against the backdrop of the friction caused by the Dubai saga, the organisation convened its third general conference in Asmara, Eritrea, in July 2018. Emotions were running high as a result of the Dubai meeting, the last Nairobi round that had further widened the division of the party and the consequent awakening of the old rivalry. An open power struggle began between an enlarged assertive Dubai group aiming to take the leadership of the organisation and an angry mass of cadres determined to deny them another victory. The former group wanted to take the chairmanship, but due to the strength of their opponents, their candidate withdrew from the competition in the end.

But the story did not end there. The Dubai group advocated the creation of a secretary-general position to reduce the heavy load of the work from, as they put it, the shoulders of the elderly chairman. Their proposal went through and the necessary amendment to the constitution of the organisation regarding the structural change of the leadership was approved. The group's candidate for the chairman position, Abdirahman Sheikh Mahdi, was nominated for the new position by the chairman. The creation of the new position had ramifications for both the positions of the chairman and the vice-chairman: it reduced the former's power and erased the position of the latter.

The organisation made a peace agreement with Ethiopia in Asmara, Eritrea, three months later (on 21 October 2018), and its leadership returned home in December 2018. The leadership of the organisation was warmly welcomed home, and despite their failure in achieving the goal they were fighting for, they took pride in avoiding annihilation and returning home with the hope of furthering the cause. The organisation returned to complete the unfished liberation work via a new approach; by abiding by the constitutional rules of the political game it was trapped in, it was determined to continue its liberation work.

Another general conference was held in Godey in November 2019. Its aim was to fill the position vacated by the retired chairman and to reform the organisation to make the necessary preparations for the shift from an insurgent group to a political party and from an exile-based leadership to a home-based administration. Holding the conference inside the region, especially in Godey after decades of conflict, was itself a victory for the organisation. The organisation headed the first regional administration elected in 1992 and made Godey its capital. It is not clear whether this was a random or deliberate choice, but the location of the conference venue in the city where the first and last ONLF-led administration was based was symbolically significant and historically interesting.

There were serious issues that the conference must handle: a new leader with the ability to handle the challenges of the new situation was to be elected to replace the retired chairman and lead the organisation. Additionally, the ONLF also needed reform and renewal to adapt to the new operational approach and subsequently constitutional and administrative changes were required. The organisation entered a new circumstance: becoming a political party that was pursuing its goals peacefully and a home-based organisation. Thus, it was adapting to a new environment in both location-based and operational terms.

On the latter issue, the conference did not attempt to make any changes to the constitution or the structural reorganisation of the party apart from the abandonment of the armed resistance, the restoration of the vice-chairman position, the consequent elimination of the general secretary position and the expansion of the central committee (that is, the organisation's parliament). No changes were made to the composition of the existing members of the central committee, but new members were added.

On the former issue of electing the chairman, the organisation messed up. There were two candidates for the position: Abdirahman Sheikh Mahdi, the secretary-general, and Ahmed Yasin Sheikh Ibrahim, the foreign secretary. The former is a WSLF movement veteran, one of the founding members of the ONLF and one of the most senior long-standing figures of the ONLF movement. The latter is relatively new in the top leadership, but he was a member of the young intelligentsia group before he joined the executive committee. Despite the big difference in experience, most of the central committee members proposed the junior to lead the organisation, but the senior rejected the proposal and wanted the conference to decide the issue. The conference elected Abdirahman Sheikh Mahdi as the chairman of the organisation.

Although Ahmed Yasin accepted the outcome, it was a contentious election in which the two rival camps exchanged accusations. The frictions resulting from the aggressive campaigns of the election and the new chairman's handling of its aftermath opened a new conflict between him and his defeated opponents, which threatens the existence of the organisation. The new row also reignited the Dubai Saga and the historical rivalry between the old guard and young intelligentsia.

Abdirahman was the leader of the ONLF delegation that attended the Dubai meeting and was amongst the top leaders that confronted the chairman over the cadre's participation in the top leadership and blocked them. Because of his leadership in the negotiations, the Dubai saga has especially damaged the standing of the new chairman and it has also overshadowed the election and its aftermath. Ahmed Yasin is one of the few of the cadre group who got a position in the top leadership. The young generation views the latter as one of their own and a progressive leader who can renew the organisation, whereas the former is seen by the same group as a single-minded old guard who wants to maintain the status quo.

The organisation is facing two interlinked major problems today: an internal conflict with unprecedented magnitude and a lack of strategic direction on how to carry the struggle forward. An organisation cannot hold together if it has persistent internal fighting or does not have something to live for.

After the election, the division of the party widened: in addition to the rivalry between the cadres and the old guard, the senior leadership is also divided, and they are quarrelling openly in the public domain. Recently, over a dozen executive members resigned due to the chairman's leadership style and the former vice-chairman left the organisation. In response to these resignations, the chairman declared the removal of six senior members, including his main rival Ahmed Yasin Sheikh Ibrahim from the central committee—a move that his opponents described as unconstitutional and led to the formation of a splinter group, which claims to have removed the chairman from his position and taken the leadership of the organisation. In response, the chairman announced the expulsion and suspension of about 30 central committee members.

Since the home return of the ONLF, the organisation also lost its direction in terms of how to carry out the struggle work going forward. It has neither articulated its strategical thinking of how to go about the peaceful struggle it opted for, nor has it acted in a manner that is consistent with its previous history or its constitutionally stated aims.

The so-called peace agreement, which in practice looks like an understanding rather than an agreement, is frozen in the sense that it was a one-off event rather than a beginning of a process that aimed to solve the major issues of contention, as it was claimed to be by the organisation. The organisation remains silent not only about the government's broken promise regarding the establishment of the joint committee, but it has so far refrained from criticising the federal government even when it crosses the line, too, as its hands are tied by an agreement that leads nowhere and that is partially broken by the other side. In other words, the ONLF is a passive onlooker even on existential issues, such as the misappropriation of natural resources and the poisoning of the resources' owners. The silence is inconsistent with the liberation goals of the organisation as well as with its past practices of dealing with the Ethiopian government.

According to the critics of the leadership, one of the main reasons the leadership of the organisation is submissive to the federal government is its leadership's ambition to take over the administration of the region and the patron-client practice through which the federal government nominates the regional administration. The desire to acquire power through the handpicking of the centre prevents the ONLF leaders from criticising the centre or raising issues of contention. As a result, the struggle for freedom has become a struggle to gain power, according to their view.

Whether the ambition of power is the cause or not, the organisation's stand on the issue of self-determination is not as clear as it used to be. In an interview with Addis Standard on 20 August 2019, the chairman, Abdirahman Sheikh Mahdi, said that the issue of the independence of the region is not on the immediate agenda of the organisation and that there is no need for secession if the fundamental rights of the Somali people are not violated. He also claimed that the organisation was fighting for the freedom of all Ethiopians because of their advocacy of human rights for all. The chairman added that they believe in Pan-Africanism, the establishment of which starts with a just and peaceful coexistence with the nations of Ethiopia, followed by the integration of the Horn of Africa region and ends with the unification of the continent. He further declared that the organisation backs the Ethiopian prime minister's efforts towards regional integration and wants to assist him in that endeavour by adding the missing Somali region's perspective to the integration plan.

The chairman's remarks are not only overly ambitious but they convey an extremely unrealistic dream given the organisation's inability to unite its members, let alone the Somali people in the Somali state, the long history of hostility between the Somali region and Ethiopia, the involuntary union of the diverse nations of Ethiopia and the lack of justice system to hold them together, the complexity of the conflict-ridden region of the Horn of Africa and the vastness of the African continent. The comments also sharply contradict the documented history of the liberation of the organisation. Whether they were the personal view of the chairman or the party's new policies, such statements put the objectives of the party into question in both cases. If they were the chairman's personal view, they put him on a collision course with liberation-minded members of the organisation and thereby split the party on the core principle of the liberation cause. If they were the organisation's new objectives, they erase their own history and put themselves in conflict with the whole society of the Somali region for misrepresenting the cause they sacrificed so much for and for reversing their view on the struggle.

The new leadership's unclear position on the core issue of self-determination and other issues of contention resulted in a further division of the organisation, adding a new layer of conflict between the allegedly power-seeking group and the liberation-minded group. The two interlinked problems of internal conflict and the lack of a visible liberation strategy have become so severe that they are endangering the existence of the organisation. Thus, to save the party from collapsing, prompt solutions to these problems are urgently needed.

As it is clear from its name and is written in its constitution, the organisation was formed to liberate the Somali region from Ethiopia. The peace deal allows the organisation to pursue its political goals in a peaceful manner and in accordance with the provision of the constitution, which also permits the right to self-determination up to secession. Given the guidance of the constitution and the peace agreement, the ONLF can declare its political standpoint freely and start the liberation efforts legally. But its political objectives are contentious, and therefore, politically, they will certainly trigger a negative political response. A political confrontation is inevitable and most likely that reality is preventing the ONLF leadership from being proactive on the self-determination issue, but sooner or later it will have to confront the central government unless it abandons the cause it was established for and fought so long for.

However, before the ONLF confronts its opponents, it must put its house in order: factionalism must end and an organisation united in purpose and human power must emerge before the stalled struggle restarts. Its resilient history of resistance under indescribable difficulties shows that it can bounce back and renew itself, and it is not too late to do that. Despite persistent internal rivalry, the organisation was able to move forward because of the common purpose that its members hold dearly and the strong fundamentals on which the common purpose was built: the dream to live in freedom and decide their own destiny is still alive. The trigger of the resistance, namely, the oppression has not disappeared, and as a result, the struggle for freedom is inevitable.

The future role of the ONLF regarding the liberation struggle depends on how the organisation clarifies its goals and strategies and gets rid of its current ambiguous approach to the core issues, which is damaging its standing, and whether it ends the factionalism that is hampering its internal cohesion. Unless the party restores its unity, articulates its goals clearly and states the strategies it wants to achieve these goals, it will lose its position as the leader of the liberation struggle, and its role will diminish further, too.

13.2 The SPP/EPP

Since the mid-1990s, the ruling party of the region had been established with the help of the federal government to counterbalance the liberation-minded forces in the region of which the ONLF was the biggest. The Ethiopian Somali Democratic League (ESDL) and a faction of the

ONLF, created by the federal government in 1995 to undermine the true ONLF, merged in 1998 and formed the Somali People's Democratic Party (SPDP). The name of the party changed several times (from SPDP to ESPDP, to SDP and finally SPP/EPP). In April 2019, it changed its name to SDP from ESPDP, which was the name of the party during the preceding administration. The present regime again changed the party's name in 2020 after it became part of the umbrella party the EPP. The branch of the EPP in the Somali region is called the SPP.

Since it was formed to counteract the liberation fronts, its main mission was to represent the federal government in the region and carry out the political instructions of the federal authorities. Of these, control of the region and the containment of unwanted forces were the paramount goals. To varying degrees, the successive SPDP/ESPDP administrations carried out the political instructions of the centre both in administrative terms and in dealing with the liberation movements. And the last administration headed by Abdi Mohamed Omar followed the federal government's policies to the letter and even exceeded the government's expectations and wishes, especially in the fight against the rebels.

Although not elected, the present administration is different from its predecessors in several aspects: the reform and the political system have become relatively more open and transparent, the insurgency ended with a peace deal and the resistance returned and there are many opposition parties and interest groups that are very keen to bring the shortcomings of the government into the spotlight. Because of the change in the political environment and the relative peace of the region, the central government can neither dictate its oppressive policies unchecked as it used to nor can the regional administration function without public support. As a result of these changes and the proactive policies of the regional authority to reform the political system and improve governance, the system is to some extent moving gradually from governorship to a government of the people and for the people.

Despite these positive developments, the patron-client relationship is still intact and the swallowing of the SDP by the EPP is to some extent counterbalancing the freedom relief that came through the reform and the ensuing peace. Whether the members of the umbrella organisation become the federal government's new instrument to reinstall and maintain the delegated provincial governor system or the regional party becomes a weighty member of the republic's decision-making body, promoting the regional interests where and when the decisions are made remains to be seen. The SPP party is optimistic about the membership of the centre party and believes that the benefits of influencing the centre's politics at the source outweigh the disadvantages of losing the entity identity and focus on local interests.

The participation of the centre's politics is not, in general, a bad idea, and having some influence in the shaping of the policies in the present volatile political environment is especially important. It might not have a decisive influence on the decisions because of the region's small proportional representation and the built-in instruments of historical marginalisation, but the presence of the regional authorities where decisions are made will certainly be beneficial. They are unlikely to get a positive response on all the region's demands, but knowing what is going on is itself important, and as each group and region seeks the support of others for the approval of their wish lists, there will be bargaining involving give-and-take types of negotiations amongst the regions. Thus, both directly on the meeting table and indirectly through bargaining, the participation will enable them to campaign for an equitable regional share on matters on the table at the right places and at the right time in a fair play situation.

Given its anti-resistance history, the joining of the EPP, and its stated position of remain on the region's future membership of Ethiopia, it will be a miracle if the ruling party suddenly becomes a liberation party campaigning for the secession of the region inside the EPP, and it seems impossible for an Ethiopian party led by proper Ethiopians to advocate self-determination for Somali people. Nevertheless, that does not rule out the possibility of advocacy of the Somali region's rights within Ethiopia by the Somali branch of the EPP party. Such an endeavour is not an ordinary liberation, but if successful, it will be a step in the right direction and a practical step towards nation-building.

Even if it does not promote Somali interests in an appropriate manner, one does not expect the new party to blindly follow the central government if the federal government decides to reimpose its repressive policies. This is because of the changes that took place regarding the composition of the membership of the party and the new political landscape generally in Ethiopia and particularly in the Somali region.

The files and ranks of the members of the new party, as well as the party leaders, are quite different from the previous members both in educational and outlook terms. Nearly all the central committee members have a university education and many of them are holding masters and PhDs. Some of them, including the president of the region, have been human rights activists and owe their prominence to the fight against oppression and human rights violations. In short, the leaders of the new party are well-educated people who know the political environment of the country and who have a relatively competitive mindset, compared to their predecessors, regarding their relationships and dealings with the rest of Ethiopia.

The political environment generally in Ethiopia and particularly in the region also prevents the federal government from single-handedly pursuing political games. The general polarisation of politics in Ethiopia, the collapse of the EPRDF system and the rise of the power of the peoples, which defeated the military powers, are new developments that limit the power of the federal government. The federal authorities' dilemma in Tigray, as detailed in chapter 14, illustrates the government's decreasing power.

The government's reluctance to intervene during the last two years, despite the regional authority's clear rulebreaking and its inability to end the ongoing war there, indicates the limited political and military manoeuvrability of the federal government.

The short record of the present ruling party shows positive signs regarding the assertion of Somali rights within the system. The demand to correct the underrepresentation of the region, the law on resource revenue sharing, which parliament passed and which the Somali region's government consider a concession to the region, the regional government's equitable distribution campaign and the subsequent increase in federal development projects are good examples of the encouraging development regarding the relationship between the centre and the Somali region. If the party maintains its present assertive attitude and continues the push for more rights and equitable shares in all aspects of life, that could be liberation work in another form and will certainly be a foundation to build the equitable membership of the federation or to advance the goal of self-determination.

13.3 The Society

The struggle for self-determination in the Somali region was always the people's struggle. It started as a reaction to the occupation and the ensuing oppression, and it began spontaneously in an unorganised manner to protest the infringement of their fundamental rights. As a result of the persistent oppression that triggered it, the struggle has never ended, although its levels have varied over the years. The level of right infringements and life circumstances were the main factors that led to its ups and downs. At times of increased repression, the ensuing resistance increased reciprocally and at times of drought and famine or relatively milder repression, it used to decrease. In other words, the higher the level of human rights abuse the higher the level of resistance and vice versa.

The government has taken positive steps in improving the human rights situation and it is promising to further improve the political system through democratisation and respect for the rule of law. The armed opposition reacted positively to the political reforms and changed their armed struggle to a peaceful one. Today, there is no fighting in the Somali region and all the former insurgent groups have made peace deals with the government and are now registered as political parties. They are pursuing their political objectives in a non-violent manner as per the rules of the political game laid down in the constitution of the country.

After 27 years of indescribable repression and nearly a decade of blockades and collective punishments, in which all the people of the region lived either collectively in open-roof prisons or in individual confinements, their desperate situation became unbearable, and the main preoccupation was whether they would be alive the next hour. While in that situation, the reform relief came and gradually the oppressive system disappeared. Just like insects springing out of their hideouts after a rainfall, people began to come out of their respective prisons, but unlike insects, they did so slowly due to their weak bodies. Due to the hopeless situation they only recently put behind them, there is no enthusiasm for a verbal confrontation, let alone an armed struggle. Additionally, the increasing level of freedom, human rights protection and respect for the rule of law are further reducing the need for a struggle of any sort.

However, there is still no agreement on the root causes of the conflict, the political environment in the country remains unstable and its future development is unpredictable. For that reason, the armed struggle is on hold but not yet over. The top leadership of the country introduced the reform due to public pressure. The Ethiopian people have become relatively more powerful since they forced the regime to reform, and the prime minister who put the reform into practice is leading the country: these two elements of political development are positive and encouraging signs. But the reform is not complete, and there is no consensus amongst the different political forces on how to further the reform processes and on what platform politics must be conducted.

From the political discussions across the country, it seems the debate regarding the future system of the government has taken centre stage. There are political forces, especially in the Amhara region, who want to restore the old unitary system and abolish the federal system. Most of the people of the country are of the view that only through a federal or confederal system can the different nations of the country be held together. The federal political forces are the majority, but they are not united. For example, the TPLF, which introduced the federal system, is at odds with all the other federalist parties because of its repressive policies when it ruled the country and its hypocritical practices regarding federalism. On the other hand, the anti-federalists are in power and are using their political position to further their cause.

Due to the fragility of the current government and the unpredictability of future political development, all regional authorities have increased their paramilitary militias. Armed militias are opposing one another in the Amhara, Oromo and Benishangul-Gumuz regions. And the Tigray region has been, in practical terms, preparing itself for a separate state since they lost power at the centre.

Given these uncertainties, the attainability of democracy and respect for the rule of law in the country, which the government promised, are in doubt; thus, the development of the political behaviour in the country is to some extent unpredictable, too. The implications of uncertainty for the Somali region and its self-determination struggle are like that of the rest of Ethiopia. Both the regional government and the opposition parties are conducting their responsibilities in the hope of gaining more freedom and rights in a transformed country with a more democratic system of government and more devolution of power. But they know that things can go wrong, and hence these expectations may not be fulfilled.

Like their politicians, the public in the Somali region are hopeful of a better day to come, but they are following the political development with apprehension, fearing the return of the old painful days. The wounds from the constant crackdown and the unimaginable dehumanisation practices of the last decades are not yet healed in physical, psychological, economical and judicial terms, and as a result, are neither prepared for a confrontation now nor do they wish for a future conflict with the government. However, if a war is imposed on them, implications drawn from their history indicate that they would resist no matter how hard it might be for them or how much they may dislike it.

The current government policies regarding natural resources best illustrate the mixed feelings of the Somali people about what to expect from the present regime. On the one hand, the passing of the law defining how to share the revenue from natural resources gave them hope in that they felt they were being listened to for the first time, and that their share of the revenue was legally upheld. On the other hand, the government has not abandoned its irresponsible policies on the ground regarding the environment, the mistreatment of the people who live around the oil field exploration sites and the exclusion of the locals who own the land where the natural resources are found. Rather than consult them about the use of their resources, they are driven from their ancestral land, which was the foundation of their shelter and the source of their livelihood, by an evil cartel who came from lands as far as China.

Today, we are witnessing the first results of the damage caused by the irresponsible policies of the government and the consequent misbehaviours of foreign oil exploration companies. The local people who were uprooted violently from their villages, and consequently lost their livelihoods in that inhumane cleansing process, are today dying in big numbers from a mystery sickness caused by toxic chemicals dumped on the ground and water sources by those exploration companies.

The response of the government to the news of the mystery disease is even more disappointing. Instead of investigating the disease, with the aim of correcting the misconducts of the government and its foreign associates in the exploration business that caused it, the federal authorities denied any wrongdoing policy-wise by claiming to have followed all of the international exploration standard procedures to the letter. To send an independent competent team to the area to investigate both the disease and its causes was the second natural thing to do after the dispatching of medical emergency relief teams. But neither a medical emergency group nor an independent expert team was sent to the area. After denying any misconduct and the existence of the medical condition in the mass media, it sent a team of government officials headed by the Ministry of Mining and Natural Resources. As expected, the team confirmed the already stated government position by denying the existence of the illness.

In conclusion, the mystery disease and the government's handling of the disaster are bringing back memories of the century-long oppression, the brutal habits of the tyrannical system of government in Ethiopia and the immense sufferings caused by the international greedy cartel united to utilise the Somali state natural resources at the expense of the Somali owners. The quest for the Somali state resources was the main cause of the occupations of the Somali region by different nations and the cause of the subjugation of its inhabitants. Unless the Ethiopian government changes its deplorable present policies regarding the mistreatment of the true owners of the natural resources and takes prompt practical rectification, the impending natural resource's debacle will no doubt be the trigger of the next armed struggle.

14

The Future Status of the Somali Region

The Somali region was forcibly incorporated into the involuntary union of the Ethiopian nations. It did not accept the imposed marriage, and since the start of its first occupation, it has been resisting the forced incorporation. Despite the long resistance, the Somali people failed to regain their freedom, but they have not given up on self-determination and are hopeful of realising that long-awaited dream. As the region was added to Ethiopia by force, the occupation was maintained by the same method, and so was the method of the consequent resistance and mainly armed struggle.

In 1994, Ethiopia approved a new federal constitution that came into force in 1995, which recognises the existence of the different nationalities within the republic and allows the devolution of power through the nationality-based federal system. The constitution also grants the member nations self-determination rights and allows them to seek secession.

In the following sections, we will examine the possible future relationships between the Somali region and Ethiopia, considering the relevant constitutional provisions, the reform and the current political situation. The likely relationships and the different scenarios of each option will be analysed using both current and historical parameters. A federation, confederation and secession are the only acceptable alternative choices, and the focus of our discussion is the circumstances that could lead to either retaining or changing the current federal system and the factors affecting the choices for an alternative system.

14.1 Federation

Ethiopia consists of 10 federated states and 2 federally administered city-states. The second largest of these states, which makes up the federal republic of Ethiopia, belongs to the Somalis who also make up most of the inhabitants in the federally administered city of Dire-Dawa. Although federalism is not the first choice of the Somali people, if implemented properly, it might have been considered as the second-best alternative to secession or at least could have divided society into two camps of federalists and separatists.

The federal constitution of Ethiopia is a beautifully written document intended, first and foremost, to resolve national conflicts. If this had been properly implemented on the ground, it would have served its main purpose and resolved other divisive issues, too. The republic consists of multiple ethnic groups with distinct cultures, languages and in some cases religions. Apart from the former Abyssinian regions (Tigray and Amhara), the ethnic groups did not join Ethiopia voluntarily. The Abyssinian kings conquered the neighbouring nations one after the other and added them to their kingdom. The annexation of other regions began in the 1830s, and Menelik II, the most recent Abyssinian king who carried out most of the conquering, nearly completed the annexation process by the beginning of the 20th century.

As detailed in chapter 2 of part I, the Somali region was gradually occupied by Menelik II, but Ethiopia lost it to Italy in 1935. Italy also occupied the whole of Ethiopia the following year. The region returned to Ethiopian hands in between 1948 and 1955 after Italian and British occupations in the periods of 1935–1941 and 1941–1955, respectively.

The Abyssinian Kingdom, which changed its name to the Ethiopian Kingdom after conquering territories and nations several times larger than its original territory and population, used to maintain the unity of the country in the same forceful way that it created it. The conquered nations were compelled to take on the Ethiopian identity as soon as they joined the kingdom, making Amharic, the language of the ruling ethnic group, not only the official language but also a requirement for Ethiopian citizenship in some places. Both the absolute monarchy and the totalitarian military regime that replaced it denied the existence of different nations within the country; therefore, it did not attempt to find political solutions to the national issues that caused persistent conflicts in many parts of the country.

For the first time, the EPRDF regime admitted the nationhood problem of Ethiopia and introduced the federal system, which it claimed to be the remedy for the problem and the only way through which the unity of Ethiopia could be maintained. The regime replaced the unitary system with a federal system and introduced a professionally written document with clear provisions granting a wide range of individual and national rights. The country has also been divided into ethnic-based states. Amharic remained the only official language at the federal level, but the federated states were given the right to use their languages for teaching and administration in their respective regions.

The different nations that make up Ethiopia are divided over the intertwined issues of the federal system and the constitution. The unitarist hegemony, which is mainly the Amhara ethnic group, opposes both the federal system and the constitution. The TPLF, which is the proponent of the system, and all the other remaining nationalities, whom we call here the underdogs because of their subordinate positions, support the country's current constitution and system of government. Although, in principle, the underdogs back the federal system, they accuse the proponent of selective implementation of the constitution and abuse of power and, for that reason, are not on good terms with that organisation.

14.1.1 The Selective Proponent

The federal system was promoted by the TPLF and the main points of the documents were in the organisation's charter, which was drafted before it took over the reign of power. The constitution was approved in 1994 by the EPRDF regime, which was dominated by the TPLF. The EPRDF merely completed the TPLF's draft constitution in a standard manner. Officially, the motive behind the introduction of the constitution was to recognise the multinational nature of the country and give the different nations self-rule over their regions within the republic, and even allow them to leave the union if they wished.

From its 27-year rule of the country and its current politically arrogant behaviour, implications can be drawn, which indicate that the TPLF was not sincere about the federal system and its stated reasons for the introduction of the constitution. The concentration of power at the hands of the TPLF, the overrepresentation of the Tigray state in parliament and all federal institutions and the nomination of regional administrations by the federal government are all examples of the TPLF's clear breach of the system and its guiding document, both of which were introduced by the same organisation. The TPLF's rejection of federal laws and directives of the federal government after losing power also shows the insular attitude and undemocratic and anti-constitutional practices of the TPLF.

Although the Tigray population is about 6 per cent of the Ethiopian population, for many years, the TPLF occupied the premiership, the foreign ministry, the chief of staff of the army and nearly all of the important positions in government. Over 60 per cent of the top army generals were from Tigray, and all the economic and commercial activities were carried out by the same ethnic group throughout the country.

Although the federal parliament has been a symbolic institution with no proper parliamentary powers, the Tigray region is overrepresented. There are 38 members of parliament from Tigray, and according to the representation formula law, the region is overrepresented by 9 members. The same number of members is underrepresented by the Somali state, which currently has 23 members of parliament.

The TPLF ruled the country through the EPRDF umbrella organisation, which consisted of four parties from four regions (that is, Tigray, Amhara, Oromo and the Southern Nations). All other regions were not allowed to join the ruling club, which the TPLF created and led. The four EPRDF regions were administrated by the EPRDF party, whereas the rest were led by TPLF-nominated administrations. Thus, the TPLF practically ruled the country using a two-tier system: through the EPRDF with other subordinate parties in the first tier and the regional state administrations in the second tier. The federal system, which was supposed to devolve powers and establish administrations with different mandates at the federal, regional and district levels, became a one-party-led system in all levels of government.

Not only did the two-tier system enhance the absolute power of the TPLF directly, but it also increased its supreme power indirectly by exclusively granting itself direct rule over the periphery regions outside the EPRDF arrangements. As the only party that could exercise its authorities in all levels of government and all regions of the country, it acquired unlimited access to everything and thereby monopolised the politics of the country.

According to the constitution, the regional governments should be answerable to elected regional assemblies. But real elections did not take place at all levels of government since the approval of the federal constitution. Although the degree of interference in regional affairs varied in accordance with their relative power, the federal government directly or indirectly controlled all regional governments and assemblies.

The degree of interference in the Somali region was exceptionally higher than in all other regions. The TPLF generals effectively ruled the Somali region. On the pretext of fighting the resistance that persisted in the region throughout the EPRDF regime's tenure of office, the TPLF put aside the regional institutions and ran the affairs of the region. The regional administrations and the local militias it created were merely used as tools to carry out the policies of the federal government.

Since the TPLF lost power, it became a vocal opponent of the system it created, daring even to break the laws it introduced when it clashed with the interests of the TPLF. After having lost the absolute power it exercised during its 27-year rule of the country, the TPLF retreated to

Tigray and began preparing the region for de facto statehood. Leaving the republic at the appropriate time was the hidden intention of the TPLF according to independent analysts, who also observed signs of political activities and institution-building efforts, indicating the preparations for statehood. Politically, the regional authorities became more assertive by taking an independent political stand on the issues of contention. Additionally, they undertook service upgrading and state institutional enhancing measures to increase their capacity and reduce their dependency on the federal government until the eruption of the war between the federal government and the TPLF. Separatist parties who were openly advocating for secession also joined the political stage.

With its open political confrontation with the federal government, the regional government was, in many ways, acting increasingly like an independent government even before the start of the armed conflict. The regional authorities challenged the federal government in many areas, too. The TPLF refused to join the EPP, which had replaced the EPRDF, and described the dissolution of the latter as unlawful. The TPLF accused the EPP of being an anti-federal party and denounced the establishment and political approach of the new EPP party. The regional government also declined to hand over former government officials that were wanted by the federal government for alleged crimes and described the persecution of the officials as a discriminatory manhunt directed against the Tigray officials. A host of more serious problems followed, which exacerbated the political confrontation.

The stalemate was aggravated by the constitutional crisis over the cancelling of the election. The government and parliamentary mandates expired in October 2020; however, because of the COVID-19 pandemic, the election could not be held on time. The government referred the matter to the upper house and gave it four options: to dissolve parliament, declare a state of emergency, amend the constitution or seek constitutional interpretation from the HoF. Parliament opted for the latter, but before the upper house began the deliberation, the TPLF government declared that it would hold the election as originally scheduled and ignored the parliamentary decision to postpone it due to COVID-19. The central committee of the TPLF also backed the decision of the regional government to hold the election on time. The prime minister vowed to intervene if the regional authority did not uphold the law.

In another development, the speaker of the HoF, Keriya Ibrahim, resigned on 8 June 2020 over the issue of the constitution. The speaker resigned on the eve of the day the meeting was called to discuss constitutional interpretation alternatives, which the house opted for, to solve the constitutional crisis over the deferred election. The resignation was prompted by the constitutional interpretation alternative, which she described to be unconstitutional. She also said that she did not want to cooperate with a dictatorship in the making. The speaker was a TPLF member and was representing the Tigray region; it is believed she had been instructed to resign by the TPLF. For that reason, the resignation did not surprise many observers who had been following the deteriorating relationship between the federal government and the TPLF.

The regional authorities refused to abide by the decision of the parliament to postpone the election due to COVID-19 and, in defiance, held the regional election in September 2020. The federal government did not recognise the election and the prime minister vowed to enforce the rule of law, though initially, he ruled out the use of force. In response, the regional authorities refused to recognise the federal institutions and recalled the representatives of the region from federal institutions. The federal government consequently took several punitive measures against the regional authority, which included the suspension of budgetary subsidiaries to the regional state of Tigray. Eventually, the political confrontation led to an ongoing military conflict and the federal government's indictment of the regional authorities.

The immediate trigger for the military conflict was an alleged attack by TPLF forces on the headquarters of the Northern Command of the Ethiopian National Defence Force (ENDF) on 4 November 2020. In response to the attack, the government declared war on the regional administration and issued arrest warrants for dozens of prominent TPLF political leaders and military officers. The government's counter-offensive started on 6 November 2020 with airstrikes and declared its termination on 28 November 2020 after the fall of Mekelle, the capital city of the region. Although the government took control of all major urban areas, many high-profile political leaders and military commanders were either captured or killed. While the prime minister declared the completion of the offensive, which the government termed a 'law enforcement operation', the military conflict has not ended. The ongoing fight has the potential to transform into a full-blown civil war that could last far longer.

Despite the government's declaration of victory and its refusal to talk to the TPLF, the TPLF is unlikely to surrender. The TPLF leaders vowed to defend their right to self-rule, and most of the people of Tigray will probably rally behind their leaders due to the external threat they feel. The TPLF's consistent defiance of the federal government during the last two years, as well as its activities on the ground, also indicate that the organisation is aiming to make the region an independent state.

Even though the TPLF did not campaign openly for succession, before the eruption of the war, it threatened to do so if the federal government did not stop what it called discriminatory policies against the Tigray region, and generally, the demand for a separate nation has been increasing in Tigray. Prior to the armed conflict, there were three separatist parties in Tigray who were explicitly promoting a nationalistic agenda. The Salsay Weyane and Baitona parties saw the separation of the region from Ethiopia as the second-best option. The independence party was very clear on the issue and advocated outright secession even before the armed conflict. The ousted regional government not only acted like an independent entity, especially after the formation of the EPP, but since it lost the power of the federal government, it also gave priority to statehood building processes in Tigray and made huge efforts in that endeavour.

As part of the preparation for statehood, the regional authorities undertook both spiritual and institutional capacity building measures. To promote nationhood consciousness, the authorities encouraged intellectuals inside the region and from diaspora communities to discuss how to enhance their economic and social service capacities, and how society as a whole could contribute to these efforts. In its capacity-building efforts, the regional government gave priority to strengthening the law and order and upgrading the capacity of the defence forces. All necessary steps were taken, and all possible resources were put in place to create a deterrent force. That force was put on display in an unprecedented manner in the last celebration of TPLF's 45 founding anniversary on 11 February 2020. The recent armed conflict between the TPLF and the federal government showed that the TPLF forces were no match for the huge Ethiopian army; however, whatever remains of that force will be expected to continue the fight in a guerrilla fashion.

The main reason for the change of direction by TPLF authorities is likely to be their long-held hidden intention to secede from Ethiopia in the event of losing power. That hidden intent is believed to be the chief reason for adding article 39 to the constitution, which permits regions to secede. The TPLF's original aim was to liberate Tigray and make it an independent state, as stated in its first manifesto. The organisation, however, changed its position by making a secession plan B in the event of the unsustainability of the rule of the union. The plan B scenario became a discussion theme in that region after the TPLF lost the leadership of the central government. The advocation for an independent state began there in a gradual manner, but that demand has been getting louder and clearer each day.

However, the sudden acceleration of the push for a separate state has been caused by an imminent perceived threat. The Tigray people were generally blamed by the Ethiopian public for the wrongdoings of the EPRDF regime because of the TPLF's domination of that government. The peace agreement between Eritrea and Ethiopia, which was done without prior consultation with the Tigray authorities and Abiy's subsequent befriending of their arch-rival President Afwerki of Eritrea made them feel encircled. The persecution of former senior officials, mostly from Tigray, for the wrongdoings of the previous government also contributed to the siege sentiment. The ongoing armed conflict will certainly strengthen the secession demand and could trigger an open struggle for independence.

Because of the prevalent siege sentiment and the pessimism about the future of Ethiopia, the Tigray region has been isolating itself. The ousted Tigray regime and the people, in general, are not optimistic about the political development in Ethiopia: they are anticipating the failure of the federal government and the collapse of the Ethiopian republic. They accuse the anti-federalist forces led by the Amhara ethnic group of undermining the system and for blaming the Tigray people for anything that has gone wrong in Ethiopia during the EPRDF regime. In their view, the anti-federalists will eventually plunge the country into chaos and create regional conflicts all over the country. As a result, they prepared themselves for a civil war, which they view as inevitable and which they anticipate emerging from victoriously as an independent nation.

Whether the Tigray prophecy regarding the future of Ethiopia can be fulfilled remains to be seen, and whether the government is blameless in its political deadlock and military confrontation with that region is debatable, but what is certain is the widening gap between the federal government and the Tigray region. Despite its perceived insincere intentions regarding the introduction of the federal constitution, the absence of the Tigray region from the centre at this critical time is not healthy for the development of political processes, especially when the discourse about the future system of the government is taking centre stage. Their absence weakens the federalist camp and strengthens the position of the federal opponents.

14.1.2 The Unitarist Hegemony

The Amhara hegemony lost its political power and some of its other hegemonic powers to the regime that ousted it in 1991; this was directly through the power grab of that regime and indirectly through the introduction of the ensuing federal constitution and the system of government that emerged from it. But still, the Amhara people enjoy cultural, economic and historical hegemonic powers and are determined to get back the political power they lost to the TPLF and the system they introduced. The unhidden intent of most of the Amhara people is to restore the unitary system and get rid of the federal system. They know their anti-federal views are not widely shared in Ethiopia, but they are blinded by the nostalgia for their historic hegemony and are keen to take advantage of the current fragmentation of federalist forces and the federal power position they hold.

The anti-federalist camp blames ethnic-based federalism for the current political conundrum and everything that has gone wrong in the past three decades. They claim that the system was introduced by narrow-minded ethnic nationalists whose aim was to promote the special interest of their group at the expense of the wider public, and they blame the current constitution for planting the disunity of the country by institutionalising the ethnic division. For that reason, they see the revision of the constitution as the first step in the political reform process. Although they are a minority in the country, the voice of the anti-federalists has been getting louder.

Despite the current political conundrum caused by the failure of the federal regime, the political crisis was not created by the system of government, but by the drivers of the system. As mentioned in the preceding section, the proponents of the federal system were not sincere about their motives and, as a result, wittingly did not implement the constitutional document as it was written. In one sense, the anti-federalists are right about the ethnic nationalistic agenda behind the promotion of the federal system. But that fact alone can neither invalidate the importance of the federal system nor it can justify the restoration of the unitary system.

What matters is the content of the document and not who brought it. Before we examine the advantages and disadvantages of the current Ethiopian constitution or the suitability of a federal system to the Ethiopian political environment in general terms, we must remember the circumstance under which it emerged. The system was introduced by liberation fronts that had fought long wars against a totalitarian dictatorship. The system they introduced as a remedy did not work well because they misused their power and not because of the recognition of multiple ethnicities. In fact, the ethnic-based federal system and the little devolved powers the different nations gained through it, gave the underdog majority a sense of belonging to the republic.

The unitary totalitarian system that the Amhara hegemony is nostalgic about cannot be an alternative to the present system. The people of Ethiopia know what to expect from a totalitarian unitary system led by people who believe in Amhara supremacy. They lived under such a system, and they do not want to be reminded of it, let alone restore it because of the chauvinistic outlook that shaped its political behaviours, the way its institutions were built and the practices its justice were based on. The subjugations of the other ethnic groups, the violations of human rights and the oppressed people's consequent resistance to the injustice led to prolonged wars in nearly all parts of Ethiopia, which eventually caused the collapse of the Amhara hegemony's absolute rule. Thus, the introduction of ethnic federalism was the result of the failure of the unitary system.

The federalists also accuse the anti-federalists of being narrow-minded nationalists, whose chief aim is to regain their lost powers. As a result of the introduction of ethnic federalism, the Amhara hegemony lost much of its powers to other entities, both directly through the takeover of its political positions by others and indirectly through the system, which reduced its sphere of influence both institutionally and geographically.

Although the system did not function well because of the driver's political malpractices, nevertheless it made some progress especially in some regions such as Oromia in terms of empowering regional governments. The Amhara hegemony used to control politics through the central government and local governments. After the introduction of an ethnic-based federal system, the territorial influence of the central hegemony was reduced to the province it originated from, as every nationality exclusively took over the administration of its region with varying degrees of federal direction. The Amhara used to live in every province of the country as the ruling elite, but their privileged position disappeared with the removal of the system that gave them upper-class status. The federalists view the lost privileges of the Amhara as the cause of their nostalgia for the old system and their anti-federal views.

So far, the anti-federal forces have not come up with an alternative system that is acceptable to the majority, and the unitary system does not have public support beyond the Amhara region. The federal system was promoted by ethnic nationalists who won the war over the central dictatorship, and the argument against the federal system was based on the ethnic outlook of the federalists, that is, the institutionalisation of the ethnic division. On the one hand, the system indeed encouraged ethnic identity alongside national identity; however, on the other hand, the devolution of power led to the empowerment of many ethnic groups to some extent, which in turn gave them a feeling of inclusiveness and increased their political participation. The support base of the old unitary system is very narrow; unlike the current system, which is treasured in most regions, it does not have support outside the Amhara region.

14.1.3 The Struggling Underdogs

The underdogs are the majority of the Ethiopian people, who share the unprivileged position of being ruled by the top dog to varying degrees. They joined the Ethiopian union forcibly, and since their annexation, they have been ruled in a coercive manner by their rulers. They are from all Ethiopian regions apart from the Abyssinian regions of Amhara and Tigray, who conquered them and have ruled them since then. As the ruled class, they did not devise any of the systems of government, and thus did not have prior motives about the systems imposed on them by the ruling class. But they have views about the systems of government, which evolved from their practical experience of these systems.

Most underdogs are in the federalist camp and their support for the system is based on their political experience as well as their desire for the revitalisation of their national identity. Through the federal system, they regained some degree of autonomy and aspire towards self-determination, including secession. They see federalism and the resulting autonomy as the minimal devolution of power that can keep them in the union; thus, they completely rule out any return to the unitary system.

Despite their unity on the view of the federal system, they are not only divided by geography and ethnicity, but they are adversaries in politics too and disagree over a wide range of issues. Some of these issues originated from the implementation of the system they all back, such as the demarcation problems of the ethnic boundaries. As a result of their diversity and their historical position as underdogs, they are not organised as a force, and they do not devise the politics of the country. They are either passive onlookers waiting for the outcome of the political game played by the historical Abyssinian regions or supporters of the players with minimum influence over the political game.

Because of the proponents' appalling power abuse during the EPRDF regime and their subsequent retreat to Tigray after losing power, the proponent wing does not have a relationship with the underdog wing of the federalist camp. The two wings of the federalist camp do not trust one another, and for that reason, they are unable to communicate, let alone forge a common front against their common rival, namely, the anti-federalist camp.

Another reason for the lack of cooperation between the two wings is the invisibility of their opponent and the consequent lack of a battleground. The TPLF and all the other ruling parties that joined the EPP declared their continued support for the federal system. Only some extremist parties and individuals in the Amhara region declared their opposition to the system and are openly campaigning for a return to the old unitary system.

Additionally, the federalists and anti-federalists are not communicating directly, as facts about the real intentions of the opposing sides are not known, despite the suspicion and stereotypes they have of one another. The battle lines are not drawn yet on the ground, and the rumour-based cold war is conducted on the airwaves through the media, in political forums and to some extent in government circles and channelled through federal agencies.

Regardless of the declared commitments of the ruling party to maintain the federal system, the federalists fear the removal of the system by the governing EPP party. Although the main Amhara ruling party—the Amhara Democratic Party (ADP)/the Amhara National Democratic Movement (ANDM)—which joined the EPP, officially supports the system like the other parties that became part of the EPP, federalist hardliners suspect that party, its supporters and the prime minister of hidden goals. They aim to gradually dismantle the system and their fear is based on signals indicating a movement towards centralisation.

The amalgamation of all the ruling parties bearing the regional names into one organisation with a national name is a sign of the centralisation of power. The regional names symbolised both the devolution of power that came with the federal system and the ethnic identity on which it was based. Besides the symbolism, the new party structure strengthens the power of the central authorities at the expense of the peripheries and undermines the authorities of the regional administrations. The pyramid structure of the party will enable the central authorities to take advantage of the hierarchical system, and hence take direct control of the regional politics. In other words, the hierarchical system allows the boss of the party to deal directly with the members of the party irrespective of their geographical location, thereby bypassing the local administration. For that reason, the establishment of the EPP is seen by the federalists as the first step in the centralisation process.

The epicentre of the anti-federalists is the Amhara region. The dream of returning to the old glory days of the absolute rule by the central hegemony is prevalent in the region, and the struggle for that cause is vividly noticeable there. There are parties such as the National Movement of Amhara (NAMA) and media outlets campaigning for the removal of the multinational federal system, and there are armed militias opposed to the federal structure who want to impose their own system of government forcibly. Because of these forces and the widespread support for the unitary system in the Amhara public, the ruling party there is under great pressure to listen to the people of the region, and the federalists suspect them of secretly working behind the scenes to undermine the constitution under the banner of the EPP.

Despite his officially supportive position, the prime minister's stand on federalism is not clear enough for the opposition, and the federalist camp is increasingly losing patience with him because of his ambiguous approach to the issue and the strong position of the Amhara in his government. They see him as a pragmatical politician whose chief preoccupation is the consolidation of power. He was propelled to power by a coalition of mainly Amhara and Oromo protesters. But after he ascended to the premiership, a difference of opinion emerged between the two ethnic groups regarding their view of the premier and his government. The increasing reliance of the premier on the support of the mainly anti-federalist Amhara people and the government's decreasing backing of the mainly federalist Oromos increased the concerns of the supporters of the current system of government.

Unlike the Oromos, most of the Amhara people support the government and are at odds with other main political players over the contentious issue of the constitution and even the extremist Amhara nationalists view the prime minister as the lesser of the two evils. The most enthusiastic backers of EPP, which is the biggest political project of the prime minister, are from the Amhara region. And the prime minister is becoming increasingly dependent on their support, particularly in federal politics.

Abiy Ahmed Ali was propelled to power by an Oromo-led alliance mainly from the Amhara and Oromo regions. However, large sections of the Oromo population deserted him after he took control because of dissatisfaction with the government's policies. Instead, they formed their own parties or joined other existing parties to promote their political goals. The Oromos, who oppose the prime minister, accuse him of failing to introduce the reforms they fought for and concentrating on the consolidation of power instead. The Oromo federalists have become more critical of the premier because of his unclear standpoint on the federal system. His declared supportive position of the federal constitution was overshadowed by his political practices. Additionally,

227

the establishment of the EPP and his recent glorification of the atrocious imperial kings by opening a memorial park for them are just more examples of his centralisation tendencies. In other words, they do not trust him, particularly on the issue of the constitution, and they fear the introduction of a unitary system by his government.

The current turmoil in Oromia following the killing of a popular musician, the ensuing crackdown of that region and the imprisonment of prominent political leaders who led the uprising that swept the premier to power have deepened the Oromos' mistrust of the premier. There is no doubt that the premier lost much of the popularity that he gained in his first year and that his relationship with his ethnic group is currently not good. Only time will tell whether that relationship is repairable; however, the development of that relationship is crucial to the future of the federal system. The defeat of Oromia will empower the anti-federalists and enable them to change the current system of the government, whereas an Oromia victory would kill their dream of reimposing the old unitary system.

Given the political fragmentation of the country, the probability of replacing the current system is not possible at least in the short term, and the commotion around it seems to be political positioning rather than a genuine drive for a fundamental change to the current system of government. However, these political positionings are signals of what to expect from the political actors, and the political muscles they exhibit in that process are also a test of their future political manoeuvrability. The current performance of the political players will be reflected in their future goals. The underdogs are not in the driving seat and are not coordinating well for the time being, but in principle, they are united in safeguarding the current constitution. Besides that, some of the conquered nations have an ongoing self-determination struggle of their own, and any move to further erode what they have of self-rule will most likely unite the historically subdued nations and trigger the drive for a common front. If the central government decides to reimpose the unitary system, it will certainly meet strong challenges from the federalists, and the ensuing conflict will likely be a long-drawn-out one with an unpredictable outcome.

14.1.4 The Somali Perspective
As part of the underdog group, Somalis are supporting the federal system, too. Though, so far, it has not been greatly beneficial to them. Although some symbolic changes were introduced such as the regional assembly, the regional government and the Somali language becoming an

official language in the region, the real power remains in the hands of the federal authorities. Besides that, as detailed in previous chapters, the EPRDF regime that introduced the system became the most brutal regime they had ever seen.

Their support for the system is purely ideological. Any step towards devolution in terms of political principles, institutional change or practical administration is seen in the region as a positive. On that basis, all the political parties support the ethnic-based federal system and view it as the minimum devolution that can keep them in the republic.

The system was introduced primarily as an answer to the conflicts between the central government and the regions—of which the war in the Somali region was the biggest and the longest. Even if implemented to the letter, it is unlikely to be a substitute for the long-held aspiration of an independent Somali state in the long run. However, for the time being, a true federal system is the main demand of the political parties. Regardless of whether the dream of self-determination is still alive, they are eager to give peace a chance and are prepared to once again explore the possibility of coexistence with Ethiopia under a federal system.

The recent tragic experience of the conflict is discouraging them from returning to the conflict, and they are encouraged by the reform wind from the centre. Because of the reform, they are hopeful of the full implementation of the federal system with real devolution of power, and they are eager to take advantage of the reform and peacefully pursue their political goals. However, they share the same concerns as the other underdogs regarding the government's alleged intention to further undermine the already eroded system or to replace it with a unitary system.

14.2 Confederation

A confederation is a union of nations that exist in a looser form than a federation. The nations forming the confederation could be sovereign states or member states of one country. The degree of cooperation and the power of the central authorities depends on the established rules of the confederation and whether the member nations are sovereign states or parts of one sovereign state. Members of a one-nation confederation usually share common authorities in certain areas such as defence and foreign policies, and decisions on these shared matters are often made in consensus.

In Ethiopia today, political discourse is dominated by the debate of whether to retain ethnic federalism or return to the unitary system. The opponents of the federal system see it as not only too loose, but they also regard the ethnic-based regional structures as divisive. For that reason, they want to recentralise the system. Since a confederation implies more decentralisation than a federation, it will not be acceptable for anti-federalists, and thus it does not seem plausible that it will be part of the political discourse any time soon.

However, given the current constitutional conundrum, the widening gap between the federal government and the Tigray region, the simmering tension between the federalists and unitarist hegemony and the fragility of the government, the survival of the federal state cannot be taken for granted. In the event of state disintegration—which is not unlikely—if the current political crises are not resolved, all methods of union formation will be under discussion in terms of how to keep the union together. Although it was not a formal confederation in the modern sense, Abyssinia was once ruled by princes. Each one controlled part of the region and that historical period (1769–1855) is called the Era of the Princes.

14.2.1 The Tigray Crisis

The ongoing armed conflict in Tigray took the political stalemate that caused the fighting to a higher level. The Tigray and the federal political actors have been at loggerheads over several issues of contention, which reinforced one another stagewise. The rift between the two began after the premier change in 2018, but it came to the surface when the TPLF refused to hand over fugitives wanted by the federal government for alleged crimes. The dissolution of the EPRDF in 2019, the refusal of the TPLF to join the EPP and the subsequent removal of TPLF ministers from the federal government further widened the gap.

The deadlock over the postponement of the election, as well as the constitutional amendments through which the government wanted to justify the delay and resolve the constitutional dilemma, resulted in the expiration of the terms of parliament and the government. However, the government delayed the election and further escalated the political confrontation. The Tigray authorities declared that they would hold the elections on time and the premier vowed to restore law and order if the regional authorities broke the law. The Tigray government defied the decision of the parliament and held the election, but the federal government refused to recognise the result. Subsequently, both the regional and federal governments designated each other as illegitimate and refused to talk to each other.

Initially, the government ruled out military intervention and instead took punitive measures, which included the withholding of federal funds to the region to enforce its authority. But eventually, it abandoned its non-violent approach after an alleged attack on a federal army base in Tigray and launched a military offensive against the TPLF on 6 November 2020 on the pretext of restoring law and order. It declared to have successfully completed its military offensive, which it termed it a 'law and order operation', on 28 November 2020 after taking control of Mekelle, the regional capital. The government is now in control of the main urban areas and it declared a six-month state of emergency in Tigray. It also nominated an interim president and began the process of administration-building in the region.

Despite the official termination of the government offensive, the military clashes continued unabated and are unlikely to end until the conflicting parties reach a political settlement. TPLF forces withdrew to the hills and mountains and the organisation's leaders vowed a guerrilla war against the federal government. For its part, the federal government sees the TPLF as an irreconcilable group and accuses the organisation of aiming either to rule or ruin the country. For that reason, it has ruled out every option apart from a military resolution. However, given the TPLF's determination to fight, the strength of Tigray's security forces, the siege sentiment there and the growing desire for an independent state, the conflict could well be protracted.

Mainly due to the issues that divided the ousted regional authorities in Tigray and the federal government in the last two years, Tigray has been acting more like an independent entity prior to military conflict. The deposed Tigray administration showed consistency in its defiance of the federal state, and its position regarding the contentious issues had hardened further since the start of the war. The ongoing war also reinforced the secession struggle, which the ousted regional government was preparing for while in power. The difficult relationship between the federal government and the TPLF before the war enabled the latter to consolidate its power in the Tigray region and to prepare the region for de facto statehood, which has been interpreted by the regional authorities as the attainment of the necessary technical capabilities to function like an independent state. The motto of the statehood-building efforts, which the regional authority embarked on, was self-reliance. According to the TPLF, in some areas such as defence and administrative capacity, the building processes for de facto statehood were either complete or in the final stages before the war erupted.

The most obvious element of the statehood building process was the defence forces, which it established. Together, the paramilitary force and the local militia were estimated at 250,000 strong before the eruption of war. Despite the defeat of that force in the first phase, the bulk of that army is believed to be intact, and the rocket attacks on Eritrea after the fall of Mekelle show that they still have enough weapons to fight with.

Because of the self-isolation of the regional administration and the siege sentiments felt by a large segment of the Tigray population, which originated from the conflation of the Tigray people and the TPLF for the latter's human rights abuses by Ethiopian protesters, and the government's persecution of former officials mainly from Tigray for the abuses of the previous government, the TPLF's accusation of the federal government of unjustly singling out the Tigray people for the misdeeds of the EPRDF regime gained ground in the region. In addition to that, the fallout from the ongoing war not only deepened that victimhood sentiment further but also drove the region towards a secession struggle.

Because of the involvement of Eritrea and the Amhara state paramilitaries in the fighting and the territorial claim both have on Tigray, as well as the double standard the federal government recently showed regarding the ethnicity issue, the people of Tigray feel encircled and more threatened than ever before.

Eritrea is not only politically backing the Ethiopian government in the fight against the TPLF but, as claimed by the latter, divisions of the former's forces have participated in the fighting. Western diplomats and the Ethiopian government also confirmed the presence of Eritrean troops in Tigray. The disputed territory that Eritrea wants to take over and that Ethiopia and Eritrea fought over between 1988 and 2000 is the main reason Eritrea is supporting Ethiopia in the fight. The disputed area was ruled for Eritrea by the independent boundary commission in 2002, and Abiy Ahmed Ali accepted the commission's decision in the peace agreement that his government made with Eritrea in 2018. However, the transfer of the land's ownership was not implemented because of the TPLF's opposition to it.

The Amhara also claim parts of Tigray and are part of the coalition that toppled the Tigray-led regime and holds federal power. The Amhara people are fighting in Tigray in two tiers: at the federal level in defence of the federal government, which they are part of, and at the regional level to take back the land they claim is theirs.

The government's handling of the sensitive issue of ethnonationalism during the conflict was disastrous. On the one hand, Amhara regional forces not only fought alongside the federal army against the TPLF in the western part of Tigray, but the government also allowed them to set up an administration of their own in the disputed part of that region. On the other hand, the government has been speaking strongly against ethnonationalism, and it is fighting the TPLF on the pretext of restoring a central authority. Because of the fusion of federal and Amhara forces, the fighting appears to be a war between the Tigray region and the Amhara region supported by the federal government. The government's contradictions on the issue of ethnonationalism, and the widely reported dismissal of Tigray army officers and other officials from government departments, strengthen the sentiment of victimhood in Tigray and to some extent validate the TPLF's claim that the Tigray people are encircled by invading enemies, aiming to wipe them off the face of the earth, and that only the TPLF can ensure their protection and survival.

The fallout from the ongoing conflict reinforced the victimhood sentiment, reignited the warrior culture there and helped the TPLF in its mobilisation of the people for what it called the defence of the homeland against the invading alliance. Given the under siege feeling that is prevalent in the region, the TPLF's history of struggle and the land grab that Tigray's eastern and western neighbours (Eritrea and the Amhara state) are contemplating, the TPLF is expected not only to fight to the bitter end but also to accelerate the process it started two years ago towards an independent state.

As the primary architect of the current system of government, the TPLF selectively implemented it. The organisation was happy with the federal system when it was holding the power, but now it appears to prefer a looser system or independence to avoid the domination of the ruling ethnic groups (that is, the Amhara and Oromo nations). Prior to the conflict, independent observers said that the TPLF was contemplating a plan B to leave the union using article 39 or derail the federal constitution to force the introduction of a confederation system in the event of no resolution to the standoff with the government. If the TPLF succeeded in plan B, both scenarios would have a domino effect on the rest of the federal member states.

Given the perceived plan B of the TPLF and the government's refusal to talk to the TPLF, as well as the government's inability to eliminate that organisation, the probability of protected war is extremely high. Also, taking into account the deep-rooted warfare mentality and the frequently changing opportunistic alliances of the conflict-ridden Horn region, the instability of the government, the nature of the involuntary union and the fragmentation of the nations that make up the republic, the limited resources of the country and the increasing unrest in many parts of the republic, the military option will not be sustainable in the long run. These difficult political circumstances will eventually force the government to talk to the TPLF. Considering the bloodshed and consequent likelihood of disintegration, the TPLF will, in the event of a peace negotiation, most likely demand secession or a looser relationship than federalism. A confederation is a more devolved system and the only alternative to independence in that regard. Any change of relationship between Tigray and Ethiopia will affect the other regional states as well.

14.2.2 The Tension between the Unitarians and the Underdogs

Another clash point, which could have existential consequences for the republic if not resolved, is the simmering tension between the unitarist hegemony and the federalists, especially the underdog wing, over the future system of government. The latter group is not happy with the present system because of the abuse of the proponent, but they want to hold on to it and improve it, especially on practical application. They do not want to go back to the unitary system because they believe going back to that centralised system will take away whatever autonomy they gained through the federal system and set the wheel of reform backwards. They fear the restoration of centralisation, and they see the EPP as the tool the hegemony wants to use for the transformation of the system.

The underdogs enthusiastically supported the prime minister at the beginning because of the reform, but that support is gradually giving way to concerns about the erosion of the system. On numerous occasions, the premier declared his support for the federal system and cited the recent acceptance of the referendum of a new federal state for the Sidama region as proof of the sincerity of the government regarding the issue. So far, there are no big discrepancies between the reform process and the government's declared policies towards democratisation in most parts of the country and that is an encouraging sign. However, the signals of centralisation manifested in the establishment of the EPP and the increasing influence of the unitarist hegemony in the government, as well as the security forces' increasing intimidation and suppression of the opposition in Oromia, which has been documented by international rights groups, remind the people of the historical path of deception taken by nearly all governments in Ethiopia; that is, a promise of democratisation at the beginning, accompanied by the consolidation of power using methods contrary to the rule of law, followed by a brutal crackdown on dissent and, finally, the removal of the regime in a violent manner.

Despite the fear of a backlash, both the underdogs and the Amhara hegemony were instrumental in the regime change and in spearheading the reform: the reform came largely through the pressure of the Oromo and Amhara protesters, and the two ethnic group's cooperation in the EPRDF system resulted in the formation of the reformist government. However, tensions have been building between the two ethnic groups especially over the contentious issue of the federal system and that tension is approaching boiling point.

A clash between the second-largest group (Amhara) and the majority of the largest ethnic group (Oromo), supported by all of the other ethnic groups in the peripheries, will probably lead to a collapse of government and chaos. In the event of state disintegration, the discussion on how to reinstate the failed state will focus on a set of alternative systems, which will include the confederation and probably start with it because of the disintegration effect and failure of other union systems. Disintegration drifts the units of the union apart and bringing the units back together is not the same as holding the parts of an existing state together. For that reason, any talk of re-establishing the union in such a circumstance will most likely start with a looser system than the one that cannot hold them together, and a confederation is a more devolved form of a union and the next stage to separation.

14.2.3 The Performance of the Federal Government

The most important factor that can keep the discourse of the political debate on the current system of government or change it from a federal to a confederal system is the federal government. All the doom scenarios outlined above take government failure as an assumption. If the central government succeeds in resolving its deadlock with the federal member state in the north (Tigray) and honours the commitments it made regarding the upholding and proper application of the federal system, democratisation and respect for the rule of law there will not be confrontations amongst the stakeholders; therefore, there will not be any need to change the system of government.

However, whether it will manage to resolve the issues of contention, paralysing the functioning of the government and the constitutional conundrum drifting the units of the union apart and threatening the very existence of the state, remains to be seen. Given the magnitude of the disagreements, the prevalent warfare mentality of Ethiopian societies and their minimal experience in peaceful political resolutions, the precarious political situation and the ongoing war in Tigray, it will be difficult to overcome the stalemates. Although it is not impossible to resolve the disputes before the conflicts explode and thereby save the country from plunging into chaos and disintegration, the danger of the collapse of the state is real.

14.2.4 The Somali Perspective

For the time being, there is no push for a confederal system from the Somali region. Their long struggle for self-determination did not achieve its goals, though the dream did not die. Anything that brings them closer to their ultimate dream or gives them some sort of autonomy is welcome there, but their immediate demand is the proper application of the current federal system.

They see that the full implementation of the current system will give them a type of autonomy that will enable them to coexist with the rest of the union for the time being. From this, they can go on to realise their aspirations for an independent state. Because of the selective practices of the proponent, the federal system was not implemented in a proper manner in the Somali region, and along with the other members of the underdog group they share the concerns of further system erosion by the government.

14.3 Secession of the Somali State

Secession has been the biggest dream of the people in the Somali state, which is also known internationally as the Ogaden region, since they were forcibly incorporated into Ethiopia. They strived hard for the realisation of that dream ever since the incorporation, but the hard-fought struggle did not achieve its goal, and the freedom they long yearned for is still out of their reach. Despite the lack of success of the long struggle, the dream did not die; the struggle is ongoing and will most probably continue until it achieves its aim.

The independence right of the Somali people living in the Somali state from a legal point of view is detailed in chapter 12 of part I. In this section, we will focus on the striving for statehood from a political and administrative point of view, the effects of the possible scenarios for political development and the future of the federal republic on the secession issue.

14.3.1 Striving for Secession

The struggle to regain their freedom started after the first incursion into the region by Ethiopia centuries ago and continued unabated, persistently renewing itself after any respite and taking both armed and non-armed forms in line with the dynamic geopolitical and generational changes. The method of the struggle for self-determination was armed most of the time, but it is now progressing in a peaceful manner due to the recent change in political environment. The current constitution of Ethiopia, which recognises the right of member nations of the federal republic to secede and requires a peaceful approach for the achievement of that goal, the reformist government in power that promises to respect that right and the fruitless long-armed struggle have been the main factors that led to the current non-violent form of the struggle.

Whether the current non-violent approach succeeds in getting what the armed struggle did not achieve depends on the genuineness of the change at the federal level, that is, whether the Ethiopian government respects the nation rights detailed in the provisions of article 39 of the constitution. In other words, whether it allows in practice the initiation of the secession process or accepts an independence outcome.

In 1994, the regional parliament overwhelmingly voted for a referendum to secede from Ethiopia, but the decision of the only truly elected parliament in the history of the region was not only rejected outright but the regional government was also sacked and replaced with an unelected regional government nominated by Addis Ababa. This was mainly due to the demand for the independence referendum. Whether the new regime will honour its commitment and allow the people of the state to exercise the right enshrined in the constitution remains to be seen. However, the recent reneging of parts of the peace agreement with the ONLF is in tune with the contradictory historical records of the Ethiopian governments' practices and stated policies.

Given the history of the Ethiopian regimes reneging on past promises and the stalled talks between the ONLF and the federal government over the contentious issues of which the future relationship between the region and Ethiopia is the biggest, the government is unlikely to permit the initiation of the secession process, let alone accept the result. Regardless of that pessimistic view, sooner or later, the self-determination issue will take centre stage because of the people's undying dream for independence and Ethiopia's denial of that right.

However, for the time being, there is no push for secession from the region. The last remaining liberation front, namely, the ONLF has signed a peace accord with the federal government agreeing to abide by the constitution and pursue its objectives in a non-violent manner. Using the constitutional nation rights, it will probably raise the self-determination issue sometime in the future, but the organisation's immediate goals are the attainment of full autonomy for the state, that is, an autonomous state with all the powers and rights enshrined in the constitution and an end to the persistent disparity in all sectors between the region and the rest of the union.

The outcome of the short-term goals will have a profound effect on the pursuit of the long-term goal of independence. The realisation of full autonomy will boost the confidence in the system of governance and will encourage the continuation of the non-violent struggle to resolve the remaining issues, whereas discrepancies between the constitutional rights and their practical implementation will have the opposite effect.

But the road to the short-term goals itself seems a long one, too, given the ONLF's absence from decision-making bodies and its inability to actualise its goals or bring them to the table for discussion. As an opposition party with no representation in the regional and federal parliaments, it can neither influence the decisions made by the governing bodies nor can it raise legislative issues in parliament. Besides that, as the region is represented both in the government and the legislature by the ruling party, and as the ONLF accepted to abide by the constitution, it cannot bypass the ruling party and claim to be representing the region in the federal bodies. Thus, the ONLF's influence in the political process depends, first and foremost, on joining the decision-making bodies. And this further depends on an election being held to see how much representation the ONLF gains as a result.

The volatile political climate, and the unpredictability of the future path of political development in Ethiopia, further complicate the situation and frustrate the efforts to reach a lasting solution to the core problem. The uncertainty surrounding the stability of the political environment and the allegation of a centralisation plan overshadowing the government's reform efforts are not also encouraging signs. As mentioned above, the proponent of the federal system did not respect the national rights enshrined in the constitution it introduced, and there is even a fear of the introduction of centralisation by the new regime; for that reason, the ONLF appears to be taking a gamble.

However, whether it is a gamble or a calculated move, it is very unlikely to lose much because of the non-violent approach. It already lost the military side of the struggle because, amongst other things, of a strategical error: confronting the federal government alone at the peak of its power. It does not want to repeat that mistake, and it wants to test the genuineness of the reform by exploring all the means of achieving its goals peacefully. In other words, it does not want to fight Ethiopia alone, and it is not prepared to confront the new regime before it exhausts all the possibilities of a peaceful solution.

The ONLF awaits the outcome of the reform, and regardless of which way it goes, it expects to play a leading role in shaping the relationship between the region and Ethiopia. It believes that a successful outcome will put her in a government position, and thereby influence vital decisions at the source. The failure of the government to honour its commitments will put her in confrontation not only with the Somali region, but also with other federated states, and such confrontation could either lead to a negotiated settlement or disintegration—both of which will affect the future relationship between the Somali region and Ethiopia. The ONLF expects to join the discussion platform in both scenarios and take a leading role in reshaping the region's future status.

However, despite the ideological ambitions of the ONLF to achieve the goal of the struggle, the party has been getting weaker and smaller in organisational terms since the peace agreement because of a deep internal conflict and the dissolution of its armed wing. Recently, over a dozen executive members resigned and the former vice-chairman, Hassan Muhumed Mo'alin, who was instrumental in reshaping the movement from an insurgent organisation into a political party left the party. A splinter group, claiming to have ousted the chairman was also formed. This internal weakness will be reflected in its dealings with the political actors at the federal and regional levels unless the organisation resolves its internal fragmentation and bounces back.

14.3.2 Preparation for De Facto Statehood

There are no political organisations intentionally preparing the region for de facto statehood. The party in power is not a secessionist party, and even though it is not in power, the leader of the ONLF made clear that his organisation is not advocating for secession now. He further said that there will no need for independence unless the government violates the rights of the people and breaks the rules of the constitution. Thus, there are no preparations for de facto statehood wittingly going on in the region.

Besides that, there is no consensus on major issues amongst the political parties in the region, and because of the contest for power amongst the parties and the patron-client relationship between the federal government and regional politicians, they are unlikely to unite on a national agenda. The ONLF is competing with the ruling regional party for the leadership of the regional government and the federal government is the power broker: whoever it picks up gets the power. For that reason, the current regional politicians are unlikely to initiate something that does not please the federal government.

However, indirectly, the region's statehood building process started with the introduction of the federal system in the 1990s. Although the federal government did not allow the federal system to take root in the region for security excuses, and the EPRDF regime directly ruled the region throughout its tenure of office, the region was a federated state in symbolic terms. A regional assembly, a regional government with all government departments, regional courts, regional security forces, regional media and more have been put in place. Since the current regional administration led by Mustafe Muhumed Omar came to power, the regional institutions became somewhat functional in the federal sense, partly due to the reform in the country and partly because of the increased competence of the regional authorities.

The reform and relative peace of the region gave the regional authorities breathing space. The reform was the main cause of the peace accord between the ONLF and the federal government, and the ensuing peace removed the excuse for security, which was the main reason for the interference of the federal government. Still, the region is not free from interference, and the federal government can dismiss the regional president, whom it appointed, any time it wishes; nevertheless, the degree of interference is less than before.

Although the new leader was constrained by, amongst other things, the time limit imposed by the need to fill the vacuum caused by the collapse of the previous regime and the rottenness of the political system in which he was to operate within, the relative freedom gained through the reform enabled the new regional president to choose his cabinet on merit and not loyalty. He gave educational qualification the highest priority over all other considerations and set up a cabinet consisting of highly educated people, most of them holding masters and doctorate degrees. As a result of the increased educational capacity, the departments of the government became more professional.

The regional government departments are now better functioning because of their increased educational capabilities, though it will take time before they can reach the standard of professionalism they should be operating with. There is a functioning system of political pluralism, and the press is becoming freer and more competitive. Judicial reform is on the way, despite a long delay, and the scrutiny on the security forces to ensure they stick to the rule of law is increasing, even though its level is still not satisfactory. The regional parliament is becoming relatively more assertive, and after the election, their representative role is more likely to be enhanced. In short, the infant regional regime looks like a government and the Somali state has the shape of a federated state.

The region's future relationship with Ethiopia depends on the strength of its de facto statehood and the survival rate of Ethiopia's statehood. The two statehoods affect one another inversely. The stronger the former's de facto statehood preparedness, the higher the chance of influencing the direction of the relationship in the way it wants. Additionally, the higher the survival rate of the latter, the lower the probability of the former leaving the union. In other words, if the federal government manages to hold the union together, the demand for secession will decrease due to the regional politician's limited political manoeuvrability, whereas in the event of the weakening or disintegration of the federal government, the demand for secession will increase and the possibility of gaining independence will be higher.

A high level of de facto statehood preparedness will be helpful to the regional state, both if it decides to exercise its constitutional nation rights and seek separation using article 39 and in the event of the collapse of the federal state. However, without the consent of the Ethiopian government or the disintegration of the Ethiopian republic, it cannot leave the union.

We outlined the current lack of political advocacy for independence and the indirect preparation for de facto statehood taking place in the region, as well as the probability of the use of constitutional nation rights. In the following section, we will briefly examine the probability of state collapse in Ethiopia and its implication for the issue on focus here, namely, the secession of the Somali region.

14.3.3 The Disintegration Scenario

In short, the future of the federal republic's existence is uncertain and disintegration is not unlikely. The union was built by force and maintained by the same method. The history of similar empires, such as the Soviet Union and, indeed, the recent political change in Ethiopia and the current standoff amongst the various political actors, all indicate that a military approach is not sustainable and force is unlikely to hold the union together in the long term. Nevertheless, the current regime is increasingly resorting to a military resolution because of the political stalemate and the dictatorial political culture of the country. The inability of the Ethiopian state to find political resolutions to its national problems and its reliance on military resolutions will eventually lead to a dead-end and, hence, the implosion of the state.

The Abyssinian nations (Tigray and Amhara) who founded the country and forcibly incorporated other nations into the union are pulling the republic into different directions; as a result, the remaining nations that make up the majority have been left bewildered. The government is led by a pragmatic leader with a mixed Amhara and

Oromo background who understands the historical grievances of the oppressed people because of his Oromo father and sympathises with them, but who is also from the ruling elite and has the ambition to lead a united and strong Ethiopia. For the attainment of that goal, he relies on the support of the Amhara hegemony, which both his mother and wife came from and which dominate his government.

The TPLF dominated the EPRDF regime, which ruled Ethiopia in the period from 1991–2018, put a federal system in place that was supported by most of the nations that make up the republic of Ethiopia; this is because of the individual and nation rights, especially the self-determination rights, enshrined in that document. However, as mentioned earlier, the TPLF was selective in the implementation of that document and grossly violated these individual and nation rights. The TPLF is using the same document in its confrontation with the government over several uses, accusing it of violating the constitution. The hypocrisy of the TPLF regarding the constitution is crystal clear, but it seems that the organisation's selective capacity persists even after it lost power. The Tigray region nearly completed its preparations for a de facto statehood before the war began; From its practices, it appears that it wants to stay in the union either on the Tigrayans' terms or secede using article 39 of the constitution. They denied that right to the Somali region in 1994 when the Somali regional assembly voted for a referendum on independence using that article; however, because of the defence deterrence they established, it seems that the Tigrayans still believe they have the exclusive right to selectively implement that self-determination right in Tigray.

The Amhara hegemony also bases their arguments with their opponents on the constitution, but for the opposite reasons. They portray the constitution as the source of the country's political problems and interpret the human rights violations and the selective implementation of the constitution by TPLF as the outcome of the ethnic nationalist agendas promoted by the ethnic-based constitution. Thus, they see the constitution and ethnic federalism as incompatible with Ethiopian nationhood in general, and they regard it as the biggest threat to their hegemony. The Amhara hegemony wants to remove the system and are actively working on that, directly and indirectly, both inside and outside the government circles.

The other nations in the union are, for the time being, apprehensive about the political development, partly because of the government's unclear position on the federal system issue, the Tigray's selective attitude towards the constitution and the Amhara hegemony's endeavours to restore their lost hegemonic powers through the restoration of the unitary system. In addition to this, they are apprehensive of the unresolved constitutional and political conundrum resulting from the delay of the election and the expiration of the terms of parliament and the government. But despite the federal system support that united them, the non-Abyssinians have not yet taken clear political standpoints on how to approach the issues of concern, and because of the national diversity in this group, it will take time to make a common front against their opponents on the issue of the federal constitution.

The ongoing war between the TPLF and the federal government, the low probability of a successful military resolution to that conflict, the irreconcilable views of the ethnic groups over the governing system and the current political and constitutional difficulties that the country is facing are all symptoms of state failure. Given these symptoms, Ethiopia is not immune from disintegration and the Somali region will probably be one of the first federated states to establish an independent state in such a situation. Time will tell how long it can hold together as one country and how many parts it will split into in the likely eventuality of fragmentation, but it will be a miracle if Ethiopia continues to exist in its current form in the long run.

14.3.4 Conclusion

Despite the suspension of the armed struggle and the lack of a political voice advocating outright independence for the Somali people in the Somali state, the prospect of regaining their independence by legal means or as a result of the collapse of the Ethiopian state is greater than at any other time in the history of the struggle. The suspension of the armed struggle was preceded by an announcement of a change in approach to the conflict by the Ethiopian government, which raised the prospect of a peaceful resolution and which was the chief cause of the option for the peaceful endeavour of self-determination.

Opting for a non-violent struggle does not necessarily indicate a change in attitude regarding the issue of independence. There is a written constitution recognising the right to leave the union and a government promising to stick to the rules and rights enshrined in that document. Therefore, considering the new constitutional and political development in Ethiopia, the non-violent approach and the lack of push for immediate independence should not be interpreted as the death of the dream of self-determination.

The independence dream is prevalent in the whole of society and does not depend on one organisation. As the history of the region shows, successive generations inherited the struggle from one another: each generation organised itself in the form that suited its situation and carried the struggle forward to the next one. The Ethiopian aggression was the cause of the resistance, and the level of oppression has been a function of the level of the resistance: the higher the oppression, the higher the resistance that follows. Therefore, since the denial of the right to self-determination—which is the fundamental cause of the resistance—is persistent, the struggle will continue whatever shape it takes.

However, both the attainability of the dream of self-determination and the maintenance of a future independent state will depend on how the people of the Somali state organise themselves and how effectively their nationhood will function internally. The clannism culture, which is prevalent in the region, is an impediment to the cohesion of society and the achievement of its goals. A persistent clan division will slow the progress of the struggle for freedom and hamper the building process of a de facto statehood. In contrast to the past, the adverse effects of internal divisions are today more harmful to the endeavour for self-rule and pose more serious setbacks to the preparation process for a future independent state, both in political and administrative levels, than the highlander's suppression and the threat of other external forces. Hopefully, they will understand that internal weakness and make the necessary changes that are needed to achieve the long-awaited goal of independence.

Appendix

The following treaty recorded by the UK government as Treaty Series No.1 (1955) was the last agreement signed between Britain and the Ethiopian government regarding the British handover over the Somali state (the Ogaden) to Ethiopia. Other treaties relating to the handover and subsequent border demarcation are presented in the appendix of the first part of this historical work.

Appendix I

AGREEMENT BETWEEN THE GOVERNMENT OF THE UNITED KINGDOM OF GREAT BRITAIN AND NORTHERN IRELAND AND THE IMPERIAL ETHIOPIAN GOVERNMENT RELATING TO CERTAIN MATTERS CONNECTED WITH THE WITHDRAWAL OF BRITISH MILITARY ADMINISTRATION FROM THE TERRITORIES DESIGNATED AS THE RESERVED AREA AND THE OGADEN

London, November 29, 1954

The Government of the United Kingdom of Great Britain and Northern Ireland and the Imperial Ethiopian Government;

Desiring to terminate the temporary arrangements provided for in

Article V11 of the Anglo-Ethiopian Agreement signed at Addis Ababa on December 19, 1944, and

Desiring to implement the provisions of the Anglo-Ethiopian Treaty signed at Addis Ababa on May 14, 1897, relating to grazing rights;

Have agreed as follows:—

ARTICLE I

The full and exclusive sovereignty of Ethiopia over the territories which are set forth in the attached Schedule (hereinafter referred to as 'the territories'), recognised by the Anglo-Ethiopian Treaty of 1897, is hereby reaffirmed. As from February 28, 1955, British Military Administration for which temporary provision was made under the Anglo-Ethiopian Agreement of December 19, 1944, shall be withdrawn from the Reserved Area as defined in the Schedule to that Agreement and from that part of the Ogaden which is at present under British Military Administration. The Imperial Ethiopian Government shall from that date reassume jurisdiction and administration of, in and over the territories.

ARTICLE Il

The right of tribes coming respectively from Ethiopia and the Somaliland Protectorate to cross the frontier for the purpose of grazing, as originally set out in the Anglo-Ethiopian Treaty of 1897 and the letters annexed thereto is reaffirmed by the two Contracting Parties who shall take steps to ensure that as far as possible tribal grazing rights in the area shall be protected.

ARTICLE III

Subject to the jurisdiction and administration of the Imperial Ethiopian Government and to their responsibility for the maintenance of public order, the facilities and powers set out below are hereby accorded within the territories by the Imperial Ethiopian Government as a special arrangement designed to meet the circumstances under which tribes from the Somaliland Protectorate utilise the territories for the purpose of grazing, which tribes are hereinafter called 'the tribes'.

(a) Without prejudice to the jurisdiction of the Imperial Ethiopian Government and whilst the tribes are in the territories, the tribal organisation consisting of the system of local authorities (Akils), tribal police (Illalos) and Elders, as set up and recognised by the Government of the Somaliland Protectorate, shall continue to function and the tribes may be given from time to time instructions on internal tribal and inter-tribal matters as appropriate from the Government of the Somaliland Protectorate; and the tribal organisation shall have the responsibility of maintaining law and order among the tribes. The tribal organisation shall not be used for political agitation within Ethiopia and nothing in this Agreement shall authorise political agitation by the tribes or members thereof. There shall be no more than 700 Illalos at any one time in the territories. Apart from the Akils, Illalos, Elders and Liaison Officer and such staffs as are or may be provided under sub-paragraphs (d) and (e) below, there shall be in the said territories no officials of, or appointed by, the Government of the Somaliland Protectorate except by agreement with the Imperial Ethiopian Government.

(b) Cases involving only persons who are members of the tribes or members of the tribes and the liaison officer or members of his staff shall, if so triable, be tried by Protectorate Courts sitting inside the Somaliland Protectorate. Cases involving both Ethiopians and members of the tribes shall be tried by Ethiopian courts but the British liaison officer referred to in sub-paragraph (d) below or a member of his staff shall have the right to be present in court. He shall be given an opportunity to provide any relevant information.

(c) Without prejudice to the full powers of arrest in the territories on the part of the Ethiopian police, the Illalos shall have full powers of arrest over members of the tribes and any other person where such arrest is necessary to prevent the imminent commission by such person of a serious crime involving members of the tribes or the liaison officer or his staff or the escape of such person immediately after the commission of a crime involving members of the tribes or the liaison officer or his staff. Any Ethiopian national arrested by Illalos shall be delivered for custody at the earliest opportunity to the Ethiopian authorities. Any person arrested by the Ethiopian police who, under subparagraph (b) of this Article is to be tried by the Protectorate Courts shall be delivered for custody at the earliest opportunity to the tribal authorities.

(d) There shall be a British liaison officer with the necessary staff appointed by the Government of the Somaliland Protectorate who may reside in and shall be permitted to move freely in the territories. The liaison officer and his staff shall hold themselves at all times available for consultation by the Ethiopian authorities, and their advice shall be sought by the Ethiopian authorities in the conduct of the latter's affairs with the tribes. While the tribes are in the territories the liaison officer and his staff shall be responsible to the Government of the Somaliland Protectorate for transmitting to the tribes the instructions of the Government of the Somaliland Protectorate referred to in subparagraph (a) above and they shall promptly inform the Ethiopian authorities of the substance of such instructions. They shall also, as and when requested by the Imperial Ethiopian Government transmit the latter's instructions on other matters when not directly or otherwise issued to the tribes by that Government.

(e) Medical veterinary and educational services hitherto provided for the tribes within the territories may continue to be provided at the existing scale during the presence of the tribes in the territories and the two Contracting Parties agree at the request of either to negotiate regarding the provision to the tribes of any expansion of or addition to these services including the provision of water supplies.

ARTICLE IV

Reciprocal facilities and powers corresponding to those provided for in this Agreement in respect of tribes from the Somaliland Protectorate shall, subject to corresponding obligations, be accorded to the Imperial Ethiopian Government in those areas of the Somaliland Protectorate which the Ethiopian tribes may enter pursuant to the provisions of Article II of this Agreement.

ARTICLE V

The provisions of this Agreement shall be subject to review at any time at the request of either Contracting Party. Unless otherwise agreed the Agreement shall remain in force for a 'period of fifteen years, at the end of which period, unless six months' prior notice of termination shall have been given by either Contracting Party, it shall continue to remain in force until six months after the sending by either Contracting Party to the other of a notice of termination. The termination of this Agreement shall not affect the grazing rights referred to in Article II.

ARTICLE VI

This Agreement shall come into force on signature and shall replace the provisions relating to the territories in the Agreement of December 19, 1944, including the Annexes and Schedules appended thereto and the provisions of the Protocol of July 24, 1948. It is further agreed that all questions concerning the administration of the territories pursuant to the provisions of the aforementioned Protocol and Agreement have been disposed of by the present Agreement.

In witness whereof, the undersigned, being duly authorised thereto by their respective Governments; have signed the present Agreement.

Done in duplicate at London, this 29th day of November 1954, in the English language.

ANTHONY EDEN.
AKLILOU.

SCHEDULE

The territories consist of a continuous belt of Ethiopian territory bounded on the West and South by a line defined as follows:—

Starting at a point on the international Frontier between Ethiopia and the Somaliland Protectorate situated mid-way between the triangulation and astronomical points of Eirile and Cuble in a line drawn from Cape Maskan to the triangulation and astronomical point of Burta Dulleti, the line follows a straight line to Burta Dulleti, thence a straight line to the village of Darimu. From Darimu the line goes to Abosa-Cololcia-Serir Gerad—Gara Garri, thence to Buloda Uen, thence to Bulo Quruh, thence Libahful—Subul Hanfele-Ghetiit Addole—Subul Neric—Subul Bar Dod—Subul Odle—Abai Folan; thence in a straight line to Gaho, thence following the thalweg of the Tug Gerer to a point ten kilometres above Dagahbur. From this point the line passes round Dagahbur following a semi-circle to the North and East of Dagahbur with the centre at Dagahbur and a radius of ten kilometres and rejoining the Tug Gerer at a point ten kilometres below Dagahbur, thence follows the Tug Gerer to a point eight kilometres North-west of the triangulation point of Bulaleh. From this point the line passes around Bulaleh following a semi-circle of eight kilometres South-east of Bulaleh Wells; thence following the motorable track to Harardighet (Biad Detta): thence the line following the old motorable track to the East of the new road to Mersin Galgalo; thence following the same track to Hara Ado (designated on the map Gabredarre KCN 4280 as Ado) leaving a well on each side of the line; thence in a straight line to meet the track from Ual Ual to Galladi at a point sixteen kilometres to the East of Ual Ual; thence following the same track to Galkayu as far as its point of intersection with the frontier of the United Nations Trust territory of Somaliland.

Glossary of Abbreviations, Acronyms, and Terms

Afder or Afdheer: the name of a zone
Al-Ithad Al-Islamiya (abbreviated to Al-Itihad) (Arabic): Islamic union
ADP: Amhara Democratic Party (former ANDM)
ANDM: Amhara National Democratic Movement
Barbaarta (Somali): a youth protest movement
Caleen, Alen or Aleen: the name of a village
Ceel Karri or El kere: the name of a town
CUD: Coalition for Unity and Democracy
Dhagaxbuur, Degeh Bur, Dagahbur, Dagahbour: the name of a city
Dhagaxmadaw or Dagahmadow: the name of a town
Dhanaan, Danan or Denan: the name of a town
Dulmidiid (Somali): an anti-injustice protest movement
DfID: Department for International Development
EHRC: Ethiopian Human Rights Commission
ENDF: Ethiopian National Defence Forces
ESDL: Ethiopian Somali Democratic League
EPP: Ethiopian Prosperity Party
EPRDF: Ethiopian People's Revolutionary Democratic Front
ERA: Ethiopian Road Authority
ESAT: Ethiopian Satellite Television
ESPDP: Ethiopian Somali People's Democratic Party
Fik, Fiiq or Fiq: the name of a town
FDRE: Federal Democratic Republic of Ethiopia
Gode or Gedey: the name of a city
HEGO: the name of a vigilante group
HoF: House of Federation
HoPR: House of People's Representatives
Harakat AlShabaab Al-Mujahidin (abbreviated to Alshabab) (Arabic): Mujahideen Youth Movement
CIC: Council of Islamic Courts
IGAD: Intergovernmental Authority on Development
ICRC: International Committee of the Red Cross
IDP: Internally Displaced Person
IOM: International Organisation for Migration
Jijiga or Jigjiga: the name of the regional capital city
Liyu Police (Amharic): special police; paramilitary militia of the SRS
MSF: Médecins Sans Frontières

NAMA: National Movement of Amhara
NEBE: National Electoral Board of Ethiopia
NISS: National Intelligence and Security Service
NSC: National Security Council
Obole or Obale: the name of a village
OCHA: United Nations Office for the Coordination of Humanitarian Affairs
OFC: Oromo Federalist Congress
OLF: Oromo Liberation Front
ONLF: Ogaden National Liberation Front
ODP: Oromo Democratic Party (former OPDO)
OPDO: Oromo People's Democratic Organisation
OMN: Oromia Media Network
POLY-GCL: a joint venture between Poly Group
Corporation and Golden Concord Holdings Limited
Qabdidaharre, Qabridahar, Kabridahar or Kebri Dehar: the name of a city
Qabribayax, Qabribayah or Kebri Beyah: the name of a town
Qalaafo or Kelafo: the name of a town
Qoriley, Qorile or Qoriile: the name of a village
SPDP: Somali People's Democratic Party
SPP: Somali Prosperity Party
SRS: Somali Regional State
Shaygoosh or Shekosh: the name of a town
SEPDM: Southern Ethiopian People's Democratic Movement
SRAJ: Somali Regional Alliance for Justice
SRTV: Somali Regional Television
Selective Proponent: the TPLF/Tigray region
SPEE: Soviet Petroleum Exploration Expedition
Struggling Underdogs: Non-Abyssinian Ethiopian nations
TPLF: Tigray People's Liberation Front
Unitarist Hegemony: Amhara Nation
UNPO: Unrepresented Nations and Peoples Organisation
UWSLF: United Western Somali Liberation Front
WSLF: Western Somali Liberation Front
WSYLO: Western Somali Youth Liberation Organisation
WSWLO: Western Somali Women Liberation Organisation
Wardheer or Werder: the name of a town

Bibliography

Unlike part I, which detailed the development of the struggle over many centuries, part II deals with the recent history of the region, starting from 2007. Because it primarily covers current events, the main references are based on information the author witnessed through observation, interviews, news bulletins and documentation of the media, rights groups and other international bodies.

Chapter 1

1. Space Daily. '74 Killed In Attack On Chinese Oil Venture In Ethiopia'. *Space Daily*, April 24, 2007. https://www.spacedaily.com/reports/74 _Killed_In_Attack_On_Chinese_Oil_Venture_In_Ethiopia_999.html.
2. Sydney Morning Herald. '74 killed in attack on Chinese oil venture in Ethiopia'. *Sydney Morning Herald*, April 25, 2007. https://www.smh. com.au/world/74-killed-in-attack-on-chinese-oil-venture-in-ethiopia-20141031-9cq.html.
3. Shuang, Xu. 'Press release: General Manager of Zhongyuan in Ethiopia, Zhongyuan Petroleum Exploration Bureau'. *Xinhua News Agency*, April 24, 2007.
4. Powell, Anita. 'Ethnic Somali rebels kill 74 at Chinese oilfield in Ethiopia'. *Guardian*, April 25, 2007. https://www.theguardian.com/world/2007 /apr/25/ethiopia.
5. Interviews of local people and ONLF militants involved in the Obole fighting with the author, 2008–2020.

Chapter 2

1. Human Rights Watch. Collective Punishment: War Crimes and Crimes against Humanity in the Ogaden area of Ethiopia's Somali Region. New York: Human Rights Watch, 2008.
2. Quinn, Ben. 'UK tenders to train Ethiopian paramilitaries accused of abuses'. *Guardian*, January 10, 2013. https://www.theguardian.com/ world/2013/jan/10/ethiopia-forces-human-rights-funding. https://www.theguardian.com/world/2013/jan/10/ethiopia-forces-human-rights-funding.
3. Rice, Xan. 'Humanitarian crisis hits Ethiopia'. Guardian, September 5, 2007. https://www.theguardian.com/world/2007/sep/05/ethiopia.
4. AFP. 'Ethiopia army claims killing around 100 Ogaden rebels'. *WebArchive.org*, November 16, 2007. https://web.archive.org/web/ 20071120040351/http:/afp.google.com/article/ALeqM5jjE3h6c4Bel630G MHcelOa0aZqFw.

5. BBC News. 'Ethiopia "bombs" Ogaden villages'. *BBC*, November 19, 2007. http://news.bbc.co.uk/1/hi/world/africa/7101598.stm.

6. Porteous, Tom. 'Ethiopia's dirty war'. *Guardian*, August 5, 2007. https://www.theguardian.com/commentisfree/2007/aug/05/ethiopiasdir tywar.

7. Bengali, Shashank. 'Ethiopia starves, kills own people, its refugees say'. *Hiiran Online*, September 15, 2007.
hiiraan.com/news2_rss/2007/Sept/ethiopia_starves_kills_own_people_its_re fugees_say.aspx.

8. Gettleman, Jeffrey. 'In Ethiopia, Fear and Cries of Army Brutality'. *New York Times*, June 18, 2007. https://www.nytimes.com/2007/06/18 /world/africa/18ethiopia.html.

9. Gettleman, Jeffrey. 'Rebels with a Cause'. *New York Times*, June 20, 2007. https://www.nytimes.com/video/world/africa/1194817118699/rebels-with-a-cause.html.

10. Gettleman, Jeffrey. 'Separatist Rebels Accuse Ethiopia's Military of Killing Civilians in Remote Region'. *New York Times*, November 20, 2007. https://www.nytimes.com/2007/11/20/world/africa/20ogaden.html.

11. Wallis, Daniel. 'West seen failing to condemn Ethiopia rights abuses'. *elEconomista*, June 12, 2008. https://www.eleconomista.es/global/ noticias/594378/06/08/West-seen-failing-to-condemn-Ethiopia-rights-abuses.html.

12. Human Rights Watch. 'Ethiopia: No Justice in Somali Region Killings'. *Human Rights Watch*, April 5, 2017. https://www.hrw.org/news /2017/04/06/ethiopia-no-justice-somali-region-killings.

Chapter 3

1. Tisdall, Simon. 'The Ogaden: a forgotten war draining a forgotten people'. *Guardian*, March 24, 2008. https://www.theguardian.com/world/2008 /mar/24/ethiopia.somalia.

2. Adow, Mohamed Ethiopia's Ogaden Rebels, Aljazeera April 15, 2008, https://www.youtube.com/watch?v=j2Is2DDD85U

3. Adow, Mohammed. 'Female fighters in Ogaden region - 16 Apr 08'. Filmed April 2008 at Al Jazeera English News Studio, Doha. Video, 2:20. https://www.youtube.com/watch?v=OO1jflVaBoE.

4. Human Rights Watch. 'Ethiopia: Army Commits Executions, Torture, and Rape in Ogaden'. *Human Rights Watch*, June 12, 2008. https://www.hrw .org/news/2008/06/12/ethiopia-army-commits-executions-torture-and - rape-ogaden.

5. Al Jazeera. 'Unrest simmers in Ethiopia's Ogaden'. *Al Jazeera*, April 15, 2008. https://www.aljazeera.com/news/2008/4/15/unrest-simmers-in-ethiopias-ogaden.

6. Human Rights Watch. 'Ethiopia: Probe Years of Abuse in Somali Region'. *Human Rights Watch*, August 20, 2018. https://www.hrw.org/news/2018

/08/20/ethiopia-probe-years-abuse-somali-region.

7. Gettleman, Jeffrey. 'In Rebel Region, Ethiopia Turns to Civilian Patrols'. *New York Times*, December 14, 2007. https://www.nytimes.com/2007/ 12/14/world/africa/14cnd-ethiopia.html.

8. Human Rights Watch. '"We are Like the Dead": Torture and other Human Rights Abuses in Jail Ogaden, Somali. Regional State, Ethiopia'. *Human Rights Watch*, July 4, 2018. https://www.hrw.org/report/2018/07/04 /we-are-dead/torture-and-other-human-rights-abuses-jail-ogaden-somali-regional.

9. Abdulkadir, Fowsia and Sam Zafiri. 'Ethiopia and the State of Democracy: Effects on Human Rights and Humanitarian Conditions in the Ogaden and Somalia: Presented to the House Committee on Foreign Affairs Subcommittee on African and Global Health at the United States Congress.' *Human Rights Watch*, October 2, 2007. https://www.hrw.org /news/2007/10/01/ethiopia-and-state-democracy-effects-human-rights-and-humanitarian-conditions-ogaden.

10. Abdulkadir, Fowsia and Elias Kifle. 'Statement by Fowsia Abdulkadir to the U.S. Congress'. *Ethiopian Review*, October 4, 2007. https:// ethiopianreview.com/content/1262.

11. Human Rights Watch. Collective Punishment: War Crimes and Crimes against Humanity in the Ogaden area of Ethiopia's Somali Region. New York: Human Rights Watch, 2008.

12. Ogaden Human Rights Committee. Series of Reports. 2006–2009.

13. Human Rights Watch. 'Ethiopia: 'Special Police' Execute 10'. *Human Rights Watch*, May 28, 2012. https://www.hrw.org/news/2012/05/28 /ethiopia-special-police-execute-10.

14. Interviews with victims of Jail Ogaden. *SRTV Documentaries*, 2018–2019.

15. Interview with a victim. *SATV*, June 21, 2015.

16. Interviews of victims with the author, 2008-2020.

Chapter 4

1. PA-X, Peace Agreements Database and Access Tool, Version 1. *The United Western Somali Liberation Front (UWSLF) on the Termination of the State of Insurgency*. Edinburgh: University of Edinburgh, 2010. https://www. peaceagreements.org/view/1080.

2. Interview with UWSLF leader. *BBC Somali Service*, July 29, 2010.

3. BBC News. 'Ethiopia signs peace deal with Ogaden rebel group'. *BBC World Service*, July 29, 2010. https://www.bbc.co.uk/worldservice /africa/2010/07/100729_ethiopia_rebels.shtml.

4. Jigjiga Herald. 'UWSLF: A Genuine Truce for Peace or Tactical Manoeuvre for Surrender to Ethiopia?' *Jigjiga Herald*, July 1, 2018. https://www.jigjigaherald.com/2018/07/01/uwslf-a-genuine-truce-for-peace-or-tactical-maneuver-for-surrender-to-ethiopia/.

5. Abukar, Hassan M. 'Ibrahim Dheere and Ethiopia: Seven Years Later'.

Wardheer News, March 13, 2017. https://wardheernews.com/ibrahim-dheere-and-ethiopia-seven-years-later/.

6. BBC News. 'Ethiopia "kills 123" ONLF rebels and surrounds 90 more'. *BBC Africa*, September 15, 2010. https://www.bbc.co.uk/news/world-africa-11315967.

7. Davison, William. 'Ethiopia-Based ONLF Denies Rebels Are Surrounded in Somalia'. *Bloomberg*, September 16, 2010. https://www.bloomberg.com/news/articles/2010-09-16/ethiopia-based-ogaden-rebel-group-denies-fighters-surrounded-in-somalia.

8. ONLF. 'Meles Zenawi Incites Genocide Again in Ogaden'. Press Conference. August 11, 2010.

9. Adow, Mohammed. 'New Fighting Force in Ethiopia's Ogaden'. Filmed September 2012 at Al Jazeera English News Studio, Doha. Video, 2:36. https://www.youtube.com/watch?v=3IDR4IJNDg8.

Chapter 5

1. ONLF. 'ONLF Statement on Oil Exploration and Security in Ogaden'. *SomaliTalk*, September 4, 2010. http://somalitalk.com/2010/09/04/ onlf-statement-on-oil-exploration-security-in-ogaden/.

2. Abebe, Bewket. 'Ethiopia: Ministry of Mines Signs Agreement With Chinese Firm for Ogaden Gas Reserves'. *All Africa*, December 2, 2013. https://allafrica.com/stories/201312031008.html.

3. Reuters Staff. 'Ethiopia and Djibouti sign deal to build gas pipeline'. *Reuters*, February 17, 2019. https://www.reuters.com/article/ethiopia-djibouti-gas-idUSL5N20C074.

4. Energy Mix Report and Radio Dalsan. 'Somali region to now receive 50% of oil revenue'. *Energy Mix Report*, June 11, 2019. https://www.energymixreport.com/somali-region-to-now-receive-50-of-oil-revenue/.

5. Cawthorne, Andrew. 'Villages deserted, burned in Ethiopia's Ogaden-MSF'. *Reuters*, September 4, 2007. https://www.reuters.com/article/idUSL04541837.

6. Bloomfield, Steve. 'Ethiopia's 'own Darfur' as villagers flee government-backed violence'. *Independent*, October 17, 2007. https://www.independent.co.uk/news/world/africa/ethiopia-s-own-darfur-as-villagers-flee-government-backed-violence-394904.html.

7. UNPO. 'Ogaden: Killing and Destruction of Communities along Somalia Border'. *UNPO*, June 1, 2015. https://unpo.org/article/18259.

8. Farah, Liban. 'Shidaalka Ogaden Basin ee dhulka Soomaali Galbeed: Khatartii ugu weyneyd oo soo wajahdey Soomaalida gumeysiga ku hoos nool'. *Warbaahinta Coldoon*, July 1, 2018. http://coldoon.net/articles/266 /Shidaalka-Ogaden-Basin-ee-dhulka-Soomaali-Galbeed-Khatartii-ugu-weyneyd-oo-soo-wajahdey-Soomaalida-gumeysiga-ku-hoos-nool.

9. Farah, Liban. 'Laughing Hyenas: Red flags the new Somali regional president should be wary of'. *Wardheer News*, August 31, 2018.

https://wardheernews.com/laughing-hyenas-red-flags-the-new-somali-regional-president-should-be-wary-of/.

10. Ali, Juweria and Tom Gardner. 'The mystery sickness bringing death and dismay to eastern Ethiopia'. *Guardian*, October 15, 2020. https://www.theguardian.com/global-development/2020/feb/20/the-mystery-sickness-bringing-death-and-dismay-to-eastern-ethiopia.

Chapter 6

1. Abdi, Ahmed. 'Ethiopia Abducts two key-ONLF senior leaders and negotiators in Nairobi, Kenya'. *Sucrifyforright.blogspot.com*, January 28, 2014. http://sucrifyforright.blogspot.com/2014/01/ethiopia-abducts-two-key-onlf-senior.html.

2. ONLF and Somaliland Sun. 'ONLF Condemns Nairobi Abduction of Two Senior Officers by Ethiopian Intelligence Agents'. *Somaliland Sun*, January 27, 2014. https://www.somalilandsun.com/onlf-condemns-nairobi-abduction-of-two-senior-officers-by-ethiopian-intelligence-agents/.

3. UNPO. 'Ogaden: ONLF Abduction From Nairobi'. *UNPO*, February 12, 2014. https://unpo.org/article/16842.

4. Ombati, Cyrus. 'Two police officers arrested over abduction of Ethiopian officials'. *Standard*, February 3, 2014. https://www.standardmedia.co.ke/counties/article/2000103807/policemen-arrested-over-abduction-of-ethiopian-officials.

5. Ombati, Cyrus. 'Police investigating alleged abduction of two Ethiopians in Nairobi'. *Standard*, January 29, 2014. https://www.standardmedia.co.ke/kenya/article/2000103474/police-investigating-alleged-abduction-of-two-ethiopians-in-nairobi.

6. UNPO. 'UNPO Calls for the Release of Abducted ONLF Leaders and Urges Ethiopia and Kenya to Resume Peace Talks'. *UNPO*, February 11, 2014. https://unpo.org/article/16832.

7. ONLF, The Release of the ONLF Negotiators abducted by the Ethiopian government, ONLF press release, June 3, 2015.

8. Black, Debra. 'Where is Bashir Makhtal?' *Toronto Star*, May 21, 2007. https://www.thestar.com/news/2007/05/21/where_is_bashir_makhtal.html.

9. Black, Debra. 'Wife despairs for man in Ethiopia jail'. *Toronto Star*, December 25, 2010. https://www.thestar.com/news/canada/2010/12/25/wife_despairs_for_man_in_ethiopia_jail.html.

10. CBC News. 'CBC report from the Ethiopian Court trial'. *CBC Radio*, March 20, 2009.

11. Cannon, Lawrence. 'Statement by Minister Cannon on Bashir Makhtal Sentencing in Ethiopia'. *Canada.ca*, August 3, 2009. https://www.canada.ca/en/news/archive/2009/08/statement-minister-cannon-bashir-makhtal-sentencing-ethiopia.html.

12. The Canadian Press. 'Canadian facing execution seeks help from PM'. *CBC News*, July 28, 2009. https://www.cbc.ca/news/canada/canadian-facing-execution-seeks-help-from-pm-1.778841.

13. Neve, Alex. 'Letter to Prime Minister Harper on the case of Bashir Makhtal'. *Amnesty International Canada*, February 4, 2015. https://www.amnesty.ca/news/open-letters/letter-to-prime-minister-harper-on-the-case-of-bashir-makhtal.

14. Multimedia interviews with Bashir Makhtal after his release in 2018.

15. Shaban, Abdur Rahman Alfa. 'Outrage as Somalia transfers citizen to Ethiopia in breach of national laws'. *Africa News*, August 31, 2017. https://www.africanews.com/2017/08/31/outrage-as-somalia-transfers-citizen-to-ethiopia-in-breach-of-national-laws//.

16. Reuters Staff. 'Somalia hands over ONLF rebel leader to Ethiopia: group'. *Reuters*, August 31, 2017. https://www.reuters.com/article/us-ethiopia-rebels-idUSKCN1BB26X.

17. Hassan, Mohamed Olad. 'Somalia: ONLF Member Transferred to Ethiopia Was Terrorist, Regional Threat'. *TesfaNews*, September 7, 2017. https://tesfanews.net/somalia-onlf-member-transferred-ethiopia-terrorist-regional-threat/.

18. Jama, Mo Ahmed. 'Somalia: The extradition of Qalbi-Dhagah was illegal, says parliamentary committee'. *Wargane*, November 18, 2017. https://wargane.com/2017/11/18/somalia-extradition-qalbi-dhagah-illegal-says-parliamentary-committee/.

19. Multimedia interviews with Qalbidhagah after his release in 2018.

Chapter 7

1. Abbink, Jon. 'Ethiopia's Unrest Sparked by Unequal Development Record'. *Global Observatory*, September 13, 2016. https://theglobalobservatory.org/2016/09/ethiopia-protests-amhara-oromiya/.

2. BBC News. 'What is behind Ethiopia's wave of protests?' *BBC Africa*, August 22, 2016. https://www.bbc.co.uk/news/world-africa-36940906.

3. Al Jazeera News. 'Ethiopia declares state of emergency over protests'. *Al Jazeera*, October 10, 2016. https://www.aljazeera.com/news/2016/10/10/ethiopia-declares-state-of-emergency-over-protests.

4. Shaban, Abdur Rahman Alfa. 'Ethiopia army suppressing new protests in Amhara: gunfire, deaths reported'. *Africa News*, January 25, 2018. https://www.africanews.com/2018/01/25/ethiopia-army-suppressing-new-protests-in-amhara-gunfire-deaths-reported//.

5. BBC News. 'What is behind clashes in Ethiopia's Oromia and Somali regions?' *BBC Africa*, September 18, 2017. https://www.bbc.co.uk/news/world-africa-41278618.

6. BBC News. 'Dozens die in clash between Ethiopian Somalis and Oromos'. *BBC Africa*, December 18, 2017. https://www.bbc.co.uk/news/world-africa-42394108.

7. United Nations Office for the Coordination of Humanitarian Affairs. 'Ethiopia IDP Situation Report May 2019'. *Relief Web*, June 13, 2019. https://reliefweb.int/report/ethiopia/ethiopia-idp-situation-report-may-2019.

8. Internal Displacement Monitoring Centre. 'Ethiopia tops global list of highest internal displacement in 2018'. *Relief Web*, September 12, 2018. https://reliefweb.int/report/ethiopia/ethiopia-tops-global-list-highest-internal-displacement-2018#:~:text=Ethiopia%20has%20seen%20the%20highest,isn't%20making%20global%20headlines.

9. International Organisation for Migration. 'IOM Report: Ethiopia Records More Than 1.8 Million Internally Displaced in 2020'. *IOM*, September 15, 2020. https://www.iom.int/news/iom-report-ethiopia-records-more-18 -million-internally-displaced-2020.

Chapter 8

1. Ahmed, Abiy and ETV. 'PM Dr Abiy Ahmed Speech in Parliament – FULL'. Filmed June 2018 at Federal Parliamentary Assembly, Ethiopia. Video, 2:35:15. https://www.youtube.com/watch?v=wJnC2aX4jP8.

2. Maasho, Aaron. 'Ethnic unrest tarnishes new Ethiopian leader's reforms'. *Reuters*, August 24, 2018. https://cn.reuters.com/article/us-ethiopia-violence-idUSKCN1L914V.

3. Allo, Awol K. 'Ethiopia's new Prime Minister has had a stellar two months, can he keep it up?' *CNN*, June 7, 2018. https://edition.cnn.com/2018 /06/07/africa/ethiopia-abiy-ahmed-transformation-intl/index.html.

4. Gebreselassie, Elias. 'Is the Ethiopian justice system on the right path of reform?' *Al Jazeera*, October 1, 2019. https://www.aljazeera.com/ features/2019/10/1/is-the-ethiopian-justice-system-on-the-right-path-of-reform.

5. Soliman, Ahmed. 'Ethiopia's Prime Minister Shows Knack for Balancing Reform and Continuity'. *Chatham House*, April 27, 2018. https://www. chathamhouse.org/2018/04/ethiopias-prime-minister-shows-knack-balancing-reform-and-continuity.

6. Reuters. 'Ethiopia reform wave rolls on, opposition no longer "terrorists"'. *Reuters*, July 5, 2018. https://www.reuters.com/places/africa/article/us-ethiopia-prisons/ethiopia-fires-senior-prison-officials-for-abuses-as-reform-wave-rolls-on-idUSKBN1JV0CE.

7. BBC News. 'Abiy Ahmed's reforms in Ethiopia lift the lid on ethnic tensions'. *BBC Africa*, June 29, 2019. https://www.bbc.co.uk/news/ world-africa-48803815.

8. Jeffrey, James. 'The challenges of navigating Ethiopia's new media landscape'. *Al Jazeera*, October 29, 2019. https://www.aljazeera.com/ news/2019/10/29/the-challenges-of-navigating-ethiopias-new-media-landscape.

9. Mumo, Muthoki. 'Under Abiy, Ethiopia's media have more freedom, but

challenges remain'. *CPJ: Sub-Saharan Africa*, April 29, 2019. https://cpj. org/2019/04/ethiopia-abiy-ahmed-press-freedom-reform/.

10. Associated Press. 'Death toll in Ethiopian protests after killing of singer rises to 166'. *CBC News*, July 5, 2020. https://www.cbc.ca/news/world/ ethiopia-protest-singer-hachalu-hundessa-killed-1.5638219#:~:text=Dea th%20toll%20in%20Ethiopian%20protests,rises%20to%20166%20%7C% 20CBC%20News.

Chapter 9

1. Africa News. 'Ethiopia PM Abiy Ahmed visits Jigjiga on Oromia-Somali peace mission'. *Africa News*, April 8, 2018. https://www.africanews.com /2018/04/08/ethiopia-pm-abiy-ahmed-visits-jijiga-on-oromia-somali-peace-mission//.

2. Fasil, Mahlet. 'News: ex-Somali region president dismisses criminal charges against him as "coordinated lies"'. *Addis Standard*, February 6, 2019. https://addisstandard.com/2021/news-ex-somali-region-presiden t-dismisses-criminal-charges-against-him-as-coordinated-lies/.

3. Jigjiga Herald. 'Abdi Iley: "I Was a Tool for TPLF"'. *Jigjiga Herald*, July 12, 2018. https://www.jigjigaherald.com/2018/07/12/abdi-iley-i-was-a-too l-for-tplf/.

4. Gardner, Tom. "Ethiopia's Somali strongman". *Africa Report*. July 3, 2018. https://www.theafricareport.com/599/ethiopia-the-somali-strongman.

5. Sisay, Andualem. 'Ethiopian army takes over Somali region security'. *East African*, August 7, 2018. https://www.theeastafrican.co.ke/tea/news/rest-of-africa/ethiopian-ar my-takes-over-somali-region-security-1399946.

6. All Things Ethiopia. 'Breaking: Federal defence forces surround Somali regional state president Abdi Mohamud Omar; situation remains tense'. *All Things Ethiopia*, August 5, 2018. http://www.allthingsethiopia.com /ethiopia-breaking-news/4026/.

7. Zelalem, Zecharias. 'THE RISE OF THE BARBAARTA: Somali protesters demand an end to Abdi Illey's reign of terror'. *OPride.com*, June 1, 2018. https://www.opride.com/2018/06/01/the-rise-of-the-barbaart a-somali-protesters-demand-an-end-to-abdi-illeys-reign-of-terror/.

8. Ethiopia Observer. 'The Ethiopia's Somali region gets new president'. *Ethiopia Observer*, August 22, 2018. https://www.ethiopiaobserver.com /2018/08/22/the-ethiopias-somali-region-gets-new-president/.

9. Solomon, Salem and Sahra Abdi Ahmed. 'Ethiopia's Somali Region Hopes New Leader Will Bring Peace'. *VOA News*, August 25, 2018. https:// www.voanews.com/africa/ethiopias-somali-region-hopes-new-leader-will-bring-peace.

10. Hagmann, Tobias. *Fast politics, slow justice: Ethiopia's, Somali region two years after Abdi Iley*. London: LSE, 2020. https://www.lse.ac.uk/ideas/Assets /Documents/Conflict-Research-Programme/crp-memos/Hagmann-Two-years-after-Iley-final.pdf.

Chapter 10

1. Addis Standard. 'News: Ethiopia, ONLF sign historic peace deal'. *Addis Standard*, October 22, 2018. https://addisstandard.com/news-ethiopia-onlf-sign-historic-peace-deal/.

2. Shaban, Abdur Rahman Alfa. 'Eritrea hosts final peace pact between Ethiopia and ONLF'. *Africa News*, October 22, 2018. https://www.africanews.com/2018/10/22/eritrea-hosts-final-peace-pact-between-ethiopia-and-onlf//.

3. Conciliation Resources. 'Conciliation Resources attends historic Ethiopia peace deal signing'. *Conciliation Resources*, October 2018. https://www.c-r.org/news-and-insight/conciliation-resources-attends-historic-ethiopia-peace-deal-signing.

4. Brooks, Aaron. 'Ogaden rebel group returns to Ethiopia following peace accord'. *East Africa Monitor*, November 22, 2018. https://eastafricamonitor.com/ogaden-rebel-group-returns-to-ethiopia-following-peace-accord/.

5. Adow, Mohammed. 'Ethiopia signs peace deal with former Ogaden rebels'. Filmed April 2019 at Al Jazeera English, Ethiopia. Video, 3:21. https://www.youtube.com/watch?v=fDww8H1F8ko.

6. Maruf, Harun. 'Ethiopia Opens Three-Day Talks with Somali Rebels'. *VOA News*, February 11, 2018. https://www.voanews.com/africa /ethiopia-opens-three-day-talks-somali-rebels.

7. Tekle, Tesfa-Alem. 'Peace talks between Ethiopia and Ogaden rebels failed'. *Sudan Tribune*, October 19, 2012. https://sudantribune.com /spip.php?article44267.

8. ONLF and Dayr. 'Peace talks between Ogaden National Liberation Front (ONLF) and the Ethiopian Government Held in Kenya'. *Ogaden News Agency*. September 8, 2012. http://www.ogadennet.com/?p=15739.

Chapter 11

1. Marshall, Alyssa. 'Ethiopia to Close Jail Ogaden'. *IR Insider*, September 26, 2018. https://www.irinsider.org/subsaharan-africa-1/2018/9/26/ethiopia-to-close-jail-ogaden.

2. Shaban, Abdur Rahman Alfa. 'Ethiopia's Somali region closes notorious "Jail Ogaden"'. *Africa News*, September 22, 2018. https://www.africanews.com/2018/09/22/ethiopia-s-somali-region-closes-notorious-jail-ogaden//.

3. Adow, Mohammed. 'Ethiopia: Former jail to become museum'. Filmed April 2019 at Al Jazeera English, Ethiopia. Video, 3:18. https://www.youtube.com/watch?v=u1Hcw_nzb84.

4. Geeska Afrika Online. 'Ex-Ogaden rebels hail Ethiopia PM for peace in Somali region'. *Geeska Afrika Online*, January 30, 2019. https://www.geeskaafrika.com/ex-ogaden-rebels-hail-ethiopia-pm-for-peace-in-somali-region/.

5. Cade, Cabdi. 'ONLF: Hope against Hope!' *Allbanaadir Online*, August 25, 2020. https://www.allbanaadir.org/?p=162877.
6. Damte, Eldad. 'Prosperity Party and ONLF Cooperating for Peace in Somali Region'. *Addis Insight*, July 27, 2020. https://www.addisinsight.net /prosperity-party-and-onlf/.

Chapter 12

1. Farah, Liban. 'Laughing Hyenas: Red flags the new Somali regional president should be wary of'. *Wardheer News*, August 31, 2018. https://wardheernews.com/laughing-hyenas-red-flags-the-new-somali-r egional-president-should-be-wary-of/.
2. Manek, Nizar. 'Ethiopia's Challenge: Overcoming "Mafia"-Style Violence'. *Bloomberg Quint*, October 1, 2018. https://www.bloombergquint.com/ politics/-mafia-state-shows-worst-of-system-ethiopia-is-racing-to-reform.
3. Ethiopia Observer. 'A plot to overthrow the president of Ethiopia's Somali region'. *Ethiopia Observer*, January 24, 2019. https://www.ethiopia observer.com/2019/01/24/a-plot-to-overthrow-the-president-of- ethiopias-somali-region/.
4. Hagmann, Tobias. *Fast politics, slow justice: Ethiopia's, Somali region two years after Abdi Iley*. London: LSE, 2020. https://www.lse.ac.uk/ideas/Assets /Documents/Conflict-Research-Programme/crp-memos/Hagmann-Two- years-after-Iley-final.pdf.
5. Jelan, Bileh. 'News: Somali regional state asks, "equitable representation" at federal parliament'. *Addis Standard*, December 23, 2019. https://addisstandard.com/news-somali-regional-state-asks-equitable-re presentation-at-federal-parliament/.
6. Ethiopian Monitor. 'ERA Launches 6bln Br Road Construction Projects in Somali Region'. *Ethiopian Monitor*, October 29, 2020. https:// ethiopianmonitor.com/2020/10/29/govt-launches-road-construction- projects-in-somali-region-at-cost-of-6bln-birr/.
7. Omar, Mustafa Muhumed and Abdihafid. 'Maxaa Caawa kala Qabsaday Wariye Abdihafid Iyo Md Mustafa M Omer'. Filmed April 2020 at SSTV Jigjiga, Somali. Video, 59:35. https://www.youtube.com/watch?v= 4TuJaFiDBv8.

Chapter 13

1. Ethiopian Monitor. 'ONLF Plans to Compete as National Party in 2020 Election'. *Ethiopian Monitor*, August 22, 2019. https://ethiopianmonitor. com/2019/08/22/onlf-plans-to-compete-as-national-party-in-2020- election/.
2. Kulmiye, Lul Araweelo. 'An ONLF Official: "We Have a Comprehensive Plan."'. *Wardheer News,* December 21, 2018. https://wardheernews.com/ an-onlf-official-we-have-a-comprehensive-plan/.

3. Jelan, Bileh. 'Breaking: ONLF vice chairman and veteran member Hassan Moalim resigns'. *Addis Standard*, November 6, 2020. https://addi sstandard.com/breaking-onlf-vice-chairman-and-veteran-member-hassa n-moalim-resigns/.

4. Addis Standard. 'Exclusive: "If we don't treat this carefully and we meddle things, it will affect the entire region": ONLF chairman on Jubaland'. *Addis Standard*, August 26, 2019. https://addisstandard.com/exclusive-if-we-dont-treat-this-carefully-and-we-meddle-things-it-will-affect-the-entire-region-onlf-chairman-on-jubaland/.

5. Nur, Hussein and SDN. 'Sirta Qarsoon: ONLF Mudane Xuseen Nuur Part Two (Ended)'. Filmed April 2020 at SDN. Video, 38:09. https://www.youtube.com/watch?v=Y1psOS2uyVA.

6. Omar, Mohamed Ismail and SDN. 'ONLF: Khilaafka Xisbiga Waraysi Maxahmed Ismaaciil 18-03-2020 qaybtii 2aad'. Filmed March 2020 at SDN. Video, 12:44. https://www.youtube.com/watch?v=pIkEU_4L 6Jw.

Chapter 14

1. Demlie, Bantayehu. 'Analysis: Deferred election, state of emergency and #COVID19 – How can Ethiopia avoid an impending constitutional crisis?' *Addis Standard*, April 10, 2020. https://addisstandard.com/ana lysis-deferred-election-state-of-emergency-and-covid19-how-can-ethiopia-avoid-an-impending-constitutional-crisis/.

2. Kebede, Messay. 'Coronavirus and Ethiopian Constitutional Crisis'. *Ethiopia Observer*, May 26, 2020. https://www.ethiopiaobserver.com/20 20/05/26/coronavirus-and-ethiopian-constitutional-crisis/.

3. Tronvoll, Kjetil. 'In-depth Analysis: Towards Tigray Statehood?' *Addis Standard*, May 14, 2020. https://addisstandard.com/in-depth-analysis-towards-tigray-statehood/.

4. De Waal, Alex. 'Tigray crisis viewpoint: Why Ethiopia is spiralling out of control'. *BBC News*, November 15, 2020. https://www.bbc.co.uk/news /world-africa-54932333.

5. Gebreselassie, Elias. 'In Ethiopia, a heated political tug-of-war sparks security fears'. *Al Jazeera*, October 19, 2020. https://www.aljazeera.com /news/2020/10/19/political-crisis-threatens-ethiopias-fragile-peace.

6. Africa Confidential. 'Citadel falls but the war goes on'. *Africa Confidential*, December 3, 2020. https://www.africa-confidential.com/article/id/ 13154/Citadel_falls_but_the_war_goes_on.

7. Omar, Mustafa. 'The conflict in Ethiopia and the TPLF's ultra-nationalist ideology'. *Al Jazeera*, December 4, 2020. https://www.aljazeera.com /opinions/2020/12/4/the-conflict-in-ethiopia-and-tplfs-ultra-nationalis t-ideology.

Photos of Resistance Leaders

Photo 1: Sayyid Mohamed Abdille Hassan (Dervish Resistance Movement Leader)

Photo 2: Garaad Makhtal Dahir (Nasrullah/OLF Chairman)

Photo 3: Abdullahi Hassan Mohamoud (First WSLF charman)

Photo 4: Mohamed Diriye Urdoh (Second WSLF Chairman)

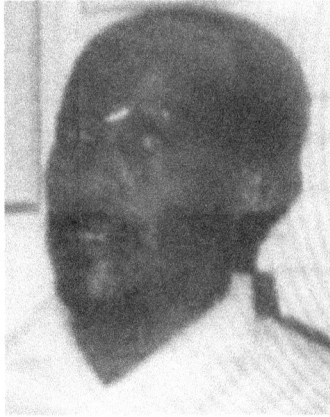

Photo 5: Sheikh Abdinassir Sheikh Adan (Third WSLF Chairman)

Photo 6: Sheikh Ibrahim Abdallah (First ONLF Chairman)

Photo 7: Mohamed Omar Osman (Second ONLF Chairman)

Index